D0849236

Evolution and Religious Creation Myths

Evolution and Religious Creation Myths
How Scientists Respond

Paul F. Lurquin and Linda Stone

OXFORD
UNIVERSITY PRESS

2007

OXFORD
UNIVERSITY PRESS

Oxford University Press, Inc., publishes works that further
Oxford University's objective of excellence
in research, scholarship, and education.

Oxford   New York
Auckland   Cape Town   Dar es Salaam   Hong Kong   Karachi
Kuala Lumpur   Madrid   Melbourne   Mexico City   Nairobi
New Delhi   Shanghai   Taipei   Toronto

With offices in
Argentina   Austria   Brazil   Chile   Czech Republic   France   Greece
Guatemala   Hungary   Italy   Japan   Poland   Portugal   Singapore
South Korea   Switzerland   Thailand   Turkey   Ukraine   Vietnam

Copyright © 2007 by Oxford University Press, Inc.

Published by Oxford University Press, Inc.
198 Madison Avenue, New York, New York 10016

www.oup.com

Oxford is a registered trademark of Oxford University Press

Library of Congress Cataloging-in-Publication Data
Lurquin, Paul F.
Evolution and religious creation myths : how scientists respond /
Paul F. Lurquin and Linda Stone.
p. cm.
Includes bibliographical references (p.) and index.
ISBN: 978-0-19-531538-7 (cloth)
1. Evolution—Religious aspects.   2. Creationism.   I. Stone, Linda, 1947–   II. Title.
BL263.L87 2007
231.7'652—dc22   2006023081

1 3 5 7 9 8 6 4 2

Printed in the United States of America
on acid-free paper

To all free thinkers, past, present, and ever to be

Human reason must never be subjugated to a dogma, or to a myth, or to a preconceived idea because for human reason to do so would be for human reason to cease to exist.
—**Henri Poincaré** (translated by L.S.)

Scientia vincere tenebras [Science will defeat darkness].
—**Motto of the Free University of Brussels** (P.F.L.'s alma mater)

PREFACE

America is becoming more and more isolated from the rest of the world. This statement is true enough politically and ideologically, with the faulty intelligence used to justify the 2003 war in Iraq, now known worldwide, and the increased influence of religious thinking in the conduct of government affairs, starting at the presidential level with George W. Bush. There is fear that our nation's separation of church and state is now threatened, considering further that some politicians are using an anti-evolutionary, creationist stance to sway their constituencies. But for a scientist, it is not just politics that is of the essence. For a person practicing and teaching science, there is now serious concern that the traditional division between science and religion is coming to an end among a growing portion of the American public, which is further promoting our international isolation. And scientific isolation from the rest of the world is a frightening, dangerous prospect.

This state of affairs is not exactly new in the United States. Many will recall the Scopes trial (also called the Scopes monkey trial) of 1925, in which John T. Scopes, a high school science teacher, was sentenced for teaching evolution to his students. Back in those days, the State of Tennessee had banned evolution from its science curriculum, a law that Scopes—who had been recruited by the American Civil Liberties Union—had evidently violated. Later, another court overturned the verdict. Regardless of this outcome, it is disturbing that a state had at that time taken the ill-inspired initiative to enact legislation regarding the teaching of science, particularly in an area perceived as questioning the validity of a literal interpretation of the Bible.

The consequences of this legislation—and the trial—were that, for a time, America was seen as a scientifically backward country, particularly in Europe. There, the issue of science potentially clashing with certain religious beliefs had been settled earlier (although not quite completely) and was certainly not expected to be legislated upon. In essence, science and faith had arrived at a state of *modus vivendi* in Europe, with the United States more or less following suit shortly after the Scopes trial. And this is indeed the way it should be, because science and religion represent very different modes of knowledge and understanding. Even though both can address similar questions (What is the origin of the universe? What is the origin of life?), they tackle these questions from very different perspectives and on completely different levels. In brief, science does not need religion, and religion does not need science. When they try to encompass one another, both become self-destructive.

Unfortunately, a renewed antiscience movement appeared in America in the 1990s, and it is becoming more and more vocal. It is also spreading to other parts of the world. This movement includes some scientists, particularly life scientists, who, again, are opposed to evolution. But this time, rather than seeking a ban on the teaching of evolution, these activists are trying to convince the public that equal time should be devoted to the teaching of divine creation stories that fall outside the realm of science. Others are advocating the teaching of "Intelligent Design," a philosophy that attempts to pass itself off as science. With a few scientists among their ranks to provide credence, creationist and neocreationist movements now claim that evolutionary thinking is critically flawed rather than being simply a-religious (or, perhaps as they see it, antireligious), as in the past. As we describe in this book, nothing can be farther from the truth: evolution rests on solid scientific bases and is in conflict not with religion as a whole, but with only a very narrow interpretation of a very small part of one sacred book, the Bible.

This is where America runs the risk of becoming isolated from the rest of the world, and not just politically. Worldwide, an enormous majority of believers in the Bible no longer interpret the Hebrew story of creation literally—only Christian fundamentalists do so. This is their right, of course. On the other hand, it is not their right to try to impose their religious views on others, especially where science is concerned. In doing so, these people, if successful, will clutter the science curriculum with misleading, unscientific issues, something our country does not need. Neocreationists and proponents of Intelligent Design usually prefer not to make reference to the Bible. But in the final analysis, their goal is the same: they want to put an end to the teaching of what they call "materialistic science" and replace it with something more in agreement with their particular Christian convictions. This strategy was discussed in the excellent book *Creationism's Trojan Horse: The Wedge of Intelligent Design*, by Barbara Forrest and Paul R. Gross (Oxford University Press, 2004).

As we know, our modern world relies heavily on science and its applications. As we also know, the state of scientific and mathematical knowledge is not a healthy one in the United States. Teaching unscientific alternatives to evolution in science classrooms would just make matters worse. In all fairness, one should recognize that fundamentalists have so far used the democratic process to further their views. But there is still a major problem: the validity of science and the scientific process cannot and should not be decided at the ballot box.

Most professional scientists, even though they are deeply irritated by all the attacks against evolution, have remained largely silent in public forums, at least in forums that involve the general public. This is a grave mistake, because these attacks and attackers will not simply go away. It is now high time to put the cards on the table and show what the game really is all about—hence this book. Here, we describe our own view of creationism and neocreationism from the perspective of anthropology and genetics and provide rebuttals to their attacks against evolutionary science. We also provide evidence that much of science is now relying on evolutionary thinking, from cosmology to biology, and even some aspects of the social sciences. Rather than being hopelessly flawed, evolutionary thinking is providing a rich framework for the advancement of scientific knowledge.

In this book we avoid the stultifying debate about whether science is (or should be) part of what philosophers call in turn methodological, philosophical, theistic, agnostic, or materialistic naturalism. This issue is entirely philosophical and has no bearing whatsoever on the enormous majority of working scientists who conduct their research in their laboratories, the field, and their observatories. These scientists use reason and the rules of science to gain understanding of the natural world, not to decide which kind of philosophical system science represents. This question is better left for philosophers to argue about because in fact, most scientists do not care about it.

This book is not against religion. Rather, it is against self-declared righteous people who, in the name of a distorted view of science and an intolerant view of religion, put the perception of science in jeopardy in America. Therefore, we have not attempted to present the problem as balanced—it is not balanced. There cannot be a balanced view when science and nonscience are clashing head to head.

As with all books, ours was inspired in large part by thinkers who preceded us. In particular, it owes much to the thinking of Ilya Prigogine (1917–2003), 1977 Nobel Laureate for Chemistry and discoverer of dissipative structures. In addition, we both found inspiration in the evolutionary thinking—biological and cultural—of Stanford University human geneticist L. Luca Cavalli-Sforza, whose scientific biography *A Genetic and Cultural Odyssey: The Life and Work of L. Luca Cavalli-Sforza* (Columbia University Press) we published in 2005. This endeavor originated a fruitful collaboration that continues to date.

We thank Harold Juli (Connecticut College) and Michael Sinclair (New York Law School), as well as three anonymous reviewers, for their help with some of the topics covered in this book. P.F.L. also thanks Kathryn Dooley, a student in his spring 2005 Origins of Life course at Washington State University, for giving him permission to quote passages from her term paper for that class. As always, all errors and omissions are ours alone.

CONTENTS

1

Creationism and Intelligent Design: The Evolution of an Idea

3

2

What Is Evolutionary Biology and Where Is It Coming From?

31

3

Creationist Purpose and Irreducible Complexity Rebutted

55

4

The Origins and Evolution of *Homo sapiens*

85

5

The Origins of Life and the Cosmos as Evolutionary Themes

109

6

Evolution of the DNA World and the Chance Events That
Accompanied It: More about Complexity

145

7

The Dangers of Creationism

179

Appendix 1
The Brusselator

195

Appendix 2
Experiments for Educators

199

Glossary

203

Further Reading

207

Index

211

Evolution and Religious Creation Myths

1

Creationism and Intelligent Design
The Evolution of an Idea

Skeptical scrutiny is the means, in both science and religion, by
which deep thoughts can be winnowed from deep nonsense.
—Carl Sagan

A 2004 Gallup Poll in the United States reported that 45% of the population
believe that God created humans in their present form within the last 10,000
years; 38% believe that humans evolved from other life-forms over many
millions of years but that God directed the process; 13% are of the opinion that
humans evolved from other life-forms over millions of years but that God
played no role in the process; and 4% have no opinion. These percentages have
remained fairly stable over the last several decades. The most prominent
opinion continues to be in favor of creationism and against evolution.

Nearly half of the U.S. population, then, reject one of the historically most
contentious scientific theories, the theory of evolution by natural selection,
often referred to as "Darwinism." Opponents of evolution claim that evolutionary biology is unfounded, undemonstrated, illogical, and possibly
un-Christian—in short, basically wrong. In 2005, the Kansas Board of Education passed a resolution giving high school teachers free reign to teach
alternatives to evolution, including so-called Intelligent Design theory
(hereinafter ID), a recent variant of creationism. This decision, and President
George W. Bush's public endorsement of it, stirred intense national debate.
A movement supporting creationism and the teaching of ID in public
schools is now spreading to other Christian countries, as well. Meanwhile,
creationists and ID advocates have become increasingly powerful in U.S.
political organizations, now representing a majority of the Republican Party
in several states. Journalist and author Chris Mooney argues in his book *The
Republican War on Science* (2005) that Seattle's Discovery Institute—an organization at the center of the ID movement—is politically and religiously
motivated. The goal of the Discovery Institute, he claims, is the destruction
of "scientific materialism" (modern science) and its replacement by a religiously imbued science based on the supernatural origin of many phenomena observed in nature (Intelligent Design). This redefinition of science,
says Mooney, is in line with the thinking of members of the conservative
Republican Christian Right and hence has serious political implications that
can affect all of us. It is therefore important to understand what ID actually

3

proposes, what its origins are, and the extent to which it can validly claim to be a scientific alternative to evolutionary science.

Intelligent Design is not really a new approach to explain life on Earth. It derives from older religious interpretations that first burgeoned many thousands of years ago and were refined in the nineteenth century. Thus, our choice of the words "evolution of an idea" in the title of this chapter is intentional and, yes, ironical. As practically all ideas in the history of humankind, ID has simpler predecessors and has clearly descended with modification from an ancestral concept: creationism. The link between ID and creationism is so clear that ID might as well be called neocreationism.

To wit, ID claims that existing life-forms and, by extension, the whole universe, perhaps, are too complex to have evolved from much simpler organisms (and physical structures) that first appeared billions of years ago. This being posited, proponents of ID make recourse to the proposition that living organisms were designed by a supreme intelligence and not by natural, undirected phenomena. By definition, such a notion calls upon a creator. Since most—if not all—supporters of ID in the United States are, to our knowledge, adherents to the Christian faith, this creator should then be named God (although a facetious, irreverent, and widely popular Web site postulates that the creator, the designer, is in fact a giant Flying Spaghetti Monster). In the view of ID supporters, God created all life-forms pretty much as they exist today, and these life-forms did not evolve—did not change over time—in any appreciable way because they are "irreducibly complex." The fixed nature of living species is already claimed and inferred in the first book of the Bible, Genesis. The principle of the unchanging nature of living species (they are called "kinds" in the Bible) created by God as in Genesis is called "creationism." Thus, ID recognizes limited hereditary variation within a "kind," as allowed by Genesis, but rejects the idea that species can evolve into other species because this concept violates the biblical precept that "kinds" were fixed by God once and for all. To avoid repetition, we give the words "neocreationism" and "ID" roughly the same meaning, whereas we reserve the words "creationism" or "classical creationism" to designate an older type of thinking, predating the idea of "irreducible complexity." The term "Intelligent Design," or ID, is used when specific reference is made to individuals who started and propagated this latest version of creationism.

ID is creationism with a twist. Indeed, gone from the present version of ID are the concepts of a universal flood, a six-day creation, and formation of the universe in 4004 B.C.E. Why is this? Its proponents claim that ID is a scientific view of nature, not just the reworking of a religious story first told a long time ago. In that light, ID supporters know very well that not a shred of geological or meteorological evidence supports the idea that the entire surface of our planet could have been under water as recently as a few thousand years ago. Even though we have not seen or heard this ourselves, we suspect that ID supporters may also know that Genesis in all likelihood evolved—derived— from the older Sumerian Epic of Gilgamesh, which already incorporated a great flood and the survival of just two human beings who later repopulated Earth.

Likewise, no serious scientist today believes that the whole universe was created in exactly six days and that this creation took place 6,000 years in the past. Further, no archaeologist accepts the biblical account that animal husbandry was invented by (or provided to) humans before they first experienced a very long period of hunting and gathering, as overwhelmingly demonstrated by the paleontological record. And finally, no credible linguist accords validity to the idea that the 6,000 or so human languages appeared all at once, as humans were building the Tower of Babel. Accordingly, books and Web sites that prescribe ID are generally silent regarding the time frames in which the origins of life and the universe, as well as the appearance of humans, took place. This distinguishes ID from old-style creationism. Also, proponents of ID no longer invoke the concept of a young Earth intentionally created to look old and thus fool naive scientists, or claims that human footprints were found in Texas running side by side with dinosaur tracks.

In this sense, ID has veered away from a *literal* interpretation of Genesis but has kept intact the *concept* of God the Creator of unchangeable species. Needless to say, mixing biblical concepts with seemingly scientific ones squarely clashes with scientific evolution, where God plays no obvious or immediate role and where species *do* change over time. But there is more. In its attacks against mainstream science, ID tries to make the case that non-ID scientists cannot (or are unwilling to) distinguish between "fact" and "theory." Indeed, it may well be this very angle of attack that most impresses the public. This makes it an important point worth discussing at some length because the public may not be aware of what these words, facts and theory, really mean in a scientific context. The following sections distinguish between fact, theory, some other scientific terminology, and the general functioning of science.

How Science Really Works: Facts and Theories

First, let us examine what a "fact" is. We can say that it is a fact that a dropped pencil hits the ground instead of flying away from it. An unobstructed midday sun is yellow-white. Microbes can be seen with the use of a microscope. The atmosphere of planet Mars contains no breathable air. Deoxyribonucleic acid (DNA), an example developed in the next section, is found in all known cellular life. These are all facts, or in other words, these are all *observations* made with our eyes and instruments. But here, already, we can see that not all observational facts are of the same nature. For example, a falling pencil and a yellow sun are obvious to all equipped with eyesight. On the other hand, microbes cannot be seen with the unaided eye, and no humans have ever been to Mars to check the claim that its atmosphere is not breathable. Finally, DNA is a molecule that must be isolated from living cells and characterized chemically. However, no one would challenge the claims that microbes and DNA exist, and we are all confident that our space probes are built in such a way as to report accurately on the physical reality that exists on other planets. But it also turns out that the reality of microbes was questioned for quite some time even after the invention of the microscope, and discussing the nature of Mars's atmosphere would have been considered ludicrous just a few decades ago. Thus, it is important to remember that facts must first be *discovered* (they are neither always obvious nor preordained) and then generally *accepted* by the scientific community. It is also important to realize that discovery these days practically always depends on the manufacturing of improved analytical instruments and not on good common sense alone.

An excellent example of a good commonsense explanation that betrayed humans for centuries is that of a flat Earth. Even though the ancient Greeks had demonstrated more than 2,000 years ago, using clever observational and mathematical techniques, that our planet is actually spherical, this knowledge was lost during the Middle Ages. Back then, the doctrine of the flat Earth prevailed because, after all, Earth *looks* flat when observed from the surface. A flat Earth is well indicated in medieval maps that have survived to the present. In these maps, continents—whose shapes are incorrect—are clustered and surrounded by a ring of water, the universal ocean that marked the boundaries of our planet. Thus, a flat Earth became an indisputable "fact" for medieval geographers even though it was a false "discovery" that is of course no longer accepted today.

In a similar vein, but this time with tragic consequences, good common sense in some rural areas of South Asia dictates that diarrhea in infants occurs when the baby gets rid of "excess water" in its body. This "fact" tells a parent not to rehydrate the sick child. One can easily imagine the results of such commonsense thinking. In summary, when people talk about "facts," they should put these in a historical, technical, medical, and so on, context and be aware that today's facts may be tomorrow's fiction. For example, the medieval belief that men have one less rib than women (to account for the "fact" that Eve was created from one of Adam's ribs) was discounted centuries ago, once early human anatomists cared to actually compare the number of ribs in men and women.

Discovery of new phenomena (new facts) is one of the aims of science. But equally important is the *interpretation* of facts or observations. It can be said that without an organization (categorization) of discoveries into *theories*, there would be no science. Theory building is absolutely central to science; without it, science would just be a boring and confusing conglomerate of facts unrelated to one another. So it is critical to understand what a theory really is. Before giving a definition of this word, let us go over how modern science interprets some of the observational facts that we listed above.

That gravity (which makes a dropped pencil fall) exists does not explain how gravity works. It took the genius of Isaac Newton in the seventeenth century and subsequently Albert Einstein in the twentieth century to explain how the force of gravity attracts objects to one another. Both theories are highly mathematical, and Einstein's in particular is completely counterintuitive. This is because Einstein's theory of general relativity equates gravity with the warping of space by massive objects. Now, try as we might, our senses cannot detect this warping of space; it takes specialized instruments to measure it. But we know that warped space exists because Einstein, using his theory, accurately predicted by *how much* space would be warped by, for example, the sun. Then, Einstein's theory was verified by quantitative measurements, which themselves constituted new facts. Or, to put it differently, a theory must be put to precise experimental tests to verify its validity. As far as we know, the warping of space predicted by Einstein's theory is a fact.

To remain in the realm of space, let us now investigate the color of the sun. We know today that the color of the light emitted by an object is proportional to its temperature. Mathematical theory and experiments tell us that given its yellow-white color, the surface of the sun has a temperature of about 5,300°C. Now, no one has ever traveled to the sun to measure its temperature with a thermometer. How, then, do we know the temperature of the sun? One might say, well, let us heat an object to 5,300°C here on Earth and let us check its color. If the color of the emitted light is yellow-white, we will have verified that, indeed, the temperature of the surface of the sun is about 5,300°C.

This is easier said than done, however, because at this high temperature, all elements exist in the form of a gas, and it is very difficult to contain such a hot gas in any kind of vessel. Rather, the temperature of the sun is inferred from a mathematical (theoretical) equation derived by German scientist Max Planck at the turn of the twentieth century. This equation was experimentally verified at lower temperatures and then extrapolated to objects such as stars. We can see that without Planck's theory we would not know the temperature of unreachable objects present in the cosmos. This example shows that a good theory should be able to make *predictions* that are consistent with observable facts already acquired or to be acquired by doing further experiments. We can say with a great degree of confidence that the temperature of the surface of the sun is indeed about 5,300°C, which is then a fact derived from a theory.

Next, let us go over an example from the biological sciences. In the second half of the nineteenth century, French microbiologist Louis Pasteur theorized that microbes could be responsible for a large number of infectious diseases. He and his successors thus developed the germ theory of disease. Originally, this theory was not well received. Even prominent scientists doubted that germs invisible to the naked eye could cause diseases such as the plague and tuberculosis. Today, nobody doubts that certain germs *do* cause disease. But how were these early scientists convinced that the theory was correct? To support their theory, Pasteur and others first had to isolate and concentrate germs from diseased animals and then inject these concentrated germs into healthy animals. When these healthy animals developed the symptoms of the original disease, and when scientists found that the injected germs had abundantly proliferated in the experimental animals, they had demonstrated the validity of the germ theory of disease. Here, again, a theory was verified by conducting appropriate experiments.

At this point, it should be clear that the words "fact" and "theory" are not at all the same and cannot be substituted for one another. A "fact" should never be taken at face value because it could simply be the result of a flawed observation. To be valid and generally accepted, a fact must first be observable and the observation should be repeatable by independent observers. Without that, a "fact" might simply be an illusion. But as we described above, facts alone do not constitute science because an isolated fact without the framework of a theory cannot lead to explanation and to the discovery of new facts, which by definition is the scientific process. Thus, "facts" and "theories" must be distinguished: these two concepts address totally different issues. We show throughout this book that creationism's (and ID's) accusation of evolution being "just a theory" shows great confusion between the notions of "fact" and "theory." And, by the way, when is the last time anyone has heard of Einstein's theory of relativity branded as being "just a theory" even by ID defenders and creationists? There seems to be a lack of consistency on their part in their assessment of the word "theory."

To sum up, a theory can be defined as "organized knowledge applicable in a wide variety of circumstances devised to *analyze* and *predict* the nature of a specified set of phenomena (or facts)." Further, one can say that, in science, progress can be achieved only through the interplay of experimentation or observation (discovery of new facts) with theory (making sense of the new facts). We will show that ID cannot be a scientific theory because it provides no framework to analyze and predict anything in the natural world. In that sense, ID (as well as a literal interpretation of the Bible) can be seen, at best, as a hypothesis (shall we say "just" a hypothesis?), that is, "a conjecture that must be subjected to verification." As we describe in this book, such verification is lacking in the case of creationist and neocreationist worldviews.

Another Misuse of Words

Admittedly, the term "hypothesis" is somewhat of a tongue twister, and for this reason, it is rarely used in common parlance. Yet, it is an important scientific concept. The dictionary definition of a hypothesis, as given above, deserves more explanation. For this, let us provide an example from biology. Everybody knows that DNA is the blueprint of life and that genes are made of DNA. What is less well known is that DNA was discovered in 1871. At the time of this discovery, nobody had any idea what the function of DNA could possibly be. Many even considered that it was just an unimportant by-product of metabolism. In addition, for decades, the accepted theory was that genes were made of protein, not DNA. This is because scientists believed that DNA was the same in all living organisms, whereas proteins varied considerably in bacteria, plants, and animals. Since bacteria, plants, and animals look very different, it was thought that this variety was due to the diversity of the proteins they harbored. We now know that this theory is wrong, but it took many years to disprove.

In fact, it was not until 1952, 81 years after its discovery, that DNA was generally accepted as the substance that actually makes up genes. But then, one should not think that the truth about DNA suddenly dawned upon scientists in 1952. Before that, over the span of about a decade, some scientists, basing their hunch on their own and others' experimental evidence, slowly started seriously considering DNA as the genetic material. This kind of hunch is called a hypothesis in scientific discourse. Thus, in the real world of the laboratory, a hypothesis can sometimes be an educated guess based on preliminary scientific observations (gradually accumulating new facts).

Little by little, as more experimental facts were gathered, it became more and more clear that DNA, and no other natural substance found in living organisms, is indeed the genetic material. What happened in 1952 was the publication of a series of convincing experiments, all based on previous observations that really clinched the issue that genes are made of DNA. This also means that, by 1952, the notion that DNA is the genetic material was no longer a hypothesis; it was now a well-supported theory: the theory of the DNA gene. This theory was further buttressed by the discovery of the double-helical structure of DNA in 1953.

This brings us back to ID. A theory starts in the form of a hypothesis (or a set of hypotheses) that needs considerable verification before becoming a credible theory. With this, it is difficult to imagine ID's position anywhere in the scientific process, especially where verification is concerned. To put it differently, since an intelligent designer of the universe must be God (or equivalent), this means that God must be at first an undemonstrated hypothesis that needs experimental verification. Very few believers in any religion would accept this understanding of God. But then, if God is not a hypothesis, God cannot be a theory, either, because a scientific theory consists of one or more verified hypotheses. The question, then, is whether God is verifiable in a scientific context. It turns out that this question has been raised innumerable times in the history of humankind and has consistently generated the same answer: God cannot be proved or disproved using any kind of rational discourse or experiment. To use one more scientific term, God is a postulate, that is, "an undemonstrated, self-evident proposition that must be accepted on faith alone." Unfortunately, many people confuse hypothesis with theory and with postulate and treat them all equally. As we just showed, the scientific definitions of these words are quite precise and should not create confusion.

Granted, science also relies on some postulates. One very important postulate is that the laws of nature were the same in the very distant past, such as billions of years ago, as they are today. We really have no way of knowing this for sure at this point in our history, but if it turned out that these laws were different a very long time ago, some of our science would have to be revised. So far, doubting the validity of this postulate has found no support in the scientific community. Nonetheless, it goes without saying that science should rely on as few postulates as possible, and it does. By contrast, we can say that ID followers and classical creationists *postulate* the involvement of a divine creator or intelligent designer because they cannot demonstrate its existence using the tools of science. In effect, these people are putting science on its head.

We conclude this section on scientific thinking with a quote attributed to the famous British mathematician and logician Sir Bertrand Russell. When asked what he would say were he to find himself before the Pearly Gates face to face with the Almighty, Russell quipped that his response would be, "Oh Lord, why did you not provide more evidence?"

Unfortunately, Darwinism Ends with "-ism"

Many words with an "-ism" ending (capitalism, socialism, Catholicism, Protestantism, colonialism, Marxism, existentialism, etc.) suggest a system of beliefs, a philosophy, a doctrine, or association with a political party. It is, of course, not Darwin himself who crafted the word "Darwinism." But the problem here is that, contrary to other scientific theories, Darwin's is the only one still referred to by the name of its author equipped with an "-ism." Even though the theory of the gene as elaborated by Mendel (see chapter 2) was called for a time "Mendelism," this expression has been obsolete for a long time. Similarly, one does not speak of "Einsteinism" or "Gell-Mannism" (the latter being the theory of subatomic quarks).

Given this -ism designation, the detractors of Darwin have an easy time characterizing evolutionary theory as being equivalent to a doctrine, even a religious one. For example, one hears people say such things as "I don't believe in Darwinism" or "I don't believe in evolution." Such people use the verb "believe" as in "I don't believe in communism" or "I don't believe in Satanism." But the fact is that nobody is asking anybody else to "believe" in evolution in a doctrinaire sense. Rather, people are asked to first study and understand evolutionary science before dismissing it as just another optional system of beliefs. We doubt that many ID defenders among the general public have gone to the trouble of doing that, which makes it a case of "what you don't know is dismissible." It remains that Christian fundamentalism, a religious movement, claims in a strange twist of logic that Darwinism is no different from a faith-based system of belief, except that here, faith is imbued with godless secular humanism. This is a grave error, because a nonreligious proposition (evolutionary theory) cannot be equated with a religious one.

What did become a doctrine was "social Darwinism," a sad invention of the nineteenth century that has lingered in various forms until the present. Social Darwinism has little to do with Darwin other than being a misapplication of the concept of survival of the fittest. This concept is just one particular aspect of evolutionary theory, but it was latched upon by early social scientists—who also misunderstood the science of genetics—to justify the brash treatment of the lower social classes. For these intellectuals, belonging (and remaining) at the bottom of the social ladder meant absence of fitness to compete in the world, and not only that, but this absence of fitness was hereditary, as well. Social Darwinism was a doctrine, not a scientific theory, and it is best dismissed.

Another unfortunate offshoot of the misapplication of Darwinism and genetics was the eugenics movement. Started in the late 1860s in England, this movement advocated the selective breeding of human beings for the intellectual betterment of the "human race." Characteristically for his time, Francis Galton, the founder of the eugenics movement, considered that people in his society were intellectually superior to Africans, which he singled out. By the early 1910s, the eugenics doctrine had reached the United States, notably through the efforts of Charles Davenport. He, too, considered Africans inferior, as he did people of southern European origins. Nordic people occupied the top of Davenport's list. Regrettably, this type of thinking was endorsed by many people, with the result that anti-miscegenation laws (limiting marriage between persons of certain "races") were established and remained on the books in some states for several decades. Davenport also recommended the sterilization of the feeble-minded and of "wayward" girls. It will surprise many that in Oregon, for example, there are still people alive today who were victims of this sterilization practice, which was outlawed only in 1981. The eugenics doctrine was pushed to its ultimate horror in Nazi Germany. As in the case of social Darwinism, the erroneous doctrine of eugenics should be dismissed or, even better, combated. Let us now turn to another issue relevant to creationism and ID: can science detect purpose in the natural world?

Notion of Purpose in the Universe

Freeman Dyson is an extremely interesting man. He gained fame as a physicist in the 1940s and 1950s for his contributions to quantum theory, the theory that explains the properties of subatomic particles, atoms, and molecules. Some even say that he should have received the Nobel Prize for these contributions. Dyson also became a professor at the Institute of Advanced Studies in Princeton, New Jersey, and thereby became one of Einstein's colleagues. What is most interesting, however, is not just that Dyson is a famous scientist and a well-known science writer. He is also a devout Presbyterian and a winner of the Templeton Prize. This prize rewards those who have distinguished themselves in reconciling (uniting?) science and religion. So, what is it that Dyson did to deserve this prize? He was one of the first modern scientists to suggest that the universe could not have appeared by chance alone: some type of universal mind must have directed the unfolding of events. Although this may be an overstatement, one can think of Dyson as having influenced present-day ID, at least in the realm of cosmology.

Since Dyson is a renowned scientist, his vision should be analyzed carefully and not be brushed off. What follows is a summary of his thinking. The Big Bang theory of the creation of the universe (developed in chapter 5) is grounded in nuclear physics. Modern physics recognizes four fundamental forces that govern the behavior of all matter in the universe. These include the strong force that determines interactions between the fundamental subnuclear particles called quarks, and the weak force, which is also a type of nuclear force. In addition, the electromagnetic force defines how atoms interact with one another in order to make chemical and biological compounds, while the force of gravity dictates how massive bodies such as planets, stars, and galaxies interact to form the large-scale systems we see in the universe. These four forces act with very different strengths, the strong force being the strongest (obviously) and gravity being the weakest by very many orders of magnitude. If the universe had been created with drastically different values accorded the four forces, the whole place would have looked very different.

For example, if gravity had superseded all other forces, the universe today would consist of a very small volume of space containing only gravitationally bound quarks and intense light. Matter as we know it could not have formed, and neither could life have appeared. Dyson then wonders about the reason why the ordering of these forces was such that matter as we know it *did* form, a prerequisite for life to appear and, ultimately, a prerequisite for sentient life-forms like humans to reflect upon this particular occurrence. Dyson sees here the action of a supernatural being or a universal mind who must have ordained the precise values of the four forces in order to allow human beings not only to exist, but also to wonder about the reason why the universe is built the way it is. By extending this type of reasoning further, one can imagine that this supernatural being (God) had a *purpose* in mind when it created our unique universe. This purpose is the creation of a universe where celestial bodies would form and where ultimately life, including human life, could appear.

But in fact, Victor Stenger, a professor of physics and astronomy at the University of Hawaii, has shown that other universes, some populated with stars like ours, are possible. To show this, he simulated putative universes where four basic physical constants, the proton and electron masses and the strength of the electromagnetic and strong forces are varied by 10 orders of magnitude, that is, by a factor of one billion-fold. In more than half of these theoretical universes, stars exist for at least a billion years and, in many cases, much longer than that (figure 1.1). Since it is now thought that planet formation is a direct consequence of star formation, and since planets are, as far as we know, necessary for the appearance of life, it is not outlandish to think that life could also have appeared in some of these other universes. Thus, the notion of a unique universe—ours—created by a supernatural being for a given purpose becomes much less tenable. But, of course, these other universes are not observable by us. Therefore, speculating about other universes and why things are the way they are—with or without God or purpose—in our only knowable universe, fun as this may be, is just that, speculation.

In fact, Dyson himself recognized this to a large extent. As a physicist, he knows and has declared that he cannot prove the existence of a universal mind or God. But as a Christian, his faith tells him that God exists and that God created the universe. In the end, Dyson came to the position that both

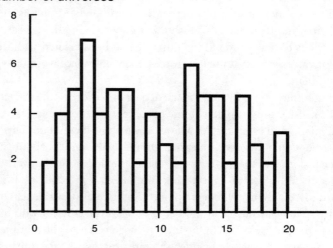

Number of universes

Logarithm of stellar lifetime in years

FIGURE 1.1
Stellar lifetimes in 72 hypothetical, random universes. Stellar lifetimes are expressed in the form of logarithms. On such a scale, a value of zero means a lifetime of just one year. Log values of 5, 9, and 10 mean lifetimes of 100,000, 1 billion, and 10 billion years, respectively, and so on. Of the 72 universes shown, 40 have stars with lifetimes longer than one billion years. By comparison, our sun is about 5 billion years old. Adapted from V. J. Stenger, *The Unconscious Quantum: Metaphysics in Modern Physics and Cosmology* (Amherst, NY: Prometheus Books, 1995).

his faith and his science are correct but that neither can comment upon, or prove or disprove, the other.

Dyson himself never claimed that God is a clever engineer who designed the fine details of living organisms. This threshold was crossed some years ago by genuine proponents of the modern version of ID, as we describe in the next section. To finish this section, we want to emphasize that Dyson is far from being a "classical" creationist in that, contrary to them, he fully espouses evolution. To wit, making reference to the famous nineteenth-century debate between Thomas Huxley (a friend and defender of Darwin) and Bishop Wilberforce (an acerbic critic of Darwin and strong proponent of divine design), Dyson wrote: "Looking back on the battle a century later, we can see that Darwin and Huxley were right." In other words, God as creator is right as a matter of religious faith, and evolution by natural selection is right as a matter of science.

Purpose and Irreducible Complexity:
The Foundations of ID

Michael Behe, professor of biochemistry at Lehigh University in Pennsylvania, is an ardent promoter of ID. Although far from being its lone proponent, Behe epitomizes the movement, and his work is fully representative of it. Behe wrote the best-selling book *Darwin's Black Box: The Biochemical Challenge to Evolution* (1996), in which he hoped to demonstrate that evolutionary biology must be wrong. For him, Darwin and Huxley were wrong, or at least they were very misguided. Needless to say, Behe's book was trounced by scientific reviewers, often in a disdainful fashion. This rough treatment was probably a tactical mistake, because ID has not gone away in shame—on the contrary. Therefore, let us examine Behe's style of argumentation in some detail. As noted, Behe is not the only neocreationist to have come up with ID to refute evolution. All members of the neocreationist Center for Science and Culture (CSC) in Seattle, with William Dembski as their philosophical leader, espouse the notion of ID, which comes in a variety of slightly different flavors that we do not discuss here. Nevertheless, position papers issued by the CSC indicate their goal: "To defeat scientific materialism and its destructive moral, cultural and political legacies. To replace materialistic explanations with the theistic understanding that nature and human beings are created by God." Further, "Accordingly, our Center for the Renewal of Science and Culture [the old name of the CSC] seeks to show that science supports the concept of design and meaning in the universe— and that design points to knowable moral order." One could not be clearer regarding the religious slant of ID and its view that the universe has a purpose.

It should also be kept in mind that Behe's book came out several years ago, in 1996. In the meantime, Behe's ideas have been largely discredited by the fast progress typical of modern biological science. Yet, curiously, *Darwin's Black Box* continues to be invoked by creationists and ID defenders who, seemingly, are unaware of its obsolescence. Behe's book can be considered their scientific "gospel," as it were.

As noted at the beginning of this chapter, ID is not a new worldview; it has evolved from old-style creationism. In the same vein, Behe also had a predecessor, William Paley, a nineteenth-century thinker. Paley is famous for his watchmaker metaphor: a watch cannot appear from scraps of metal and glass alone; to make a watch, a watchmaker is needed. And, indeed, he is right. Other anti-evolutionists have equated evolution to throwing metal and glass into a bag, shaking the mixture well, and ending up with a Rolex watch. Others yet have given the example of a tornado hitting a heap of aluminum, rubber, plastic, and glass, thereby building a Boeing 747. These are all excellent examples of statistically implausible phenomena, but with respect to evolution, these comparisons are all flawed. We show in chapter 2 how evolution really works and that the examples given above are irrelevant to discrediting it. For now, let us just say that our book gives *chance* a prominent place in the process of evolution. However, we will show that evolution is in fact a *cumulative* process that relies entirely on the laws of nature and not on what author Richard Dawkins calls "untamed chance." In his words:

> "Untamed chance," pure, naked chance, means ordered design springing into existence from nothing, in a single leap. It would be untamed chance if once there was no eye, and then, suddenly, in the twinkling of a generation, an eye appeared, fully fashioned, perfect and whole.... The same applies to the odds against the spontaneous existence of any fully fashioned, perfect and whole beings, including—I see no way of avoiding the conclusion—deities. (*The Blind Watchmaker: Why the Evidence of Evolution Reveals a Universe Without Design* [1986])

We will show that this "untamed chance" is exactly what creationism and ID wrongly imply in their refutation of evolutionary phenomena while in fact, as Dawkins shows, it is creationists who invoke the highly improbable! Further, to support their position, ID proponents focus on what they call "irreducible complexity" or variants thereof. For them, all living creatures are equipped with biological properties that must be "just right" and "irreducibly complex" for life to continue to exist. Believers in ID strongly imply biological "perfection" because, they claim, just one slightly out-of-place component of an irreducibly complex system would cause it to fail. Examples usually invoked are the complex blood clotting system of mammals, the mammalian eye, the immune system, and bacterial flagella (these are used by bacteria to propel themselves—swim—in liquid environments). For neo-creationists, none of these biological characteristics could have evolved from simpler ones because they are "perfectly" designed for the roles they play in nature. In other words, something perfect cannot evolve from something imperfect. For example, a structure such as the eye, they say, must be perfect from the very beginning because an imperfect eye (without a retina, for instance) would be useless. The same goes for imperfect bacterial flagella and an imperfect blood clotting system. Thus, evolution as a theory cannot be valid because these perfect, irreducibly complex organs and metabolic systems could not possibly have originated in the distant past as less complex, less perfect, in a sense more primitive, biological properties.

Like Paley before them, neocreationists make heavy use of metaphors. For example, Behe discusses at length how it is impossible for a perfect bicycle or a perfect mousetrap to evolve from an imperfect one. Take away the pedals and the bicycle no longer works. Take away the spring and the mousetrap is now useless. And to equip the bicycle with pedals and the mousetrap with a spring takes a designer. And so it goes for all living systems, they claim. This is the origin of the intelligent designer doctrine. We show in chapter 3 how science rebuts this claim—and we also show that mousetraps *can* evolve—but for now, let us examine how well metaphors apply to scientific concepts.

Simple metaphors can be very helpful to illuminate complicated concepts. But by their very nature, they are limited precisely because they simplify reality. This does not necessarily make them useless, however. What is much worse, as in the examples of the watch, the bicycle, and the mousetrap, is that the metaphors used by neocreationists all imply a *purpose* determined by the designer. Bicycles without riders, watches without time keepers, and mousetraps without mice (or without humans who want to trap mice) are irrelevant. Therefore, ID supporters are caught again in a situation where the designer (God) knew exactly how, when, and for whom flagella, eyes, and blood clotting systems needed to be created. This type of thinking is called *teleological*, a philosophical belief system that we develop later. For now, suffice it to say that many biological systems are quite imperfect (even though they are complex), and further, nobody—including neocreationists—has ever been able to read the mind of the "designer" and decide *why*, for example, mammals have the type of eyes they have whereas insects have different eyes. Evolutionary science does not answer this "why" question, but it shows very well that irreducible complexity is incorrect because it shows "how," for example, it is possible for a mouse gene to make flies grow strange eyes, as we show later.

In all fairness, we must also say that some ID defenders have now somewhat veered away from the untenable position that living organisms were created perfectly. Whether this represents an evolutionary or political step in their thinking is unclear. However, since perfection was originally an important implicit concept in the development of ID, we find it necessary to devote some space to its discussion.

Before moving on, one last point needs to be firmly established. Arguments against ID and for evolution are not comments on the existence or nonexistence of God or any supernatural force. These are metaphysical matters beyond science, upon which science cannot comment. Evolutionary scientists themselves may personally be theists or atheists or agnostics—it does not matter as far as their science is concerned. What science *can* comment upon, however, is natural process, and its view of this process is very much in conflict with teleology-oriented ID thinking.

The final parts of this chapter move to discussion of religion, broadly speaking, in relation to questions of evolution. We begin with discussion of origin myths in general—what are they? Are they universal? And how similar is the creation story in Genesis to origin myths in countless other cultures?

Creation Myths and Mythology

All cultures of the world have origin myths, or religious stories of how the world, life, and especially human life, or the existence of a particular people, came to be. Collected from around the world, these stories constitute rich oral traditions and creative human expressions. They are a form of verbal art, sometimes later written down in religious texts.

Often, origin myths reflect a peoples' view of nature and their place within it. For example, anthropologist William Haviland discusses how an origin myth among the Abenaki (an indigenous group in New England and Canada) reflects the Abenaki cultural idea of the unity among all living things. In this myth, a supernatural being, Tabaldak, created all life. As for humans in particular, at first he mistakenly tried to make them out of stone, but this did not work because it left their hearts too cold. Then Tabaldak tried again, using living wood, "and from this came all later Abenakis. Like the trees from which the wood came, these people were rooted in Earth and (like trees when blown by the wind) could dance gracefully." To Haviland, this mythological sanction of a unity in all life, symbolized in the necessary origin of humans from living wood, is related to the Abenaki's special respect for all nature and other animals.

The creation account in Genesis also reflects a view of humans in relation to nature, one quite different from that of the Abenaki. Here humans are apart from and dominant over nature. God said of humans, "Let them have dominion over the fish of the sea, and over the birds of the air, and over the cattle, and over all the earth, and over every creeping thing that creeps upon the earth" (Genesis 1:26, King James version). Fish, plants, and beasts were given by God to humans for food.

Beyond accounting for the origin of the world and life, myths can also provide explanations of why life is as it is or how many things came to be as they are. For example, the Nuer people of East Africa provide a mythological account of why some people have white skin and others have black skin. Here, a high god, Kwoth (spirit of the sky), gave Europeans white skin as punishment for an act of mother-son incest committed by a pair of their ancestors. In Nuer mythology, we also have an explanation for death. At one time there was no death. Earth was connected to heaven by a rope; when people became old, they climbed up the rope to reach Kwoth in heaven, where they were rejuvenated and then returned to Earth. But then one day a bad hyena managed to climb the rope and reach heaven. Kwoth commanded the hyena to never return to Earth since He knew the hyena would only cause harm if he did so. One night, however, the hyena escaped and descended down the rope. Nearing Earth, the hyena cut the rope and the portion of rope above the cut spiraled back to heaven. The link between heaven and Earth was gone, and from that time all those who grew old had to die on Earth.

The origin story in Genesis also accounts for various aspects of life. Here we have an explanation for why women suffer in childbirth. As a result of Eve partaking of the forbidden fruit, God said, "I will greatly multiply your pain in childbearing; in pain you shall bring forth children" (Genesis 3:16). We also find an explanation for why man must till the soil, for Adam also disobeyed God's command. God said to Adam, "Cursed is the ground because of you; in toil you shall eat of it all the days of your life" (Genesis 3:17–18).

Origin myths from around the world often share common themes. Floods, for example, are frequent. Also common are explanations for human suffering through people or animals disobeying divine commands, as described above. Many origin myths also make statements about the nature of men and women or the relationship between the genders. The Genesis account is quite clear about this; God said to Eve, "Your desire shall be for your husband and he shall rule over you" (Genesis 3:16). Some Nuer myths blame women for earthly ills; for example, it was women who in mythological times brought mosquitoes to Earth. Among the Navajo, an origin myth describes how Navajo deities (Holy People) lived in worlds below this one. Then one day, escaping a flood, they reached the surface of Earth and became the Earth Surface People, the first Navajo. In one story, before this emergence to Earth's surface, First Man learns of the adultery of his wife and hits her. His wife complains to her mother (Woman Chief), who scolds First Man, telling him that she, not he, is ruler of all things. In retaliation for this insult, First Man calls all the other men together, and they decide to leave all the women and live separately on their own. Both sexes suffer from the separation, especially from frustrated sexual desire. Yet as time passes, women fail at growing food, but the men are successful. The men are thus victorious over women in this battle of the sexes, but they realize they must reunite with the women in order to procreate and perpetuate their group, and so they do so.

This Navajo myth has been interpreted in different ways. Some scholars suggest it may have developed as the Navajo were shifting from hunting and gathering to agriculture. In this idea, agriculture was initially conducted mostly by women, depriving males of their roles in subsistence. Later, men were active in agriculture, and the myth might represent men's attempts to regain their status as providers. Other scholars see in this myth the Navajo cultural theme of a complementarity of the sexes. It was a woman's adultery that caused the trouble, but in the end both sexes suffer from the separation and reunite, realizing they need each other. Either way, as with all myths, this one reflects the history and culture of the mythmakers.

Anthropologists have also found that origin myths, like folktales and other oral and written literature, are commonly structured through binary oppositions—pairings of contrasts such as good and evil, male and female, culture and nature. The account in Genesis abounds with such binary oppositions—Earth/heaven, dark/light, night/day, land/sea, man/woman, to name a few. Anthropologist Claude Lévi-Strauss considered that binary oppositions are so common in humans' oral and written expressions because the human mind itself is organized to think this way. We find these myths and stories attractive because they "fit" the way our minds are constructed and we can use binary oppositions to symbolically generate meaning.

Origin myths are wonderful, meaningful stories that reflect both universal human concerns and distinctive cultural conceptions. But to what extent have people actually believed them, in the sense that creationists believe in a literal interpretation of Genesis? This is a difficult question. The nature of "belief" in myths is no doubt variable, from literal interpretation to what is undoubtedly more common—an understanding of myths as symbolically relevant or spiritually significant, but not as literal truth. Another aspect of origin myths that does appear to be unique to Christian creationism (and perhaps also Judaism) is the concern to pin down an exact time (in real, calculated human time) when creation occurred. This has led creationists to propose the "young Earth" idea, far out of line with scientific evidence. In most other cultural traditions, as far as we know, there is not a concern with a real-time framework for acts of creation. Creation is considered to have occurred in some cosmic time, outside a sense of time as we know it.

Creation Versus Evolution in Other World Religions

As we mentioned above, ID proponents and creationists in the United States are followers of particular versions of the Christian faith. But Christianity is far from being the only religion accepted and practiced by people on Earth. Therefore, let us now see how major religious traditions, other than Christianity, view the process of evolution. Not all religions or religious accounts of divine creation conflict with evolution. Thus, before moving on to the science of evolution, we end this chapter with a section addressing an interesting question: aside from Christianity, how do other major world religions view the issues of scientific evolution and divine creation? To what extent are

FIGURE 1.2
Representatives of some of the major non-Christian denominations in
the world. Clockwise from top left: a Jewish woman celebrating
Hanukkah with a "nouveau" menorah; Nepalese women celebrating the
Hindu festival of Teej; a Buddhist monk in Thailand; a Muslim bride-
groom from Bangladesh (from Linda Stone's collection).

there conflicts between the two in these religions? And are creationist
movements present within world religions outside Christianity? In what
follows, we discuss these matters in relation to Islam, Judaism, Hinduism,
and Buddhism.

Islam

"Islam" is an Arabic word meaning both "submission" and "peace." At the
core of the Islamic faith is the idea that a Muslim submits to Allah (God),
thus finding spiritual peace. Islam emphasizes the oneness and unity of
Allah, that Muhammad was his final prophet (in Arabia in the seventh

century C.E.), and that the Quran is Allah's divine word recited by Muhammad. The general belief is that the Quran is to be fully understood only in the original Arabic. Lives of Muslims are governed by the Five Pillars of Islam: (1) the witness—"I witness that there is no God but Allah; I witness that Muhammad is His Prophet"; (2) five daily prayers to Allah; (3) the giving of alms to the less fortunate; (4) fasting, as an expression of gratitude to Allah, especially during the month of Ramadan; and (5) a pilgrimage, if feasible, to the holy sites in the city of Mecca in Saudi Arabia once in one's lifetime.

As with Christianity, there is within the vast world of Islam a wide spectrum of opinions on evolution versus creationism or ID. On the one hand, many Muslims around the world maintain that there is no conflict whatsoever between evolution and the tenets of Islam. At the other end of the spectrum, the teaching of evolution is forbidden in the Islamic nation of Saudi Arabia. In addition, Muslim followers of Wahhabism (the dominant version of Islam in Saudi Arabia) reject evolution, holding that it is incompatible with Islam. This movement (now more often called Salafism) is named after a person who lived in Saudi Arabia in the 1700s. It has sought to restore Islam to its original form. Other than this, we are aware of only one creationist movement in the Muslim world. This movement is based in Turkey and goes after the name of Harun Yahya, which is apparently the pen name of Adnan Oktar, an author known for his writings about "Zionist racism." According to Oktar's Web page, "Harun" is translated as "Aaron" and "Yahya" means "John." These, according to Oktar, are his two favorite prophets. Taner Edis of Truman State University in Kirksville, Missouri, has written a cogent critique of this movement (see Web site listed in Further Readings), so here we only summarize the main characteristics of Harun Yahya.

Like the Bible, the Quran declares special creation without evolution. In the past, Muslim clerics rarely bothered to dismiss evolution, the concept of which they saw as a sign of moral decrepitude of the West. According to Edis, this attitude started changing in the recent past in the most industrialized Muslim country, Turkey, in reaction to modernization. Much like conservative Christians in the United States, says Edis, a fraction of Turkish society has found it necessary to reaffirm traditional religious values in the midst of scientific and technological advances of which they are suspicious. Interestingly, Harun Yahya takes advantage of modern electronic technology in that it produces videos and CD-ROMs, in addition to having sophisticated Web sites in a variety of languages. For this reason, it is difficult to believe that Harun Yahya is a one-man operation, Oktar's alone, given that he is also credited for having written "hundreds of books." Rather, Harun Yahya has all the characteristics of a well-designed organization.

The Quran is less detailed than the Bible in its account of the origins of life and the universe (the Quran mentions Adam and his spouse—who is not referred to as "Eve"—but does not specify how the universe was created). As a result, Muslims generally have no qualms with the idea of an old Earth. On the other hand, Islam can be fertile ground for ID principles, as much as Christianity is.

Harun Yahya's anti-evolution Web page is extremely similar to Christian creationist and ID pages. These might as well be copies of one another. The same misrepresentations of evolution are offered, in the same sequence, and using the same examples. Also, Harun Yahya vilifies Darwinism, making it responsible for, among others, terrorism and fascism. Of course, American creationists usually do no go that far, although some U.S. evangelical leaders have blamed the 9/11 attacks on our materialistic society, no doubt further vitiated by Darwinian ideology. Harun Yahya promulgates that school-children be instilled with the fear of God, a fear supposedly diminished by pernicious and godless Darwinism.

Judaism

Judaism is the oldest monotheistic religion still in existence today. Like Islam, but unlike Christianity, it rejects any pictorial representation of God. But unlike both Christianity and Islam, Judaism does not affirm that Satan is the inventor of evil.

Jews and Christians alike recognize the Old Testament, in particular, its first five books, called the Torah in Hebrew. Thus, there exists in Judaism also the potential for a literal interpretation of the Genesis creation myth. On the other hand, Jews do not recognize Jesus Christ as the Messiah, and the Christian view of the New Testament is not shared by them. Nonetheless, Jews, Muslims, and Christians alike are "people of the book"; that is, all believe in revealed religions. It is probably safe to say that God (Gott in German, Θεος in Greek, Deus in Latin, Dieu in French, Dio in Italian, Бor in Russian, and so on), YHWH, and Allah are very similar if not identical concepts.

One complication in the Jewish interpretation of Genesis, however, is the existence of several main branches of Judaism: Orthodox, Conservative, and Reform, as well as many other variants such as Reconstructionist and Ultra-Orthodox. Another complication is the absence in Judaism of a centralized authority in matters of doctrine, leaving it up to potentially many religious leaders to offer their own interpretation of the sacred texts. And there is the old joke: "Three Jews, four opinions."

Historically, the general attitude of Judaism has been that the creation account in Genesis should not be taken literally: it is symbolic rather than descriptive of an actual fact. The great medieval Jewish philosopher

Maimonides even wrote that only ignoramuses would take Genesis literally. On the other hand, the age of Earth, how life-forms came to be, and the timing of the appearance of humans are still very much debated by Jewish scholars. For example, there is no general agreement on what is meant by "days" in Genesis. Be that as it may, many Orthodox rabbis see the theory of evolution as being compatible with the Jewish faith. Some, however, do not. On the other hand, expectedly, all agree that God played and plays a role in the events that unfold in the universe. One can say that observant Jews *believe* in the spirit of the Torah but do not necessarily equate it with actual fact. Further, Jews consider that the Old Testament should be read and understood in conjunction with Jewish scholarly texts such as the Talmud, for example. Interestingly, many Jewish people understand that science, too, evolves and that, for some Jews, current scientific knowledge simply represents our best understanding of what ultimately God did.

Concerning the teaching of ID in public schools in the United States, several Orthodox and Reform rabbis in Kansas City made their views crystal clear. In 2005, these rabbis showed their total opposition to the teaching of ID in science classes, which, at that time, had been recommended by the Kansas Board of Education. Intelligent Design, they said, is not science; it is theology. Therefore, teaching it in public schools would violate the separation between church and state. Apparently, this opinion represents the general stance of American Jewish leaders.

But even so, things are not that simple. In a radio interview just after the Kansas decision, Rabbi Brad Hirschfield, vice president of the National Jewish Center for Learning and Leadership, complained that American society sees the ID/evolution issue in a much too polarized fashion. In his words,

> Most creationists relate to evolutionists as if they have no soul, and most evolutionists relate to the creationists as if they have no brain. Since according to Jewish tradition we all possess both, this is where our discussion should begin—no small feat in a culture in which the absolute obliteration of the other side's views is often the only basis for thinking that one's own position is correct. (Quoted from the NPR Web site)

This, Hirschfield says, "is totally inconsistent with the Jewish intellectual tradition of healthy debate, the acceptance of multiple positions on complex issues, and the awareness that even those claims judged to be incorrect still have a great deal to teach us." Further, for Hirschfield, "both the positions of Darwinian evolution and those of the intelligent design theorists can fit with classical Jewish thought."

From the above, we can see that some leaders in the Jewish community are divided regarding the intellectual value of ID: some reject it outright, whereas others are willing to give it a chance.

Hinduism

Hinduism is a religion of diverse gods and goddesses, elaborate ritual, and a striking tolerance for diversity, or the possibility of different spiritual paths for different people and at different times in their lives. Amidst all the diversity within Hinduism are the unifying concepts of *dharma* and *moksha*. Dharma refers to the religious duty to maintain and perfect the world and society. Moksha refers to spiritual release from this world, often by renouncing society. There are various ways and means within Hinduism to both maintain the world and seek ultimate release from it.

Contrary to monotheistic Judaism, Islam, and Christianity, polytheistic Hinduism has a plurality of religious texts. Such books as the Rig-Veda, the Upanishads, and the Bhagavad-Gita come to mind. Likewise, Hinduism has more than one myth of creation. One version restricts itself to saying that some sort of substance, *prakrit*, is at the origin of all that exists in the universe. Another version is much more descriptive; it explains how the universe is reborn multiple times in cycles of destruction and creation. In this story, each new creation originates from a vast ocean that washes upon the shores of nothingness. In the middle of this ocean, Lord Vishnu, asleep in the coils of a giant cobra, is awakened by the sound of Om, the sacred syllable. This is how the dawn of creation breaks. From Vishnu's navel appears a lotus flower, within which is Brahma, the god of creation. Vishnu then orders Brahma to re-create the cosmos, and he and the cobra disappear. Brahma uses parts of the lotus flower to build the universe, including Earth, which he then populates with humans. Fascinatingly, Brahman, The One (extremely approximately, more or less the equivalent of God, the universal essence, in monotheism), plays no role in the cycling of the universe.

Interestingly, the Rig-Veda, the oldest Hindu sacred text, wonders whether the story of the primal ocean interacting with nothingness is just speculation and, if so, whether this speculation is valid. After all, even the gods appear after the cosmic principle emerges. Therefore, the Rig-Veda does not present its version of the creation of the universe as fact. Nonetheless, as with many religions, there is the potential for Hinduism also to generate its own fundamentalism.

Hindu fundamentalism does in fact exist. It is probably best represented by the large Bharatiya Jananta Party (BJP), which was recently voted out of power in India. The BJP is an ultra-nationalist movement whose aim is to show and teach the ascendancy of all things Hindu, from history to science. In particular, the BJP advocates the development of "Vedic science" based on the posited scientific superiority of Hindu sacred traditions. These traditions include astrology, transcendental meditation, faith healing, and the antiquated (and wrong) humoral theory of diseases. For the BJP, all these traditions could easily be meshed with modern science, where, for example, quantum indeterminacy is seen as supporting the Atman (universal spirit)/Brahman (creative principle) duality mentioned in the Upanishads. Following a curious combination of physics, religious philosophy, and medicine, some even speak of quantum "healing"! In addition, the BJP equates nuclear explosions with some events described in the Bhagavad-Gita, thereby proving that nuclear physics was already known to ancient Indo-Aryans. The BJP has not yet succeeded in imposing its views on a significant fraction of the Indian public. Also, the BJP does not advocate ID or anything like it. The BJP has not singled out the theory of evolution as a threat to Hindu values.

Hindu fundamentalism, then, is not interested in detracting science (including evolution) or proving it wrong but in integrating Vedic and Hindu traditions within the main body of science. This may reflect the enormous power of syncretism in Hinduism. As David Kinsley put it in his book *Hinduism: A Cultural Perspective* (1982), Hinduism historically has been an "incurable collector," incorporating a great diversity of ideas and rarely discarding anything. The result has been Hinduism's renowned tolerance for a diversity of religious ideas and practices.

Yet even in India, there is a small battle between science and creationism: Western fundamentalist Christian organizations are currently proselytizing there. One of these organizations is the Creation Science Association of India Trust, based in West Bengal but coordinated by individuals in the United Kingdom and in the United States, where donations should be sent. This creationist association is indistinguishable from its American counterparts. Christianity has never made significant inroads in India, and it is likely that Christian creationists will not be any more successful than were traditional missionaries.

One can see that in Hinduism there is little, if any, conflict between creation and evolution. For one thing, Hinduism can easily reconcile the idea of creation (through Brahma the Creator) with that of change (evolution) as represented by the 10 incarnations (Dash avatars) of Vishnu, the Protector. In addition, as a colleague from Hindu India pointed out, the idea of humans descending from a long line of animal ancestors would not be a problem in Hinduism, where there is such a high value on animal life and some animals (cows, for example) are considered sacred. One great god, Hanuman, is a monkey. Hindu mythology is also replete with animals taking human forms and vice versa. In addition, the Hindu idea of reincarnation includes humans reincarnating into animals and animals reincarnating as humans in endless cycles.

Buddhism

Buddhism is an offshoot of Vedism (the precursor of Hinduism) that appeared between 600 and 500 B.C.E. It is traditionally associated with Nepalese Prince Sakyamuni Gautama Siddharta, the historical Buddha, who was himself preceded by many other Buddhas, at least in the major Mahayana (the Greater Vehicle) religious tradition. Like Hindus, Buddhists believe in the concepts of *samsara* (cyclical rebirth, reincarnation), *moksha* (spiritual release or salvation), *karma* (the accumulated effect on the soul of morally important deeds), and The One. However, they reject the Hindu pantheon, and Buddhism is in fact a religion without a defined deity or deities. As with Hinduism, change and transformation of the universe are familiar concepts in Buddhism. Buddhism is probably best known in the West for advocating an end to human suffering through several cycles of reincarnation and ultimate enlightenment.

The teachings of Buddhism are collectively known as *Dharma*, which includes the Four Noble Truths that Buddha realized upon his own Enlightenment: (1) *Life is full of suffering.* Everyone experiences or witnesses pain, sickness, loss of loved ones, old age, and death. Moments of pleasure or happiness are always impermanent, fleeting. (2) *The cause of suffering is desire.* Desire is egoistic attachment. People are focused on their selves and their cravings. (3) *Life's suffering can be stopped by stopping desire* (transcending egoistical attachment). (4) *Desire can be stopped by following the Eightfold Path,* which is basically following a moral, compassionate, and selfless style of life.

After this very brief introduction to Buddhist philosophy, let us see whether it is compatible or not with evolutionary science. First, we should point out that, contrary to what is happening with Judaism, Christianity, Hinduism, and Islam, there is no such thing as Buddhist fundamentalism, nor are there political parties based on Buddhism. In addition, Buddhism does not recognize any particular myth of creation, making it impossible for evolutionary science to conflict with Buddhist texts. In other words, Buddhism does not have the equivalent of Genesis and its counterpart in the Quran, or the equivalent of Hindu sacred texts explaining our origins.

There are, however, local origin myths in many of the areas to which Buddhism spread and adapted. One interesting example is an origin myth from Korea, where a Siberian tiger and a bear sought to become humans. The son of the king of the eastern heavens (Hwan-ung) told them he would bring this about if they could endure harsh austerities in a dark cave for a number of days. The tiger gave up before the deadline and left, so he remained a tiger, but the bear endured to the end. This bear was then transformed into a beautiful woman. When the woman went to thank Hwan-ung, he was so struck by her beauty that he married her. Their child was later the ancestor of a main branch of the Korean people. While Korean people know and enjoy this story, they understand it as a myth, not a literal account of their origin. It may actually be based on historical fact—two clans, one worshipping a bear totem and the other having a tiger totem, may have fought in ancient times, with the bear clan winning.

We saw that a literal interpretation of the Bible and the Quran must preclude any kind of evolutionary continuum between all life-forms: humans have a God-given soul whereas animals, plants and others do not. This belief is not held in Buddhism (or Hinduism), which, through the doctrine of reincarnation, posits that a mind (or soul) can occupy many types of physical bodies. Further, for Buddhism, in contrast to Christianity, there is no idea of a supreme divine force influencing events in the world or impinging upon the lives and destinies of humans. On the contrary, what happens in the world and what happens to us all follows from within us: our destinies follow from our own karma. In a sense, we are solely responsible for our fate. On a larger scale, what happens in the world is ultimately a product of mind, and there is no creator of mind.

What can we conclude from this admittedly brief foray into the reception of evolution in non-Christian world religions? First, it appears that evolution can be a problem in the more orthodox or fundamentalist portions of three world religions—Christianity (mostly Protestantism but more rarely Catholicism), Islam, and Judaism. All three are monotheistic religions with the idea of one God as creator. Further, these are "revealed" religions. Possibly, then, a powerful single creator God with a strong message about the origin of life sets a frame for some within these faiths to see evolution as a threat to religious conviction. By contrast, neither Hinduism nor Buddhism is monotheistic or revealed, and neither sees evolution as a threat. No supernatural force within polytheistic Hinduism reveals one divine Truth. Buddha's teachings are not revelations of a higher supernatural power; they are the result of Buddha's own Enlightenment, and they do not address the origin of Earth, life, or humans. In addition, Hinduism and Buddhism contain strong ideas of change, transformation (for example, reincarnation), and impermanence that make evolution less of a new and unfamiliar view of life.

In the United States, both Intelligent Design, a new creationism, and classical creationism may have another dimension aside from monotheism and revelation. A wonderful film called *In the Beginning* (2000) covers the evolution versus creationism debate in the United States, making every effort to be as objective as possible. In this film, the narrator asks a creationist, "What is the basis for your belief in a literal Genesis account of creation?" One expects the creationist might say that he believes the Bible is the literal word of God, or something to that effect. But what he answers is: "Just look at this country!" Note he does not refer to the world, but only the United States. He goes on to deplore the moral degeneration of the country, referring to such issues as widespread drug use and alienated, hedonistic youth. He and other creationists in the film feel that scientific evolution is the cause of this deplorable state; it is the enemy because it is a secular account of our origin that strips away spiritual meaning from our existence and fosters immorality. These concerns about the United States and its many social problems are understandable. But is evolution *really* the cause? Or is evolution an easy scapegoat? Would it not be wiser to search for economic, political, and cultural roots of what troubles us in our contemporary world?

After this introductory chapter, we next turn to what evolutionary science really says. As we show in chapter 2, Darwin did not invent evolutionary theory. He, too, had predecessors. What is more, modern evolutionary biology incorporates several concepts that were unknown to Darwin, making this branch of science much more complete and compelling than original Darwinism.

Things to Think About

This section recaps the main points made in this chapter. This summary can also be used as a basis for further discussion.

1. Intelligent Design and creationism are not that different as far as their basic premises are concerned. Both invoke the intercession of a supreme being in the unfolding of natural events. Both claim that life-forms were created basically in their present form; they did not evolve. However, ID—at least superficially so far—has veered away from a literal interpretation of Genesis.

2. The words "fact," "theory," "postulate," and "hypothesis" assume very specific meanings in scientific language. Plain English often conflates these terms, with confusing results that are often exploited by ID thinkers and creationists.

3. Scientific theories are frameworks for the discovery of new facts. Similarly, new facts potentially lead to the formulation of new theories.

The interplay of new experimental facts and new theories is at the core of the scientific process. The expression "this is just a theory" makes no sense at all in science. Similarly, the expression "I believe (or not) in such and such a theory" makes no sense, either, because science relies on evidence and reason, not faith.

4. Nature (or the cosmos at large) has no obvious purpose discernable by science. Nature and the cosmos simply *are*. Wondering whether things exist for a particular reason is not a scientifically answerable question, because, for one thing, such a question has an infinite number of possible answers. For another, ideas about a purpose in nature cannot be objectively tested. Ideas about nature's purpose are, however, valid in metaphysical or religious realms that seek spiritual understanding. What is your opinion?

5. Faith and beliefs in divinities do not belong in the scientific world. Nor do scientific concepts and methods belong in the world of religious faith. Why is it that some people want to merge the two, in spite of countless unsuccessful attempts in the past centuries?

6. Monotheistic religious fundamentalism seems to be at the root of both creationism and ID. Thus, these movements do not represent the majority view of the great world religions.

7. Of the five major world religions examined in this book, only Buddhism and Hinduism seem united in their acceptance of evolution. Why is this so?

2

What Is Evolutionary Biology and Where Is It Coming From?

Evolution is a tinkerer.
> —François Jacob, 1965 Nobel Laureate

The notion that living species of animals and plants are immutable is probably as old as humankind. A casual observation of the natural world does not readily suggest that species evolve or, for that matter, that the surface of our planet also changes over time. This is because human life spans are too short to witness these events directly, except in cases of catastrophic volcanic explosions and earthquakes. Nevertheless, the concept that life-forms could evolve may first have been formulated in ancient Greece by the sophist Empedocles. This idea was quickly abandoned. It was not until the late 1700s that scientists (they were called naturalists in those days) realized that the apparent fixity of species and a seemingly mostly inert surface of Earth are illusions. At this time, several thinkers began to revisit the dogma of a young Earth and immutable living species. Five naturalists stand out in their overturning of the old ideas and their introduction of the notion of *transformism* in biology and the earth sciences: Georges Louis de Buffon (1707–1788) and Jean-Baptiste de Lamarck (1744–1829) from France, and Charles Lyell (1797–1875), Charles Darwin (1809–1882), and Alfred Russel Wallace (1823–1913) from England. Through their works and those of their followers, we now know that Earth is very old, that its surface has been (and is being) constantly reshaped, and that living species change over time. In other words, these scientists introduced the idea of dynamic natural effects acting over long periods of time, overturning the old theory that nature is essentially static and "fixed" in time.

Buffon, Lamarck, Lyell, Darwin, and Wallace

Buffon was the first naturalist to propose that living organisms evolve, although he could not provide a mechanism for this evolution. Lamarck, his intellectual successor, picked up where Buffon left off and did propose an explanation for the evolutionary change of life-forms. He published his thoughts on the topic in 1801, followed by a more extensive book that came out in 1809, the year Darwin was born. Lamarck was a naturalist interested in comparative anatomy. This led him to categorize animals based on their anatomical similarities or differences. While doing this, he hypothesized that relatedness between animals could be construed as relatedness *in time.* In other words, he proposed that the closer two species were anatomically (such as cats and dogs), the closer was their appearance in time. Anatomically very different species (such as worms and horses) were seen as having appeared in eras much separated by time. But Lamarck went further than that. He also imagined that species could transform into others over long periods of time. On the other hand, for Lamarck, extinction of species did not take place; old species disappeared because they evolved en masse into new species. This is no longer the view of modern science—we know today that most species that have populated our planet in the last 3.8 billion years or so are now extinct, having left no descendants.

Also, Lamarck envisioned that species evolution was not driven by chance. For him, evolution resulted in increased complexity, gradually moving toward "perfection," the most "perfect" state of evolution being represented by humans. In that sense, Lamarck viewed evolution as somehow having been driven toward a "goal," the appearance of human beings. Again, modern evolutionary thinking has abandoned the notion of evolution being "guided" by some mysterious principle toward what we could call biological "progress," with humans at the top of the scale. Likewise, evolutionary science no longer considers that humans are more perfect than, say, worms. Yes, humans are more complex than worms, but they are not more perfect than worms in an absolute sense, and certainly not more adapted to their natural habitat than are worms.

In fact, the notion that there exists a natural scale measuring "perfection" is an old one. What is called the "Great Chain of Being" was first proposed by ancient Greek philosopher Aristotle and was further developed by the medieval scholastic thinker St. Thomas Aquinas (1225–1274). Its corollary, the idea of biological, and even moral, "progress," is a concept that survived into the nineteenth century (and quite possibly is still alive today in some quarters). This concept seems to have influenced Lamarck. The Great Chain of Being ranks all things according to their absolute "value" or "essence." At the top of the Great Chain stands God, and at its bottom stand rocks. The Great Chain can be simplified as follows:

God
Angels
Kings/Popes
Archbishops
Dukes
Bishops

Barons
Knights
Ladies-in-waiting
Priests
Pages
Merchants
Landowning farmers
Soldiers
Servants
Shepherds
Beggars
Actors
Thieves
Gypsies
Animals
Worms
Plants
Rocks

This structure immediately suggests that the "value" of a plant is less than that of a priest, for example. In other words, going up from the bottom of the ladder, the "value" of things—living or not—"progresses" from, to use other examples, that of a Gypsy to that of a baron and, even more so, to that of an archbishop. Of course, many people today, especially soldiers, might not agree that their "value" ranks lower than that of ladies-in-waiting, as per Aquinas's construction. This whole line of reasoning is in fact a very slippery slope. Indeed, this type of scale has been used in the past to "prove" the inferiority of women to men and some ethnic groups to others, and often, such unacceptable discrimination was sanctioned by religious authorities.

Going back to Lamarck, he is best remembered for his proposition that characters *acquired* by animals over their lifetime can be transmitted to their progeny. According to this proposition, the neck of the giraffe, for example, would get longer over generations because giraffes, in their quest for tall tree leaves for food, continually stretched out their necks to reach these leaves. This acquired character, according to the Lamarckian view, was then inherited by the progeny of these neck-stretching giraffes. We now know that acquired biological characters (whatever they may be, such as the acquired ability in humans to jog for long distances) are not heritable.

Briefly summarized as it is above, Lamarck's record may look negative, but we must remember that he was the first to develop a theory of evolution, primitive as it was, and can be rightly regarded as one of Darwin's intellectual predecessors. Darwin himself acknowledged this. We describe in a later chapter how the thinking of Lamarck has been revived in the social sciences, because Lamarckian transmission of acquired characteristics applies quite well to human *cultural* evolution, if not biological evolution.

Charles Lyell was also a predecessor—and friend—of Darwin's. At first interested in mathematics, Lyell soon turned his attention to geology. For him, as for Lamarck, Earth could not possibly be as young as just a few thousand years. He realized that processes such as erosion by wind and water, as well as the formation of geological layers, are extremely slow, meaning that visible features of Earth's surface must have taken considerable periods of time to materialize. In addition, Lyell was very interested in fossils and stratigraphy, the order in which rock layers are laid down. He realized that in many cases fossils found in rock layers close to the surface were relatively abundant and resembled the skeletons of contemporary animals. By contrast, fossils found in deeper layers were much scarcer and did not look anything like modern animals. The deepest layers often contained no fossils at all. Lyell hypothesized that deep rock layers were much older than superficial layers, which also led him to hypothesize that fossils found in deep layers were older than those present in layers near the surface. This thinking led Lyell to hypothesize further that, over long periods of time, living species diversified and became more complex. Lyell thus went beyond Lamarck because he empirically determined a temporal sequence during which the evolution of species had taken place. Of course, Lyell could not measure the age of the geological formations he had studied, but he could establish a *relative* ordering of the appearance of new rock layers and new species. The *absolute* dating of rock formations and fossils became possible only in the twentieth century, thanks to the discovery of radioactive dating techniques. These techniques—and others—confirmed Lyell's vision.

As for Darwin, he was well aware of the thinking of Lamarck and Lyell, and he continued in the footsteps of his predecessors. It is well known that Darwin undertook a long voyage to South America aboard the *H.M.S. Beagle*, that he collected finches in the Galápagos Islands, that he was independently wealthy, and that he developed his theory in an 1859 book titled *On the Origin of Species*. As we described above, Darwin did not invent evolution—others before him had already come up with this concept. Rather, Darwin invented the concept of *descent with modification* and proposed that new species arise from older ones through a branching process. This concept was then joined to a second principle, that of *natural selection*. These are the two great innovations that we owe to Darwin. These concepts are so important, and often so misunderstood, that it is worthwhile to explain them in some detail.

Although it now seems that Darwin's extensive study of finches in the Galápagos Islands is apocryphal, when he returned to England Darwin brought back several specimens that were later categorized into different species by one of his colleagues at home. That apparently is when the notion of descent with modification germinated in Darwin's mind. Since twentieth-century researchers actually *did* study the evolution of finches in the Galápagos, and since finches are so iconic, we concentrate here on this example.

Descent by modification means that different species of organisms, for example, different species of finches, *diverged* over time from a common ancestor through a *random* process that introduced variation in some of the physical characteristics of these finches. For instance, some species of Galápagos finches have a stubby beak while others have a fine beak. Such different physical characteristics were supposed by Darwin to be heritable. How, then, can one understand that these heritable characteristics are maintained in different finch populations and not lost as randomly as they appeared?

It turns out that stubby-beaked finches feed on hard seeds, which they can crush easily, while fine-beaked finches prefer soft seeds. One can then imagine that, at some time in the past, variants of finches that had randomly developed a stubby beak became more *adapted* to feeding on large seeds, while the fine-beaked variants restricted themselves to feeding on small seeds. This also means that, wherever large seeds were prevalent, stubby-beaked finches had greater *fitness* over fine-beaked finches, meaning that stubby-beaked finches found better nutrition and hence reproduced to a greater extent than did fine-beaked finches. This situation was reversed in niches where small seeds were prevalent. This is the essence of natural selection: ecological circumstances dictate which species (or individuals) prosper and proliferate (they are the best fit) as opposed to other species (or individuals) that dwindle in numbers because they are less fit under the same natural conditions.

The mechanism of natural selection, which in this example is simply the nature of the food found in a certain environment, would "decide" which finches would survive and proliferate best. It should be noted that this type of "decision" is completely undirected and entirely dictated by natural circumstances. This notion is very different from the one invoked by Lamarck, in which evolution is somehow "driven" to achieve perfection.

Thus, according to the idea of evolution by natural selection, there is a tight interplay between ecological conditions and either proliferation or potential extinction of biological variants within populations of organisms. Given enough time, deeply changing ecological circumstances, and/or physical isolation of subpopulations, entirely new species—that is, populations of organisms that can no longer interbreed—would appear.

Those who claim that Darwin's idea of natural selection has never been verified are wrong. American scientists have observed populations of "Darwin's Finches" in the Galápagos for over a decade and have concluded that, indeed, beak shape is heritable. Even more significant than that, as the Galápagos experienced cycles of droughts and wet weather, the availability of small versus large seeds cycled back and forth, which caused the different finch subpopulations (thin vs. stubby beak) to cycle accordingly in real time. Many other experimental observations, discussed further below, have confirmed the process of evolution by natural selection.

For natural selection to act, not only must variation be present spontaneously in a population of living creatures, but this variation must also be heritable. Darwin did not know how this inheritance worked, but he noted that *artificial selection* exercised by pigeon breeders for certain types of plumages *did* lead to the production of lineages where the desired type of feathers was inherited. Darwin then reasoned that in the case of the wild finches (and other organisms, for that matter), natural selection replaced the intervention of the breeders, but that the result was the same: a certain type of variant proliferated more than another one.

There are, of course, many other cases of evolution by natural selection. For those who find the evolution of finches insufficiently compelling, here is an example involving mammals. There are two basic types of mammals: placental mammals whose embryos are nourished by a placenta (as in humans), and marsupial mammals (or pouched mammals) such as kangaroos. Both types of mammals have evolved from a common ancestor. Wherever these two varieties of mammals meet, placental mammals tend to outcompete the marsupials. How, then, does one explain that marsupials have existed and proliferated for a very long time, particularly in Australia? It turns out that many millions of years ago, the continents were grouped together to form a single supercontinent. Through the process of continental drift, which is still observable today, the supercontinent broke up, one result of which was that Australia became a vast island isolated from the other continents. Marsupials were spreading in the direction of Australia before it became an independent continent, while most placental mammals were spreading in other directions. Therefore, marsupials found themselves separated from their placental competitors and were able to thrive and continue to evolve as soon as Australia broke free from the supercontinent. Elsewhere, such as in North and South America, marsupials would either become extinct or remain a small minority. We can thus see that geography, including continental drift, which isolates landmasses from one another, also plays an important role in evolution.

Other excellent examples of evolution by geographic isolation can be found in Madagascar, the large island located 300 miles east of southern

Africa. Much of the fauna and flora found there are unique to the island and are not found elsewhere in the world. Geologists think that Madagascar once was connected to Africa but started to drift away from it about 150 million years ago. As is widely known, Madagascar is home to several species of lemurs, primates that are ancestral to both monkeys and apes. It is thought that the ancestors of lemurs first appeared in Africa and that some individuals were then somehow carried to Madagascar, perhaps on floating logs. Interestingly, lemurs no longer exist in continental Africa, where they were presumably outcompeted by monkeys and apes. However, monkeys and apes did not evolve on Madagascar, and neither did large predators, allowing lemurs to evolve there into several subspecies. In the same vein, it is estimated that 90% of the 13,000 or so plants species found in Madagascar are indigenous, including more than 1,000 species of orchids.

Finally, evolution by natural selection explains well the common presence of flightless birds on remote islands. Flying creatures are obviously able to colonize islands that are not normally reachable by terrestrial mammals. For example, New Zealand has only one native mammalian species: bats. This means that New Zealand had no predatory mammals until the arrival of humans and one of their food sources, rats, about 1,000 years ago. It so happens that New Zealand has several species of ancient flightless birds, including the well-known and endangered kiwi and kakapo. We know that the islands of New Zealand separated from a large landmass that included Australia at least 80 million years ago. Thus, the ancestors of the kiwi and the kakapo were either trapped in the New Zealand islands when they drifted away from Australia, or they flew over the growing expanses of ocean separating the two landmasses. Once established in the New Zealand islands, given the existence of an easily accessible source of food on the ground and given the absence of predators, one can see how these birds could have evolved to a flightless species. First, flightless variants would have appeared in the population by spontaneous mutation. Subsequently, these variants would have survived and proliferated because no predators would have taken advantage of their inability to escape by flying away. Over time, these variants could have turned into entirely new species, such as the modern kiwi and kakapo.

We show in chapter 4 that geographical circumstances also played a role in the evolution of *Homo floresiensis*, an extinct dwarf member of our own genus, *Homo*. In fact, dwarfism (reduction in size) is observed when mammals migrate out of their original niches to reach isolated islands, as happened to the Nile basin hippopotamus (very large animals) after some of them swam across the Mozambique Channel to reach Madagascar a long time ago. Hippos in Madagascar are known as "pygmy" hippos, in reference to their reduced size. More examples of new species formation, independent from geographic isolation, are discussed in chapter 6, after we provide a thorough description of the molecular mechanisms of evolution at the level of DNA.

Going back to Darwin, a major problem that would nag him was that he did not know how variants (different beak shapes in finches, different feathers in pigeons, and different embryonic development in placental and marsupial mammals) could spontaneously appear, nor did he know how these different characteristics were inherited. This problem was solved by Gregor Mendel and many others in the next few decades, thanks to the development of the science of genetics.

As we mentioned above, Darwin hypothesized that new species appear through a branching process. Recall that this mechanism is different from that imagined by Lamarck, for whom species evolved en masse from pre-existing species, making extinction impossible. For Darwin, only *some* members of a species would gradually evolve, literally branching out from the main trunk of the rest of the species, leaving the other individuals unchanged and able to continue to multiply and potentially evolve in a different direction, or go extinct. To use just two examples, Darwin's view agrees with the fossil record that all dinosaurs are now extinct, but their evolved descendants are still with us: they are birds. Similarly, our biological—and anatomically distinct—predecessors *Homo erectus* are also extinct, but we *Homo sapiens*, their descendants, are still very much around. This is what the concept of *descent with modification* means.

Figure 2.1 gives a very simple representation of this process. Here, species A is ancestral to species B, C, D, and E but has itself become extinct. In other words, species A evolved into B and C, which still exist today. In turn, some members of species D branched out from B, and E branched out from some members of C at a later time. Both D and E also still exist. This type of representation, called a cladogram, whose groups of species are called clades, immediately suggests that some species are older than others, a concept fully supported by modern genetics.

As is often the case in science, great discoveries do not come alone. As Darwin was mulling over his field observations and was building his evolutionary theory in his mind, Wallace, another naturalist, had come to the exact same conclusions as Darwin. Wallace had traveled extensively in the Amazon (in South America) and the Malay Archipelago (in Southeast Asia). He collected tens of thousands of biological specimens during these travels. He was also well aware of Lyell's work on fossils and geological layers. And it so happened that Wallace, too, stumbled upon the idea of evolution by natural selection. The existence of a competitor spurred Darwin to speed up

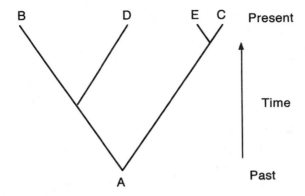

FIGURE 2.1
The representation of descent with modification. Species A existed in the past and evolved into species B and C before becoming extinct. Species D then evolved from B, and later, E evolved from C. Species B, D, E, and C are alive today. Such a figure is called a *cladogram*, in which the grouping of species E and C, for example, is called a *clade*.

the writing of his opus magnum, *On the Origin of Species*. Nonetheless, the theory of evolution by natural selection is usually called "Darwinism" by its detractors, instead of "Darwinism-Wallacism" (admittedly an awkward expression). Scientists, on the other hand, often refer to the theory of evolution as the Darwin-Wallace theory.

It should by now be clear to concerned readers that evolutionary biology does not claim that humans directly descend from apes as they are today. Rather, and referring back to figure 2.1, humans and apes shared a common ancestor a very long time ago (for example, ancestor A). This ancestor is now extinct, but it evolved into what would become ancestral humans (for instance, *Homo habilis* and *Homo erectus*) and then modern humans (*Homo sapiens*), on the one hand, as well as the great apes (orangutans, gorillas, and chimpanzees), on the other hand. Modern genetics and DNA studies fully confirm this view.

Mendel and Others

Darwin always felt that his theory was incomplete because of the lack of mechanisms to explain the existence of variants in natural populations and the transmission of these variations to offspring. Going back to the finches, how is it that some finches have long beaks and other have short beaks? In addition, how is it possible that finches with long beaks have offspring with long beaks and finches with short beaks have offspring with short beaks? Today, we have answers to these two questions: biological variants are genetic mutants, and genes are transmitted in stable fashion from parents to offspring.

Before describing gene mutation and gene transmission, we wish to debunk the claim that mutations are always deleterious. This misconception is widespread among the public and probably stems from the fact that genetic diseases are indeed due to mutations and that some are severe and negatively affect the lives of some of us. Diseases such as sickle cell anemia and phenylketonuria (PKU) may come to mind. But it should be remembered that these diseases are rare, and what is more, some of these seemingly deleterious mutations turn out to be *advantageous* under certain circumstances, in accordance with the theory of evolution by natural selection, as we show further below. Moreover, we now know that the great majority of mutations have no effect on our health because they affect portions of our DNA that play no role in our well-being. These mutations are called *neutral* mutations. They are neither beneficial nor detrimental.

Gregor Mendel (1822–1884) is rightly seen as the "father" of genetics. Mendel was a Catholic monk trained in physics and biology who lived in the city of Brno, then part of the Austro-Hungarian Empire and now located in the Czech Republic. As many people know, Mendel established his laws of genetics based on the work he did with pea plants. He was a contemporary of Darwin, but Mendel and Darwin were completely unaware that their respective studies were of great relevance to each other.

At first sight, one might wonder what pea-plant genetics has to do with the grand scheme of evolution. It turns out that Mendel's laws of genetics are applicable not only to plants but also to reptiles, mammals, birds, and so on, and yes, human beings. This is not the place to give a detailed account of Mendel's discoveries, however. Rather, we focus on just two of Mendel's conceptual approaches. First, Mendel concentrated on the breeding of pea plants that showed sharp, visible differences (these are called contrasting traits by geneticists). Some of his plants were tall, and some were dwarf. Some set yellow seeds, and some set green seeds. Some set round seeds, and others set wrinkled seeds. Today, we would call these plants mutants or variants of one another (for the purpose of this book, these two words are equivalent). For example, wrinkled seeds are the result of a variant in a gene that determines the formation of some compounds necessary to make the seeds look round. The variant gene no longer produces this compound, and as a result, the seeds look wrinkled.

Mendel then mated plants bearing green seeds with plants bearing yellow seeds, as well as tall plants with dwarf plants, and he studied the properties of the progeny plants. This was his first great insight: he used as experimental objects plants that were easy to differentiate by the unaided human eye. He observed in the offspring of his mating crosses that progeny plants continued to show—in very precise proportions—the visible properties of the parents. For example, a cross between tall plants and dwarf plants yielded both tall and dwarf progeny plants in the second-generation offspring. This result contradicted how heredity, as it was understood in those days, was supposed to function. For breeders at that time, the idea was that heredity resulted in the *blending* of parental characters. In that view, Mendel's experiments with tall and dwarf plants should have yielded intermediate-height plants. They did not. From this first observation, Mendel concluded that units of heredity are particulate, whole units of inheritance. They did not blend in offspring; they stayed the way they were in the original parents.

Next, and without entering into details, the precise proportions between two variants (green vs. yellow, etc.) that Mendel observed in his crosses led him to infer that units of heredity (which we now call genes) in individuals come in *pairs*. In other words, each individual contains *two* copies of each gene, one received from the mother, and one received from the father. The following example helps to clarify this concept, using the *Rhesus (Rh)* gene, a gene important in blood transfusions in humans. The Rh blood group was first detected in rhesus monkeys, hence its name. Evidently, rhesus monkeys and humans share this blood group and the genes that determine it, which, by the way, is a first hint of an evolutionary mechanism at work. Note that we italicize the names of genes, a standard practice in genetics.

The *Rh* gene comes in two variants, *Rh* positive (*Rh+*) and *Rh* negative (*Rh−*). Let us assume that Mendel was right and that each individual possesses two copies of each gene. In this example, we assume that both parents each harbor one copy of the *Rh+* variant and one copy of the *Rh−* variant. Thus, they both are *Rh+/Rh−*. Mendel also hypothesized that when reproductive cells form, the two copies of each gene separate, meaning that germ cells, eggs and sperm cells, end up containing a *single* copy of each gene. Thus, the mother in our example will produce 50% eggs containing the *Rh+* variant and 50% eggs containing the *Rh−* variant. For the father's sperm cells, these proportions will be the same. A simple matrix shows what kinds of results can be expected in the progeny of these two parents:

		Mother's eggs (*Rh+/Rh−*)	
		Rh+	*Rh−*
Father's sperm cells (*Rh+/Rh−*)	*Rh+*	*Rh+/Rh+*	*Rh−/Rh+*
	Rh−	*Rh+/Rh−*	*Rh−/Rh−*

Each box in the matrix represents a potential baby resulting from the fertilization of a particular egg by a particular sperm cell. We see that when eggs and sperm cells combine, there is a 25% chance (one box out of four) that the baby will be genetically Rh+/Rh+, a 50% chance (two boxes out of four) that it will be Rh+/Rh− (and thus identical to both parents for that trait), and a 25% chance (one box out of four) that the baby will be Rh−/Rh−.

This is exactly what is observed in countless other examples in an enormous variety of plants and animals. Mendel was right, and his theory complemented Darwin's, accounting for how variation appears and is transmitted. Darwin's theory of evolution by natural selection and Mendel's theory of the gene are the only two formal (amenable to mathematical analysis) theories that exist in the biological sciences.

Thus, in one fell swoop, Mendel had demonstrated how the transmission to offspring of genes and their variants occurred in a predictable manner. He had also demonstrated that traits are transmitted whole and not in a blending fashion. These are the mechanisms that Darwin needed to buttress his theory but that he did not know at the time. The synthesis between Mendel's theory of the gene and Darwin's theory of evolution was achieved many years later, starting mostly in the 1920s, with early attempts already made at the turn of the twentieth century. But before describing this synthesis, it is worthwhile to examine what mutations and mutants (variants) are and how they come into existence.

It is only after the discovery of the DNA double helix in 1953 and the molecular understanding of genes (starting in the late 1950s and continuing to date) that researchers have had a good grip on the nature of mutations. DNA is a very long, double-stranded molecule containing in its center a succession of pairs of units called bases (adenine, A; thymine, T; cytosine, C; and guanine, G) that form the "rungs" of the DNA "ladder." In DNA, an A in one strand always faces a T in the other strand, and a G always faces a C. Human DNA contains about 3.1 billion such base pairs, the *sequence* of which is known. It is the sequence of the base pairs in DNA that constitutes the blueprint of life, our genes. Through a succession of complicated mechanisms, the genetic instructions present in the DNA base-pair sequence are converted into proteins, compounds largely responsible for the traits we can see (such as yellow or green color in pea seeds, eye color in humans) and, more often, cannot see (such as the nature of our *Rh* blood group, which takes laboratory procedures to determine).

It is thus easy to understand how a change in DNA base sequence sometimes results in a changed trait. This change is heritable and is by definition a mutation. Base-pair changes in DNA occur naturally and spontaneously or can be the result of a chemical (such as a carcinogen) or physical (X-rays, ultraviolet rays) attack. Figure 2.2 shows how a base-pair change is inherited by the descendants of a mutated DNA molecule. In essence, mutations are heritable because DNA molecules are duplicated through the copying of each strand of the double helix. This copying mechanism thus ensures that a base pair modified by mutation continues to be represented in the offspring of the mutated DNA.

However, as we mentioned above, most mutations have no effect on traits. This is because 95% of our DNA is not expressed in the form of traits. We do not know for sure what this large portion of our DNA does, but it does not contain genes as we understand them. Recent discoveries indicate that some of this DNA is involved in the regulation of gene activity. Nevertheless, we know that significant portions of our DNA are free to mutate without known consequences, creating new variants that cannot be distinguished through visible traits but can be detected by DNA analysis. In many cases, it is the nongenetic portion of DNA that is used to study evolution, including human evolution.

Today, we know the sequences of hundreds of thousands of genes from hundreds of organisms. Many mutant and variant traits have a known molecular basis. For example, the disease cystic fibrosis is due to the lack of a functional protein that regulates the uptake of one of the atoms present in

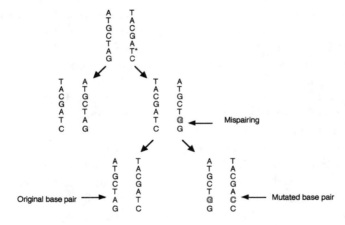

FIGURE 2.2
Mutation in a DNA double helix. Affected base pair is identified by an asterisk. Top and middle: as the two strands of DNA separate and replicate, the T in the right-hand strand (top) mispairs with a G, instead of an A (middle), in the newly formed strand. When the DNA molecule containing an abnormal T-G pair replicates, the strand containing the G will produce a G-C pair (bottom). Thus, an A-T pair present in the top DNA molecule has become a G-C, mutated pair in one of the daughter molecules.

salt, chlorine. As another example, some humans carry a mutated hemoglobin gene that gives their blood a higher affinity for oxygen and hence makes them more adapted to life at high altitude. Many humans in societies where milk is an important source of nutrition are tolerant to the sugar present in milk, lactose. The latter two are examples of beneficial mutations.

Moreover, a gene responsible for the production of long or short beaks in Darwin's finches has been identified. In 2006 it was shown that a gene—the calmodulin *CAM* gene—that controls the activity of other genes involved in tissue development is hyperactive in the embryos of the Cactus finch, which has a long, thin beak. This *CAM* gene is much less active in the embryos of finches with stubby beaks. When the Cactus finch hyperactive *CAM* gene is introduced into ordinary chicken embryos, the chickens so produced have long, thin beaks. Therefore, we know now that a variant (mutant) version of the *CAM* gene is present in Cactus finches and that this gene controls, at least in part, beak shape in these birds. We can now understand the finch story much better. Finch variants with different beak shapes due to the higher or lower activity of their *CAM* gene appear spontaneously in natural populations through the phenomenon of mutation. This mutation is then transmitted to the progeny of these finches in a stable, predictable manner. Then, depending on which types of food in the form of seeds are available, finches with a variant (mutant) beak will find themselves better or less fit for survival and reproduction compared with the nonmutant finches. If they are better fit, given enough time and unchanging ecological circumstances, the mutated variants will outcompete other finches for food, with the consequence that the variants will reproduce preferentially and become more numerous. This is, in a nutshell, how evolution by natural selection works. Given enough time (often millions of years or more), mutations accumulating in individuals and subject to natural selection can profoundly change many different traits and lead to the formation of new species.

With our understanding of how gene variants appear, how variants may show differential fitness, and how enhanced fitness is transmitted to progeny, we have come nearly full circle in the explanation of evolution. Nearly, but not quite completely. Evolution is also determined by factors other than natural selection, something that Darwin never envisioned. Let us now see what these factors are and how their existence was discovered.

The New Synthesis: Moving Beyond Darwin

Mendel's laws of genetics are statistical in nature. We showed above that it is possible to predict the *chances* of a baby carrying a particular set of gene variants, although it is impossible to predict *which* baby among successive births will inherit any given specific set of variants from its parents. Thus, when thinking in genetic terms, one should keep in mind that genetics is essentially based on probability. Since evolution takes place over time in populations of individuals that vary in size, and since mutations also occur in a probabilistic way (it is impossible to predict exactly which individual will mutate and when), it is not surprising that evolutionary biology was sooner or later to incorporate statistics. In fact, the branch of genetics called population genetics, which deals with evolution, is highly mathematical. Unfortunately, this makes it more difficult to convey the modern aspects of evolutionary theory to the general public in a simple and convincing way.

The few professional life scientists who have joined the ranks of creationism or Intelligent Design (ID) do not discuss this mathematical aspect of evolution in their books and web sites, perhaps because they do not know it, or they do not understand it, or they think the public will be bored and confused by abstract concepts. In reality, Michael Behe, the famous defender of ID, is a biochemist who prefers not to engage in discussions involving the mathematical aspects of evolutionary theory. This is not a particularly convincing stance for someone who claims that evolutionary theory is wrong, but ignoring the most sophisticated, mathematical aspects of evolution also allows him not to alienate (and by the same token, to misinform) the public.

In what follows, we show that evolutionary thinking, like life itself, also evolves with time. This is not to say that Darwin had it wrong: he simply laid down the foundations of a great theory that was subsequently broadened and refined by hundreds of his followers. Significantly, five of these followers were Sewall Wright (1889–1988) in the United States, Wilhelm Weinberg (1862–1937) in Germany, and Godfrey H. Hardy (1877–1942), J. B. S. Haldane (1892–1964), and Sir Ronald Fisher (1890–1962) in England. These five couched evolution by natural selection in mathematical terms, a process that enabled the quantitative estimation of the outcomes of evolution. This new approach is sometimes referred to as the "New Synthesis." Although we do not present any equations in what follows, we discuss some of the central mathematical points of population genetics that are relevant for the understanding of evolution.

First, population geneticists view populations of living organisms as gene pools (bags of genes, if you will) characterized by certain gene variant *frequencies*. To understand this, just think about the frequency of the human *Rh+* gene variant in the whole world (it is about 84%) and compare it with the frequency of the same gene in Europe (it is only 64%) or in Asia (where it is a high 95%). Clearly, Europe ranks well below the world average, while

Asia ranks well above. This is because European and Asian populations moved in different evolutionary directions regarding the $Rh+$ gene variant.

Another interesting example is that of a human gene variant known to *enhance* susceptibility to malaria, often a fatal disease. In sub-Saharan Africa, where malaria is endemic, the frequency of this variant is essentially zero, as evolution by natural selection predicts. In Australia, where malaria does not exist, the frequency of this variant is 99%. Here again, the reason for this big difference is natural selection: a gene favoring the incidence of malaria is rapidly selected *against* in regions where the disease exists. Where malaria is absent, the frequency of this gene can become high without consequences for the population. Differences in frequencies among human populations are known for hundreds of gene variants, and of course, such differences are also known for nonhuman populations. Knowledge of gene variant frequencies is crucial for the study of evolution.

Another very interesting example of natural selection is sickle cell anemia, a human genetic disorder of the blood. The molecular basis of this disease is very well known: it is a single base-pair mutation present in the gene that determines the blood protein hemoglobin that is responsible for ferrying oxygen to our cells. The mutation strongly decreases the affinity of hemo-globin for oxygen and is of course deleterious, even lethal. To understand the evolution of sickle cell anemia, let us first go back to Mendelian principles. Remember that humans carry two copies of each gene, except that males have only one copy of genes located on the X chromosome. Females, how-ever, have two X chromosomes. Males also have single copies of genes lo-cated on the Y chromosome. On the other hand, females do not have a Y chromosome at all.

In our sickle cell anemia example, let us also call the normal hemoglobin gene variant A and the abnormal (mutant) variant S. Since these genes are *not* located on the X or the Y chromosome, all humans possess two copies of this gene. Thus, humans can carry the combinations A/A, A/S, and S/S, depending on which variant(s) they received from their parents. A/A indi-viduals are of course normal, but S/S individuals are very sick and, without treatment, die at a young age. But what about A/S individuals? They, too, are normal, because the presence of a single A variant provides enough normal hemoglobin for its carrier to live a normal life. But then, how is it that this deleterious gene variant, S, was maintained in the human population rather than being quickly selected against given its lethal effect? The answer again is evolution by natural selection.

It turns out that, in spite of its deleterious effect in S/S individuals under all circumstances, the presence of a single S variant in A/S individuals *protects them against the effects of malaria.* This is because the red blood cells of *A/S* individuals are less susceptible to the effects of the malarial parasite than are the red blood cells of *A/A* individuals. Thus, normal *A/A* individuals will get infected with malaria more often and more severely than will *A/S* individuals. This also means that the former will die from malaria more easily than the latter and thus reproduce less frequently. This is another classical case of natural selection in humans. In an environment where malaria exists, the malarial parasite negatively selects *A/A* individuals by killing them, whereas *A/S* individuals are favored for survival and reproduction because they are more resistant to the disease. This is exactly what Darwin predicted could occur, and it confirmed his principle of natural selection through differential reproduction. And indeed, the frequency of the *S* gene variant is much higher in areas infested with malaria (as in Nigeria) than it is in areas of the world where malaria does not exist.

Another case of genetic disease caused by a defective gene variant, phenyl-ketonuria (PKU), seems to have had a positive effect in human evolution. It is present at reasonably high frequency in northern Europe but is rarer in the rest of the world. Let us call the abnormal gene variant *p* and its normal counterpart *P*. As with sickle cell anemia, *P/P* and *P/p* individuals are normal. On the other hand, *p/p* individuals are affected and afflicted with mental retardation, unless they are put on a strict diet low in the amino acid phe-nylalanine. So again, how does one explain the presence today of this defective, deleterious variant? It seems that here also, individuals carrying a *P/p* gene combination were at an advantage over normal *P/P* individuals. A *P/p* genetic makeup seems to have made humans more resistant to toxins produced by molds growing on spoiled foods, a common occurrence in the wet climate of northern Europe. Now, in periods of famine (frequent in the European Middle Ages and even later), spoiled food was better for survival than no food. *P/P* individuals, being more sensitive to the mold toxins, died more frequently after consuming moldy food and thus reproduced less. This did not hold true for *P/p* individuals, who could eat spoiled food without suffering dire consequences. The selective agents here that caused this evolutionary trend were toxic molds that grow in humid and cool climates, which explains why the PKU variant is found at higher frequency in northern Europe than in other parts of the world.

The few—among many—examples given above undeniably demonstrate that natural selection is a "force" that has shaped and is shaping gene frequencies in human populations, which by definition means Darwinian evolution of these populations. Of course, populations of animals and plants also evolve in a Darwinian fashion.

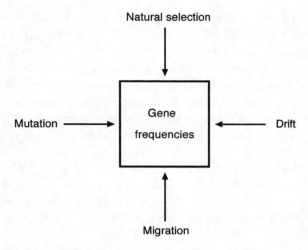

FIGURE 2.3
The four evolutionary forces that act on gene frequencies in populations
of organisms.

Let us now go back to the notion of populations of living organisms
defined as groups where gene variants exist in particular frequencies—gene
pools. Figure 2.3 represents such a population as a square, showing four
different factors that can modify gene frequencies in populations. As described above, mutations can alter gene frequencies by acting at random on
preexisting genes and thereby creating new variants. However, mutations are
very rare and so will create new gene variants at a very slow pace. Nevertheless, the constant creation of random gene variants is critically important
in evolutionary biology because mutations are the raw material of evolution.
Without the random creation of mutations, evolution would not take place.

As also described above, natural selection, the second evolutionary factor,
will "decide" whether newly created variants are more fit or less fit under a
given set of environmental circumstances and hence will proliferate more or
less. Therefore, so far, our population in figure 2.3 is subjected to two natural
"forces": mutation and natural selection. Darwin had of course discovered
natural selection, but it is only well after his death that the nature of mutations was correctly understood. In addition, Darwin never knew and hence
never took into account the existence of two additional natural forces:
migration and genetic drift. The later addition of these two new forces of
evolution completed evolutionary theory as we know it today.

The notion of migration is self-explanatory: individuals from one population migrate into another population or leave an existing population to

colonize new grounds, carrying their genes, present in particular frequencies, with them. For simplicity, the effects of migration on evolution are discussed in chapter 4, which considers human evolution in the past several million years. For now, let us just say that migration, when it involves small numbers of individuals, can result in genetic *bottlenecks*. The word "bottleneck" means here that such a small number of individuals do not necessarily represent the average genetic composition of their original population. For example, let us assume that gene variant *A* is present in 90% of the individuals of a population numbering 10,000, and that variant *a* is present in only 10% of these individuals. If only 10 members of this population migrate elsewhere and become isolated, with such small numbers they could *all* carry *A* or *a*, or any other ratio between 90% *A* and 10% *a*, purely by chance. There is no reason to believe that nine individuals (90%) will be carriers of variant *A* whereas only one (10%) will carry variant *a*. Thus, a genetic bottleneck can deeply influence gene frequencies in small, migrating groups that become reproductively isolated from their original population and then start multiplying independently. This phenomenon then leads to genetic differentiation between subgroups, which, by definition, is evolution. An associated concept is that of *founder effect*, whereby a small migrating group founds a new population that, over time, becomes very different from the original population, particularly if the new group cuts all ties with the original group and so no longer interbreeds with it.

Let us now concentrate on genetic drift, also called random genetic drift, or simply drift. This is another aspect of evolutionary theory characteristically avoided by creationists and believers in ID. Today, it is thought that drift has played and is playing as important a role in evolution as is natural selection. Thus, evolution is a process more complex than Darwin had imagined. But the existence of drift refines (and indeed, makes more complex, including mathematically) evolutionary theory without negating Darwin's great contribution. What then, is drift?

Drift and Evolution

Population geneticist Motoo Kimura published in 1968 a revolutionary article that delighted both creationists and mainstream biologists. This article laid down his "neutral theory of evolution." Creationists were enthralled because they thought that Kimura had proven Darwin wrong. Their enthusiasm was of short duration, however, because Kimura did nothing of the sort, and he made this very clear right away. Biologists were enthused because Kimura was incorporating into his theory newly obtained results on the molecular nature of mutations. As we mentioned above, most mutations are neutral: they do not affect the functioning of genes in negative or positive ways and thus have no effect on fitness. However, this does not mean that these mutations do not take place. They are very much recognizable at the DNA sequence level, but they do not influence the fitness of organisms. In other words, these mutations are not susceptible to natural selection. How then, do these mutations play a role in evolution? The answer provided by Kimura is drift.

To understand this concept, let us think again in terms of populations of individuals. At any given time, only a certain percentage of individuals in a population engage in reproductive activity. By and large, this number is about one-third of the members of a population because old people and children do not reproduce. This, then, means that gene variants (recall that changes in gene variant frequencies over time constitute evolution) passed on to progeny represent only a *sample* of the gene variant frequencies present in the *total* population. Just what sample of gene variant frequencies is passed on is purely a matter of chance. Mathematical population genetics shows that, depending on the size of a population, some gene variants can become extinct (representing a frequency of 0%) while other variants can become fixed (representing 100%) over time. For small populations, this effect can take place in just a few generations. This is what drift means: some gene variants can quickly disappear and other gene variants can take over a population purely by *chance* alone because of the *chance sampling of re-producing individuals.*

Thus, evolution takes place because of Darwinian natural selection, which depends on the interplay between carriers of gene variants and their fitness in a given environment. But in addition, evolution is also dependent upon purely statistical factors such as drift. A natural habitat changes constantly (and hence so does natural selection), and on top of that, chance factors— such as mutation and drift—are also operating. So it is no surprise that people who believe that some type of creation act should lead to "perfect" and "irreducibly complex" organisms through some "guided" mechanism feel uncomfortable with evolution. Evolution relies too much on chance and unguided natural events. To paraphrase the title of one of evolutionary biologist Richard Dawkins's books (*The Blind Watchmaker*), the watchmaker— the designer, if one exists—must be blind.

And finally, why do detractors of evolution mostly discredit Darwin but not all his followers, who are as guilty, if not more so, of evolutionary thinking? As we showed above, Darwin discovered and explained only one aspect of evolution. This brings us to the next step, the notions of tautology and teleology, the first used by creationists to discredit Darwin, and the second used by mainstream scientists to criticize creationists.

The Two Big Ts

Creationists accuse evolutionary biology (in its simplest, original Darwinian form) of being *tautological* or, in other words, circular. The word "tautological" refers to an explanation that seems true whether or not the parts constituting the explanation are true or false. One good example of a tautological statement is "All crows are either black, or they are not black." This sentence is a tautology because it is true no matter what color crows are. In the case of Darwinism, the expression "survival and reproduction of the fittest" is seen by some as a tautology because, indeed, it can be said that the fittest survive and reproduce simply because they are the fittest. Looked at in isolation, this phrase is a typical circular argument. But is this all that evolution has to say? We think not.

A scientific circular argument can be resolved by looking at it from the outside. If this argument conflicts with experimental data, it should be rejected, like any such argument. In the example of sickle cell anemia described above, in regions affected by malaria, the proportions of individuals carrying the *A/A*, *A/S*, and *S/S* gene variant combinations have been measured. These proportions are skewed in favor of *A/S* individuals (who are resistant to malaria) and skewed against *A/A* (sensitive to malaria) and *S/S* (lethal because of the presence of two *S* variants, with or without malaria) individuals. We also noted that the malarial parasite is a selective agent in the case of the *A* and *S* variants.

There happens to be a mathematical equation, called the Hardy-Weinberg theorem, which allows one to calculate gene frequencies in populations in the absence of any selective factors. When this equation is applied to populations where malaria is absent (for example, African Americans living in the United States, many of whom are descended from West African populations), the observed ratios between the three gene combinations conform to the theoretical equation, taking into account the lethality of the *S/S* combination. Not so, however, with Nigerians who live in malaria-infested areas of West Africa, who have a ratio strongly skewed in favor of the *A/S* type. The comparison between theoretical and observed numbers, then, actually allows one to obtain a *quantitative* estimate of the fitness of the different gene combinations under natural selection by malaria. In conclusion, "survival of the fittest," in a real-life context is no longer a phrase used to summarize and simplify a concept; it becomes a measurable quantity. Also, the fitness of various gene combinations in humans, plants, and animals has been measured on innumerable occasions, and all results concur that fitness is a fact of life.

And now for *teleology*. Nothing in science should be teleological. This notion is in fact antithetical to the way science works. Teleology is a rarely used term, and it helps to provide a good definition of it. According to the *American Heritage Dictionary of the English Language*, second edition (1985), teleology is "the philosophical study of manifestations of design or purpose in natural processes or occurrences, under the belief that natural processes are not determined by mechanism but rather by their utility in an overall natural design."

Even a casual reading of this definition reveals that creationism and ID are teleological. As we discussed in chapter 1, creationism (sometimes referred to as "creation science") and ID espouse the view that natural processes, which are the ones studied by science, are designed and hence have a purpose. Further, teleology also implies utility rather than mechanism. Utility, in this particular instance, means the achievement of a goal, such as the formulation of "perfect" types of structure, for example, the human brain or the bacterial flagellum. In addition, evolution is a mechanism and hence contradicts the idea of utility in natural phenomena. Clearly, evolution must be rejected in a teleological, creationist or neocreationist (ID) context because evolution is unguided—it is blind. But is it only evolution that is anti-teleological in the whole of science? After all, this is the branch of science that creationists and ID proponents have attacked all along. The answer to this question is a resounding no.

Assuming teleology in any scientific activity is tantamount to saying that chemistry and physics also have a purpose and were also designed. It turns out that creationists and ID proponents carefully avoid the notion of design in the physical sciences (except cosmology). We described in chapter 1 how physicist Freeman Dyson comes close to the idea of a "designer" when he discusses the fabric of the universe. But Dyson's idea of a "designer" does not include the notion of a designer's goal, at least not in a way that is analyzable by science.

Then, one must assume that ID and creationism are slanted against the life sciences in general and evolution, in particular. This is not too surprising, because it is easier to imagine the works of a "designer" when one contemplates the complexities of living organisms and the capabilities of the human brain. But how valid is the claim that a "designer" manufactured living species? Is this a religious issue, or is it a scientific one? This question is tackled in chapter 3 and beyond. We also show in the following chapters how scientists have repeatedly confirmed the reality of evolution, making it one of the greatest scientific theories ever formulated.

Things to Think About

1. Like all solid scientific concepts, the theory of evolution has benefited over many years from the input of many scientists. In the process, the theory of evolution has also evolved. This type of change over time holds true for all good scientific theories. Even Einstein's theories of

relativity have evolved and were never seen by their discoverer as immutable views of the physical world. This is a sign of scientific good health because incorrect theories eventually perish.

2. Modern evolutionary theory incorporates much genetics. This fact is generally ignored by ID enthusiasts. It is legitimate to wonder why.

3. Mutations are completely *chance* events. No one has ever been able to prove that mutations are *driven* or *directed* toward a particular goal by any external forces, including a designer. Most mutations are neutral, others are unfavorable, and some are favorable, depending on where and when they appear in a population.

4. Strong data back up the phenomenon of natural selection, including in humans. Feel free to come up with science-based counterexamples.

5. Teleology, the notion that natural events occur for a predetermined reason imagined by a designer, is unscientific and unprovable.

3

Creationist Purpose and Irreducible Complexity Rebutted

Such is our grand synthesis at the turn of the millennium, not a replacement for religion as much as a scientific philosophy in its own right, combining testable ideas, penetrating observations, and veritable inspiration while trekking along that everlasting path toward heightened understanding.
—Eric Chaisson, *Cosmic Evolution*

Make everything as simple as possible, but not simpler.
—Albert Einstein

It is often said that professors learn as much from their students as their students learn from them. One of us has occasionally had creationist students enrolled in his course on the origins and evolution of life at Washington State University and has learned from them about creationist thought. One student distinctly made fun in his class presentation of scientists dating bone material with the carbon-14 radioactive technique, which he called naive. This was impossible, he said, because everybody knows that bones do not contain any carbon—they are purely mineral structures. Of course, he was wrong there. Fossil bones contain plenty of carbon deriving from bone marrow cells and bone-forming cells called osteoblasts. What this student lacked was good scientific information.

Unfortunately, it is easy enough for anyone to convince a poorly informed public that scientists do not know what they are doing and what they are talking about. Frankly, scientists have not helped here; most of them are and have been reluctant to engage in debates with people they consider religious extremists and ignorant of even the simplest scientific basics. This attitude worked for a long time. But with the appearance of Intelligent Design (ID), things have changed. Today, a few people with academic credentials are challenging mainstream science in a way that is seemingly convincing to a significant fraction of the public. In particular, they aim to show that evolution does not exist by trying to rebut some aspects of evolutionary theory and the empirical evidence that supports it. In this chapter, we rebut their rebuttals by providing a critique of their views of the natural world. We also describe how it is that scientists can study the past, not only by studying its relics but also by studying the present.

The Dating of Fossils and Artifacts Is Reliable

The critique of scientific experiments and their interpretation is at the core of the scientific process. It is only when a consensus among scientists is reached that a particular theory can be considered valid, and this happens only after gathering a considerable amount of experimental evidence. This means that, invariably, some theories will be rejected. But a severe problem with creationists and believers in ID is that their critique of existing theories does not follow the methodology by which a theory should be rejected, that is, only if it is contradicted by experiments.

Basically, these people reject theories because these theories do not agree with their religious beliefs or their agendas. Worse, they offer very little in terms of alternative explanations of natural phenomena that they think have been misinterpreted. One case in point is the rejection of dating techniques by many creationists (but not necessarily by ID followers).

Classical creationists do not accept any of the techniques used to date rocks and biological specimens, especially if the ages of the samples are found to be more than 10,000 years old. These dates would indeed conflict with a literal interpretation of the Bible. Two typical rebuttals are offered by creationists: on the one hand, they say that dating techniques do not work because scientists are incompetent; or on the other hand, they claim that a designer created Earth just a few thousand years ago but made it look much older. Surely, some scientists are incompetent. But *all* of them? As for a young Earth looking old, why, for what purpose, would a designer want to create such a thing?

In fact, dating techniques are very reliable, and in many cases, totally different techniques confirm each other's results. For many years, the only available dating techniques relied on radioactive elements present in mineral or biological specimens. These elements decay at known constant rates, accurately measured in the laboratory. This is how specimens are dated: the less radioactivity a sample contains, the older it is, because, as time elapses, more radioactive decay will have taken place. Based on this type of technique, we know that Earth is billions of years old, not thousands of years old. Another tactic used by detractors of the scientific method to discredit these observations is to claim that radioactive elements may not decay at the same rate at all times. In other words, these elements seem to decay at a certain rate *today*, but they did not decay at the same rate in the past, particularly under different physical and chemical conditions. If true, this would indeed make dating impossible. But is there any evidence for this? The answer is no. Scientists have checked radioactive decay rates of elements under a variety of conditions, such as variable pressure, temperature, and many different chemical combinations, and have come up empty handed. Radioactive decay rates are invariable under all conditions tested. Granted, it is impossible to travel back in time and check the rates of radioactive decay as they may have been thousands or millions of years ago. But then, it is up to the detractors to prove their point. They have not done so.

One interesting twist regarding variable rates of radioactive decay has to do with the dating of the Shroud of Turin (Italy). This large piece of cloth is purported to have been used to wrap the body of Jesus Christ after his crucifixion. Not everybody necessarily agreed that the shroud was genuine, regardless of their faith. In a courageous move, the Catholic Church allowed three independent laboratories to use the carbon-14 dating technique on small samples of the shroud. This particular technique works well with samples of biological origin, such as cloth, if they are not older than about 60,000 years. All three labs agreed: the Turin shroud was made in the four-teenth century. In other words, it is a medieval forgery.

Many people were upset by this result, including creationists, who called the scientists who did the dating "radiocarbonists," as if the latter were members of a religious sect or a political party. One creationist explanation for the recent date of the shroud that we heard ourselves was that the "flash" of resurrection somehow "reset" all the carbon-14 atoms in the shroud. Well, who knows? But this is an explanation that is difficult to prove. To do so, one would have to observe a few resurrections (to make sure the phenomenon is repeatable) and see if they are accompanied by such flashes. Moreover, one would have to monitor carbon-14 decay rates in shrouds before and after these resurrections. This has not been done, for obvious reasons. But as someone once said, extraordinary claims require extraordinary evidence.

The carbon-14 dating technique is not the only one that relies on the steady decay of radioactive elements. Different radioactive elements possess different rates of decay; some decay quickly and some decay slowly. Carbon-14 decays fairly rapidly, and this is why it is used for samples that are not older than a few tens of thousands of years. Other radioactive elements, such as potassium-40, decay much more slowly and can date samples that are hundreds of thousands of years old. Others yet, such as uranium-238, are used to date samples that are billions of years old, such as rock samples deposited when Earth had recently formed from the collisions of smaller bodies in orbit around our then young sun.

Nor is radioactivity the only available technique to date natural objects. Another technique is tree-ring dating. Tree growth can be measured by the counting of annual ring formations in their trunks. Some trees, depending on their location, are as old as 2,000 to 3,000 years. Cores from these trees have been used to calibrate the carbon-14 method by measuring the radioactivity in their rings. Thus, a method that few would object to, the counting of tree rings, has been used to validate carbon-14 dates. Further, another nonradioactive dating method based on the chemical properties of amino acids—the building blocks of proteins—is called amino acid racemization. This method can date biological specimens that are between 50,000 and 200,000 years old. Finally, two more nonradioactive techniques, based on the effects of cosmic rays (a type of energetic radiation that pervades the cosmos) on biological and nonbiological specimens are also used to determine their age in the range of about 1,000 to 500,000 years.

The take-home lesson here is that various dating techniques, based on entirely different chemical and physical properties of materials, overlap in their respective time ranges *and thus validate each other*. This means that *all* dating techniques, radioactive or not, would have to be refuted by creationists and *all* proven wrong by them by doing the appropriate experiments. Needless to say, this has not happened. Short of that, our only choice is to accept the conclusions reached by scientific methods: Earth is very old, and fossils—as well as artifacts such as stone tools and the Shroud of Turin—can be dated accurately. As always, there are some cases where dating is uncertain, for example, when samples are contaminated or are too small for accurate analysis. But a few exceptions should not be latched on to in order to refute a whole analytical system proven to be accurate over and over again.

The Eye, the Immune System, and Bacterial Flagella as Irreducibly Complex Systems

As we mentioned in chapter 1, today's neocreationists (ID believers), unlike classical creationists, generally no longer mount frontal attacks on dating techniques. Rather, their contention is that properties of living systems, such as the existence of sensory organs (the eye), bacterial movements made possible by a structure called a flagellum, and the immune system are too complex to have evolved from simpler structures through unguided biological mechanisms. In other words, these properties must have been created as whole, "just right" units; otherwise, they would not work. To explain these complicated properties, neocreationists invoke the existence of a "designer" who, by any stretch of the imagination, cannot be any different from the designer invoked by classical creationists to support their claims for a young Earth and the invalidity of dating techniques. But this time, neocreationists no longer take on the whole of science. They restrict their attacks to only one small but tremendously sensitive area of science: evolution.

As mentioned, the ID contention is that living systems are too complicated to have evolved gradually. There is no such thing as half an eye or half an immune system, they say, although this is yet another very crude metaphor. But why do they stop at just these few examples? Let us take a look at a metabolic pathway chart (which summarizes many biochemical reactions taking place in living cells) and decide whether this chart is reducibly or irreducibly complex. Metabolic charts, familiar to all life sciences undergraduates, reveal a tangled mess of biochemical compounds linked by arrows, some linear, some circular, and many merging. Surely, *any* portion of a metabolic pathway chart looks irreducibly complex! But, of course, this is just a visual *impression*, not a fact.

An excellent example of this is the Krebs cycle (named after its discoverer, Sir Hans Adolf Krebs), also called the citric acid cycle. The Krebs cycle consists of a complicated series of cyclical biochemical reactions that metabolize sugars and fats in order to produce cellular energy. This metabolic pathway has not escaped the attention of commercial companies that sell dietary supplements promising weight loss concomitant with an enhanced energy supply. Indeed, Krebs cycle "boosters" are available over the counter. Whether they work is, of course, another story. But interestingly, some of the manufacturers of these "boosters" use a simple graphic metaphor to publicize their product. This metaphor looks like the drawing shown in figure 3.1, where the Krebs cycle is represented by a circle with arrows going up and down. Now, compare this with the well-understood real Krebs cycle as determined by biochemists (figure 3.2). A comparison between the two representations would make one think that, indeed, the Krebs cycle is irreducibly complex because it is so complicated, and therefore must have been "designed." But we now know that the Krebs cycle is *not* irreducibly complex: it has evolved from the combination of a series of simpler pathways. Why, then, some people think that an eye is more irreducibly complex than, say, a chloroplast (the cellular body where photosynthesis takes place) or the Krebs cycle escapes us. Anyway, their choices are theirs.

Since books defending ID principles have already developed their favorite examples (for instance, the complexity of the eye, the mechanism of blood coagulation, bacterial flagella, and cell membranes), we restrict ourselves for now to very brief discussions of the ID interpretation of the appearance of the eye, the immune system, and the bacterial flagellum. As far as the eye is concerned, the old argument against evolution is that the eye is just too complex not to have been designed. Added to that is the fact that the insect and the human eye, being quite structurally different, must have been created (designed) separately for each type of organism in which they are found. This

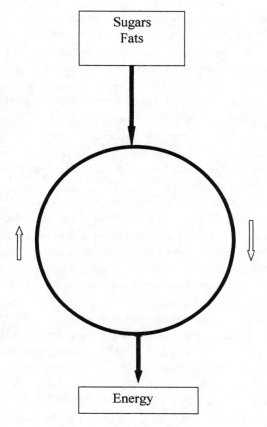

FIGURE 3.1
An artist's rendition of the Krebs cycle. Courtesy of Paul Lurquin.

makes superficial sense for anyone who has taken a look at the compound eye of a housefly. But unfortunately for ID believers, we know now that "master genes" responsible for the development of eyes are very similar across evolutionarily distant species.

As complicated, if not more so, is the functioning of the immune system. This system protects us from microscopic invaders, particularly bacteria and viruses, collectively called antigens. The immune system reacts to antigens by synthesizing specific antibodies that bind the antigens and so allow specialized cells to destroy these antigens. This system is extremely complex and integrated. Michael Behe, the ID biochemist introduced in chapter 1, claims that this system is so complicated that nobody has the faintest idea as to how it could have evolved from simpler components.

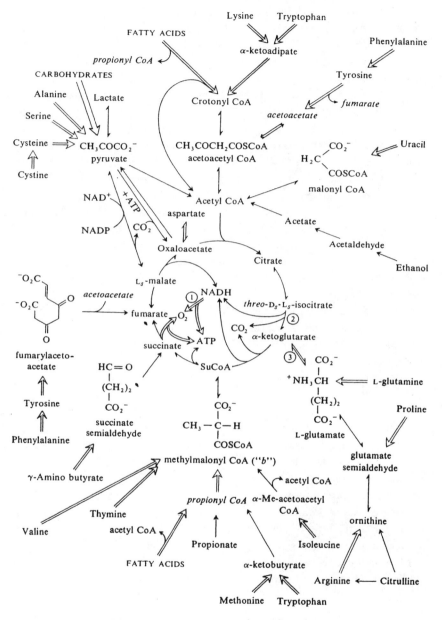

FIGURE 3.2
The real Krebs cycle.

In his book *Darwin's Black Box*, Behe attempts to explain to a lay audience how the immune system works. This is a laudable effort, of course, but unfortunately, his brushstrokes are so broad that he barely scratches the surface of what is actually known about the immune system. In a way, this is understandable because a lay audience would be quickly turned off by discussions of arcane minutiae of biochemical mechanisms. The same caveat applies to a thorough discussion of evolutionary biology, which we addressed in chapter 2. But let us remember Behe's goal: he is trying to convince the public that evolution does not work. Given that he chose extremely complex examples to defend his thesis, Behe should have been much more thorough than he was, even at the risk of boring his readers. Further, Behe all but ignores the genetic aspects of immunity in his presentation, and it is legitimate to wonder why. Also, some of his assertions are wrong. The same holds true for his discussion of the bacterial flagellum. Further, he uses inadequate metaphors in his attempts to demonstrate the irreducible complexity of the immune system. Einstein's quote given at the beginning of this chapter warns us that oversimplification is tricky. This lesson is generally not heeded in ID publications.

Behe compares an incomplete (that is, not designed) bacterial flagellum with an outboard motor that turns at one revolution per day and hence does not have even minimal function. He also compares an incomplete (also not designed) immune system with Viking marauders laughing at toy guns aimed at them. This metaphor aims to show that one single isolated part of the immune system is inadequate for function; a real gun is thus needed! These comparisons may be slightly amusing, but they are totally irrelevant. And here again, Behe's pronouncement that we know nothing about the evolution of the immune system is false, as proved by many scientific articles published before and after Behe published his book.

However, before seeing how science rebuts the claims of neocreationists, we must first explain how modern biology views the general functioning of all living cells and how genetic technology helps unravel the process of evolution at the level of DNA molecules and beyond. It is only through an understanding of modern molecular genetics that one can correlate the evolution of species with the mechanisms that led to this evolution. We then go back to discussing the three examples listed above.

The General Blueprint of All Life on Earth

There exist today fast and reliable techniques that allow us to determine the base sequence of DNA molecules. In fact, the full base-pair sequences of the total DNA (also called the "genome") from dozens of organisms are now known, including simple viruses, bacteria, fungi, plants, animals, and humans. The lengths of the sequenced genomes range from a few thousand base pairs (as in viruses) to 3.1 billion base pairs (as in humans) and more (as in rice). The knowledge of all these sequenced genomes, as well as the knowledge accumulated by geneticists and biochemists over decades of research, gives us the opportunity to answer the following questions: (1) how do organisms work at the molecular level, and (2) how similar or different are the genomes of different organisms?

The answer to the first question is that we know today that all life is one. All organisms, from single-celled bacteria to complex plants and animals, are programmed by the genetic information coded in their DNA in the form of base-pair sequences. One can think of DNA as the software of an organism. As in computers, the information stored in software must be executed by the hardware and the operating system. The hardware (mostly proteins) and operating system (RNA—a close cousin of DNA—and proteins) of living organisms, even though they are in their details orders of magnitude more complicated than the most sophisticated computer, can still be summarized as follows. First, the genetic information present in DNA is *transcribed* into RNA (ribonucleic acid), and this RNA is subsequently *translated* into proteins. RNA is very similar to DNA: it also contains bases arranged in a linear fashion, but it is mostly single stranded, contrary to double-stranded DNA. It should be noted that the step called *transcription* does not change the nature or meaning of the genetic message present in DNA. This is because messenger RNA, as it is called, which is produced in the transcription process, is an exact copy of DNA. We can say that DNA and RNA speak the same "language": both contain information stored in the form of strings of base sequences. That this seemingly unnecessary step exists in all living cells may be a relic of mechanisms first evolving at the dawn of life (see chapter 5).

The next step, *translation*, is extremely complex but functions basically in the same way in all organisms. In it, messenger RNA is decoded by a multitude of proteins and small RNA molecules (themselves coded for by DNA) into proteins, which are strings of chemically bound amino acids. Proteins are thus at the end of the line as far as the flow of cellular genetic information is concerned. They can be seen as the ultimate result of a manufacturing process whose detailed instructions are stored in DNA. Proteins can also be conceived as a combination of operating system and hardware. They are used to replicate DNA and make messenger RNA, but they also play a critical role in metabolism, the hardware of cells. Metabolism is what makes cells "tick."

Metabolism is responsible for energy transactions in cells, their growth and division; it makes the building blocks of cells and generates waste products that are excreted. Metabolism involves hundreds of proteins catalysts, referred to as *enzymes*, which help perform cellular chemical reactions. Enzymes are all coded for by DNA. And yet, in spite of the great variety of lifeforms that exist on Earth, living organisms have in common hundreds of metabolic reactions. Obviously, organisms belonging to different species have some metabolic pathways not shared by all species. For example, wheat is green because its DNA encodes the instructions necessary to perform photosynthesis, which involves the green pigment chlorophyll. Lions are not green because they do not possess the genes necessary for photosynthesis, but contrary to wheat, they have genes that determine the formation of one head, one tail, and four legs. In many ways, however, a lion and a wheat plant are much more similar than either is to, say, a rock or a cloud. This is because lions and wheat are both life-forms based on the same fundamental blueprint centered on the transcription of DNA into RNA, and the subsequent translation of this RNA into proteins.

Given the great similarities between all life-forms at the level of metabolism, as well as the way genetic information is processed by all life-forms, it is reasonable to think that a very long time ago, there appeared the first cells, processing genetic information as described above, from which all life is descended. These cells then would have left descendants that changed through an evolutionary process involving mutation, natural selection, drift, and migration, eventually branching out into new species. This is indeed the view of science: life started a long time ago, in the form of simple cells that gained complexity through natural processes.

At this point, creationists will protest that all these complicated mechanisms shared by all life-forms actually prove that life was designed. But this a specious argument, because why would a designer be restricted to creating just one type of life-form based on the same software (DNA), one extensively shared operating system (RNA and proteins), and one type of hardware (proteins)? And who can answer this type of question anyway? This would be equivalent to trying to read the mind of God, something that creationists may think they can do by using teleological dogmatism. In contrast, we show next that science offers logical and solidly verified explanations concerning the common characteristics shared by all life-forms.

Evolution of Gene Sequences and "Genetic Archaeology"

It is now time to answer the second question we asked above: how different or similar are the genomes (the DNA molecules) of widely different organisms, given the great similarities of their software and hardware? As mentioned, the genomes of even simple organisms contain extremely large numbers of DNA base pairs. Computer scientists have generated sophisticated algorithms that allow the scanning and comparison of millions of DNA base pairs by computers. Thus, it is no longer difficult to compare thousands of gene sequences from hundreds of organisms. Whenever DNA sequences are compared, it is now possible to determine accurately their degree of *homology*, that is, how much they look alike at the base-pair sequence level. Remember that it is the DNA sequence that ultimately determines the biological characteristics of organisms.

The application of DNA sequence comparisons has revealed one clear correlation: the closer two organisms are on an evolutionary scale determined by the fossil record, the closer their DNA sequences. For example, if we consider a random 10,000 base-pair-long DNA region shared by chimps and humans, we find on average that chimps differ from us by about 145 base pairs. On the other hand, if we compare the same segment of human DNA with that from rhesus monkeys, we find 751 differences. The difference between chimp DNA and rhesus monkey DNA is 606 differences. This means that humans are closer to chimps than they are to rhesus monkeys in terms of DNA homology.

This also means that humans and chimps diverged in evolutionary time more recently than the ancestors of *both* human and chimps diverged from rhesus monkeys. How can we claim this? First, we know from the fossil record that the ancestors of humans and those of chimps diverged about 5 million years ago. And indeed, we also know from the fossil record that ancestors of rhesus monkeys appeared about 35 million years ago. But then, it is not possible to retrieve DNA from such old fossils because DNA degrades over periods of only thousands of years, not millions of years. How, then, can one reconcile dates provided by the fossil record and similarities or differences (degrees of homology) between DNA extracted from modern humans, chimps, and rhesus monkeys? We can do this by looking at DNA isolated from existing organisms.

One amazing finding of research on DNA homology is that *the present can explain the past*. Many people have problems with this concept. How is it possible to do "genetic archaeology"? The crucial principle at work is that DNA mutations (changes in base pairs) *accumulate over time*. Thus, if the direct ancestors of a given species appeared a long time ago relative to a species whose ancestors appeared more recently, the DNA of the older species will have had a longer time to accumulate mutations and will have a decreased homology with the DNA of the species that appeared at a later date. Based on DNA sequence alone, we can now see why chimps and humans share greater DNA homology (only 145 differences) than either shares with rhesus monkeys (human/rhesus = 751 differences and chimp/rhesus = 606 differences): of the three species, rhesus monkeys have been around longer than chimps and humans, and this is why their DNA shows more accumulated differences.

In conclusion, by measuring the DNA base sequence homology between species alive today, and by calibrating the appearance of these species with the fossil record, it is possible to date the origin of species alive today, even if they left no trace in the fossil record. This is done by extrapolating or interpolating differences in base sequences of these extant species with those whose fossil record and dating are well known.

This method is used to build what are called *phylogenetic trees*, which can be based on DNA sequence alone. These trees look exactly like the theoretical tree shown in figure 2.1 except that here, the times since divergence of species can be measured by counting the differences in DNA base-pair sequences among various species. In fact, scientists have so much confidence in these DNA-based phylogenetic trees that they use DNA homology data to predict the functions of genes in organisms whose genomes were newly sequenced, and they can even tell which genes from which organisms are ancestral relative to others. This is done by using a computer to compare the new sequences with that of a known, previously sequenced and better understood organism. Very often, but not always, this methodology works just fine.

When does this methodology not work? As we described above, wheat and lions, even though they both possess all the genes necessary for life, differ in many characteristics. Therefore, one does not expect to find photosynthetic genes in lions or genes responsible for brain formation in wheat. The message here is that lions and wheat should not be used as comparators for genes they obviously do not share. For wheat, one should use another plant genome, and for lions, one could use any sequenced mammalian genome.

By extending the study of DNA homology from so-called higher organisms (plants and animals) to so-called lower organisms (sponges, fungi, and bacteria, for example), and thus going deeply back in time on the evolutionary scale, scientists have been able to build what is called the *tree of life* (figure 3.3). This tree looks exactly like a classical evolutionary tree with points of divergence and branches. What is special about this tree, however, is that it retraces the history of all life on Earth. Thousands of biologists have sequenced tens of thousands of DNA segments to arrive at this result. The tree shows that life consists of three big domains: the Eukarya, whose DNA is enclosed in a structure called the nucleus, and the Bacteria and Archaea, whose DNA is not confined in a nucleus.

The domain Eukarya harbors single-celled organisms such as fungi and multicellular organisms such as jellyfish, tigers, and humans. The Bacteria and Archaea are both single-celled microscopic organisms. The domain Bacteria

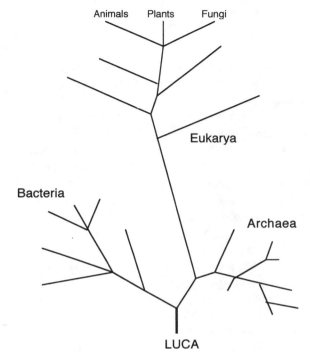

FIGURE 3.3
The universal tree of life showing the three domains of life: the Bacteria, the Archaea, and the Eukarya. The LUCA (last universal common ancestor), the ancestor of all DNA-based life on Earth, is located at the root of the tree. Animals, plants, and fungi are all Eukarya. The branch containing humans is not shown at this scale. It derives from the main branch that contains all animals.

is composed of what we call in everyday language "germs." The Archaea are more exotic. Many of them live in environments that we consider inhospitable, such as boiling water in volcanic fumaroles; near-freezing water such as that found near the Arctic and Antarctic regions; very salty water, as in the Dead Sea; or under enormous pressures, such as those found at the deep bottom of oceans.

The tree of life shows that all life-forms are descended from a population of organisms (in all likelihood, they were single celled) that lived when DNA-based life appeared, about 3.5 billion years ago (see chapter 5). This age for the appearance of life is supported by the fossil record that has kept traces of microorganisms that old. Thus, all life evolved and diversified from the last universal common ancestor (LUCA) located at the root of the tree. Intriguingly, the tree of life also shows that Eukarya (including humans) are more closely related to Archaea than they are to Bacteria. Further, the LUCA itself must have evolved from simpler organisms that appeared from noncellular structures, right at the dawn of life. We discuss in chapter 5 what the ancestor of the LUCA may have been. In summary, the tree of life allows us to establish evolutionary relationships in time *among* species alive today.

DNA sequencing offers yet finer evolutionary information. By looking at subtle base-pair differences that exist in different populations of the *same* species (for instance, trout that live in Montana vs. trout that live in California), it is possible to determine which population appeared before another. Therefore, it is possible to establish genealogies (phylogenetic trees, really) *within* a given species and decide which population evolved first. Fascinatingly, this principle applies to human populations, as well, as we discuss in the next chapter.

Needless to say, the tree of life and evolutionary divergences revealed by DNA sequences are anathema to creationists and ID believers alike because they represent the ultimate in evolutionary thinking. But in the end, the onus is on creationists and ID supporters to prove that the tree of life is a figment of the imagination of thousands of scientists. They should also tell us where, if not from evolution, DNA homologies come from. Again, nothing has transpired other than the usual mantra that the designer designed DNA sequences his own way and gave lions and wheat, and all the other life-forms, the DNA they deserve.

Back to Irreducible Complexity

The subtitle of Behe's book *Darwin's Black Box* is *The Biochemical Challenge to Evolution*. As is clear by now, modern evolutionary biology relies on a combination of many different branches of science: biochemistry, anatomy, paleontology, and first and foremost, genetics. Unfortunately, ID incorporates very little, if any, genetics. This is disturbing because, after all, genetics is the science of heredity that studies the passing down of genes, their expression in the form of traits, and their modification (mutation) over time. Given that life appeared at least 3.5 billion years ago, many changes must have occurred in DNA sequences, and hence, many changes must have taken place at the level of cells' hardware, the proteins.

Let us now review the three examples, taken from genetics, that challenge the interpretations of ID thinkers and their notion of irreducible complexity: the eye, the immune system, and the bacterial flagellum. In passing, it should be acknowledged that "irreducible" complexity has been converted recently into "specified" complexity by some ID aficionados. Whether or not this means that a designer specified complexity but no longer made it "irreducible" (perhaps because the notion of irreducibility is untenable) is only known to creationist factions and is not considered here. Rather, we stay with "mainstream" and original ID propositions.

If the eye is an irreducibly complex structure designed as a "module" that cannot withstand changes without destroying itself, it should be impossible for a fly, for example, to develop eyes using genes that are not its own. Flies and other insects have compound eyes composed of many facets. By contrast, vertebrates—such as reptiles, mice, and humans—do not possess compound eyes. If each type of eye was designed to appear in a species for which it was specially designed, a fly should not be able to grow eyes under the control of vertebrate genes. We now know this is not true.

Since the early 1970s, geneticists have developed and perfected our ability to *clone* individual genes, that is, to isolate and purify individual stretches of DNA that contain single genes. These genes can then be sequenced and even introduced into completely unrelated organisms to study how they are expressed—what they do—in different biological environments. Single genes determining eye formation have been cloned from humans, mice, and fruit flies called *Drosophila melanogaster*. These three genes are called *aniridia* in humans, *Pax-6* in mice, and *eyeless* in *Drosophila*. It turns out that when the human *aniridia* and mouse *Pax-6* genes were injected into *Drosophila*, they directed the formation of *extra compound eyes* in these flies! Indeed, these human and mouse genes had been engineered to be expressed not only in the heads, but also in the legs of the flies. Thus, the flies injected with the mouse and human genes developed extra compound eyes on their heads but also on their legs.

When the DNA of *aniridia*, *Pax-6*, and *eyeless* was sequenced, it was obvious that all three genes shared extensive homology. Taking into account that flies and mammals have evolved separately for more than 500 million years, these experiments show that the development of the eye, probably at first a very simple light-sensing organ, has remained very much the same for at least that long. We now know that these three genes are control genes, master switches of sorts that control many other genes involved in eye development. These control genes "tell" organisms to just "make eyes," while the other genes under their control fill in the details in a species-specific manner. In brief, this experiment destroyed the biochemical argument about specific design developed by Behe. Ironically, and most unfortunately for Behe, his book and the revolutionary findings regarding eye formation were published within a year of each other! What is more, we now know that an invertebrate, the sea urchin, has genes that code for light-sensing proteins (opsins) and retina development. But there is a twist: sea urchins have no eyes. What this means is that components necessary for vision in vertebrates appeared in invertebrates well before anything resembling a vertebrate eye developed. This shows again that the irreducible complexity of the eye is a simplistic myth unsupported by scientific evidence.

Behe's assertion in his book that we understand nothing about the evolution of the immune system is equally wrong. First, Behe's statement that almost nothing has been published on this topic is simply not true. Second, he fails to mention that DNA homology studies have clearly demonstrated that portions of the immune system are present in sea urchins, animals that are members of a phylum that appeared about 1 billion years ago. This observation was fully confirmed in 2006, when the complete sequence of the sea urchin genome was published. This confirmation demonstrates that this invertebrate has a complex "innate" immune system also present in vertebrates (including humans). Yet sea urchins do not produce antibodies that are part of the "acquired" immune system, which allows vertebrates to develop long-term immunity to pathogens.

In addition, even insects and simple worms called nematodes possess some elements of an immune system. But it was 450 million years ago that what we would consider a "modern" immune system (which includes acquired immunity) first appeared in jawless fish. This more complex system was passed on an evolutionary path all the way down to mammals, including humans. Thus, phylogenetic studies show that the immune system *did* gain complexity in an incremental fashion over a period of at least one billion years of evolution. In the end, Behe's mistake is that he failed to provide a critical and full analysis of all the facts well known by professional immunologists. He also did not take into account the fact that scientific knowledge progresses over time and is never limited by the pronouncements of naysayers.

As for the bacterial flagellum, the response of science is the same: it is not irreducibly complex, and its evolutionary history has been documented. For example, some pathogenic bacteria use some elements of what was to evolve into a flagellum to inject toxins into their infected host cells. In other words, these bacteria use certain components of the flagellum, but do not use these components to swim. Further, some non-pathogenic bacteria also harbor genes coding for flagellar proteins even though they *do not* rely on flagella for their motility. This was clearly demonstrated by studying the DNA sequences of homologous genes in bacteria. Further, some bacteria use their flagellum in an "on-off" manner to change directions rather than the more common directional "switching," where the flagellum does not stop beating. The existence of these two different modes of propulsion also shows that the bacterial flagellum is not irreducibly complex, because at least two types of flagella have evolved in different directions. In conclusion, the ID statement that "proteins in the flagellar motor are unique to the motor and are not found in any other living system" is not true. To convince themselves, interested readers are invited to consult the first three Web sites and references given in Further Reading. These sites provide many technical details on the evolution of the eye, the immune system, and bacterial flagella. Unfortunately, given their technical nature, these sites and articles may not be easy for everyone to follow.

Some will object that evolution by natural selection, especially the formation of new species, is not directly observable. Indeed, no one has ever seen a fish sprout legs or a lizard develop wings. But, of course, one should not expect leg or wing development to happen all at once in single organisms. These are gradual transformations that take a very long time and hence, yes, are not directly observable under natural or laboratory conditions.

This last point brings up the notions of macroevolution and microevolution. Some ID proponents are willing to accept the reality of microevolution, that is, evolution *within* species, which they incorrectly consider of little significance for evolutionary biology. However, they all reject macroevolution, the appearance of new species from preexisting ones. Most scientists do not think that a sharp distinction should be made between the processes of microevolution and macroevolution. The topic of macroevolution is addressed in chapter 6, which describes in more detail how the science of genetics views evolutionary pathways that can lead to the formation of new physiological and morphological functions. Meanwhile, major evolutionary transformations are taking place in the bacterial world right as you are reading this, and these changes both *are* directly observable and *do* have important implications for a correct understanding of evolutionary biology.

Bacteria Are Evolving Right in Front of Our Very Eyes

Anyone who has had the misfortune of being infected by a multi-drug-resistant species of pathogenic bacteria should not deny that evolution by natural selection takes place. When the first antibiotics—penicillin, streptomycin, neomycin, and tetracycline—went into use in the 1940s and 1950s, there were no human-infecting pathogenic bacteria resistant to these antibiotics. By the late 1970s, several pathogenic bacterial species had become resistant to all of these antibiotics and had started to cause serious problems in hospital settings. What happened during this 30-year period?

To understand the phenomenon of antibiotic resistance in bacteria, recall the notions of spontaneous mutation and natural selection. Bacteria, including pathogenic types, reproduce very rapidly, sometimes as rapidly as every 30 minutes or so. This rapid rate of multiplication means that bacterial populations consist of very large numbers of individuals in which random mutations take place at a significant frequency and hence generate significant numbers of mutations in each generation. Some of these mutations, through well-understood mechanisms, lead to the appearance of antibiotic-resistant mutants. Things get nasty when a person becomes infected with a mixture of resistant mutants and their antibiotic-sensitive partners. When antibiotics are given to a sick patient, the sensitive pathogens are killed. But the resistant mutants, even if they are initially present in small numbers, thrive and multiply in the presence of the antibiotic, and as a result, the patient becomes sicker. This is a typical case of natural selection where the selective agent, an antibiotic, blocks the proliferation of one type of organism (the sensitive type) but leaves the other type (the resistant mutants) untouched.

The result of the selective action of the antibiotic is that, from a small minority, the antibiotic-resistant pathogens eventually represent 100% of the pathogen population in the affected individual. And the patient releases many of these numerous mutants into the environment through bodily fluids. Ideally, if the patient is affected by a pathogen resistant to a single antibiotic, the use of another, unrelated antibiotic will save his/her life. But this is not the end of the story.

Imagine different patients treated for different bacterial infections with a different antibiotic in each case. Potentially, different pathogens may then become resistant by mutation to a variety of single antibiotics, then be naturally selected by each single antibiotic in each patient, and finally be released into the environment. As we detail in chapter 6, bacteria possess efficient mechanisms that allow them to exchange genes in a number of settings, such as a patient's body, on hospital bedsheets, in the soil, and even in the sewers. When these pathogens, each so far resistant to one single antibiotic, start exchanging and combining their antibiotic-resistant mutant genes, multidrug resistance appears; the pathogens have now become resistant to a cocktail of antibiotics instead of being resistant to just one. Today, bacterial strains that cause tuberculosis, gonorrhea, syphilis, and urinary, respiratory, and severe skin infections, for example, have become resistant to a whole catalog of antibiotics. Multi-drug-resistant urinary and respiratory infections are particularly troublesome in hospitalized postsurgical and immunocompromised patients. And this has happened all over the world within a period of only about 30 years, thanks to the powerful action of natural selection exercised by antibiotics. This is an example of rapid evolution.

The microbial world has taught us even more lessons on fast evolution by natural selection. The widespread use of synthetic herbicides started about

60 years ago. These herbicides were manufactured in laboratories and bore absolutely no resemblance to any natural compounds. Nonetheless, in just a few decades, there appeared soil bacteria able to degrade these herbicides and use them as food, even though these chemicals had never existed before in nature. The genes responsible for these new properties are mutant forms of preexisting genes that give the host bacteria a selective advantage, namely, the ability to survive and multiply by consuming completely artificial herbicidal compounds delivered by farmers. In this case, however, the action of natural selection is beneficial to humans: herbicide-degrading microbes prevent the accumulation of these chemicals in our fields and pastures.

And finally, many bacterial species have become adapted naturally to survival and proliferation in human-made noxious environments heavily polluted with toxic elements such as copper, mercury, cadmium, lead, cobalt, and selenium (mine tailings, for example). The genes responsible for these properties are well known. Fascinatingly, these heavy-metal-resistant bacteria are not found in simpler mining environments older than about 250 years. This means that it took less than two and a half centuries for mutation and natural selection to produce these strange organisms. Here again, we have an example of fast evolution imposed on microorganisms by human activities.

Alternatively, if we were to deny that evolution by natural selection exists, what would a designer's purpose be in creating these pathogenic, antibiotic-resistant mutants, herbicide-degrading mutants, and heavy-metal-resistant mutants? Did an omniscient teleological designer predict that the use of antibiotics and herbicides and the practice of mining would become common on Earth? Or rather, should we not accept the fact that adaptation to a given environment through natural selection is a better explanation? Nonetheless, it is not only microbes that teach us much about evolution. We describe next how phylogenetic trees coupled with sophisticated laboratory techniques have allowed us to physically re-create genes that went extinct millions of years ago.

Resurrecting Ancient Genes

As we just described, the analysis of DNA homologies allows scientists to study the past by looking at the divergence of DNA base pairs among existing species. In recent years, biologists have gone much further than just building phylogenetic trees based on DNA data: phylogenies have been used to re-create ancient, extinct genes and produce in the laboratory the proteins coded for by these genes. In order to resurrect extinct genes, scientists sequence homologous genes from a variety of widely divergent species such as humans, birds, amphibians, fish, and invertebrates. The DNA sequences are then compared using computer algorithms, and by applying sophisticated statistical methods, a gene sequence ancestral to all modern sequences is determined.

The next step is to synthesize the ancestral gene in the laboratory. This is achieved with advanced cloning techniques that allow the production of gene-size stretches of DNA in the test tube. The final step is to introduce the ancestral gene into living cells in order to study its function, for example, the production of a particular protein. To date, at least a dozen extinct genes have been resurrected. One of these genes determines the production of rhodopsin, an eye pigment involved in dim light vision. Based on phylogenetic tree dating, this gene would have been present in dinosaurs at a time depth of about 240 million years ago.

When introduced into living cells, this re-created gene performed well and produced rhodopsin. This observation tells us several things. First, it is now possible to reconstruct functional, extinct genes in the laboratory and study ancient life-forms in a manner not possible with conventional paleontological methods (fossils). For example, we can now infer that dinosaurs were able to see well in dim light. Second, the fact that these genes can be reconstructed at all validates phylogenetic trees. Indeed, if phylogenic trees were wrong, it is extremely unlikely that a functional protein—rhodopsin—would have been produced from the reconstructed gene. Instead, one would have obtained no protein at all or a totally incorrect one sharing no resemblance with rhodopsin. Third, this experiment shows that, at least at the molecular level of rhodopsin, some functions of the eye are not irreducibly complex, in which case it would not have been possible to reconstruct the ancient rhodopsin gene based on evolutionary data. Finally, the successful reconstruction of the rhodopsin gene based on DNA sequences from widely divergent species demonstrates the genetic continuity of gene function during macroevolution.

Gene resurrection techniques have also shown that a hormone receptor gene homologous to mammalian genes existed as long ago as 600 million to 1 billion years in the past. Here again, the argument from design, because it negates macroevolution, cannot be correct because the time depth corresponding to the resurrected hormone receptor gene shows that this gene was present in animals even before flatworms and sea urchins diverged from a common ancestor.

Moreover, researchers have demonstrated that a particular hormone receptor gene appeared much earlier in the past than the hormone it binds today (the steroid hormone aldosterone). How is this possible? Should not a specific hormone and its receptor appear together in a "modular" fashion, as per ID thinking? It so happens that, in the past, the ancestor of this hormone receptor was able to bind chemically similar but more ancient molecules. Only two mutations were needed for this ancient hormone receptor to bind more modern aldosterone. This defeats the argument from irreducible complexity that complex systems, whose components are seemingly "just made for one another," such as a hormone receptor and its specific hormone, must have appeared together and not in a progressive, Darwinian fashion. In fact, the ancient hormone receptor was "recruited," through mutation, to perform a new function.

Returning to the present, in what follows we show again that irreducible complexity does not exist, as demonstrated by a mutation that makes some people resistant to AIDS. In addition, we provide a couple of examples (among many) of poor natural design, making the putative designer little more than a beginner or an amateur.

AIDS and a Designer

This is not the place to discuss whether a putative designer was benevolent or malevolent. Yet, since ID believers claim that the immune system is irreducibly complex and hence designed by a supernatural being, one may wonder why the scourge of AIDS exists at all. Indeed, the human immune system is rendered inoperative in AIDS sufferers; it just does not work any longer. Why is this so? The causative agent of AIDS is the virus called human immunodeficiency virus (HIV). The human immune system cannot defeat this virus because HIV infects and destroys the cells that are part of the immune response. Without these cells, the immune system is incapacitated. In fact, AIDS patients do not die from viral infection; they die from rare cancers or from bacterial or fungal infections that people without HIV are resistant to because their immune system is intact.

The human immune system, complex as it is, was certainly not "designed" to fight HIV, in which case AIDS would not exist. Then what happened? We know from phylogenetic studies based on DNA homologies that HIV is a recent mutant of an ape virus that appeared perhaps as late as the 1960s. Twenty or so years later, it started propagating worldwide in humans. If this is not evolution of a virus, then what is? Further, why did a designer not design an irreducibly complex immune system that encompassed the ability to defeat an attacker on itself such as HIV? The response of immunogenetics is that this supposedly irreducible complex system cannot respond to a new, mutant virus that attacks the cells where this very system operates.

But there is more. As we mentioned in chapter 2, the word "mutant" is usually seen as a negative, sometimes meaning crippled, unfit, or weird in the popular imagination. This definition certainly does not apply to human mutants who are resistant to HIV and thus cannot contract AIDS. It so happens that some humans who *should* get AIDS simply do not. These are individuals who practice unprotected promiscuous sex with known AIDS sufferers and yet remain unaffected by the disease. Analysis of their blood reveals the presence of extremely low levels of HIV (meaning they were exposed to the virus) when high levels are expected. What is happening? Analysis of their immune system cells and their DNA reveals that the cells that are normally targeted by HIV cannot be infected in these individuals because of a *mutation in one of the components of these cells' membranes*. The cell membrane is the envelope that confines all the internal cellular material and that forms the boundary between a cell and its environment. Before entering any target cells, viruses must bind to the cell membrane through specific membrane docking sites, usually proteins. AIDS-resistant individuals do not possess functional docking sites for HIV on their cells because of a mutation in these docking sites. This makes them immune to HIV. It can be said that these human mutants possess high fitness in an AIDS-ridden environment because they cannot die from it, whereas nonmutants do and are thus less fit.

Ironically, the cell membrane is sometimes used by ID thinkers as another example of an irreducibly complex system, meaning that changes occurring in it through mutation, for example, can only lead to grave defects and total loss of function. The example above shows that this not the case. In addition, researchers now predict that, if the AIDS epidemic cannot be stopped, the mutant gene that renders individuals resistant to AIDS will increase in the human population, in particular in sub-Saharan Africa. While the frequency of this mutation is 13% in European populations, it is extremely rare in Africa. Since HIV is a powerful selective factor—it kills unmedicated people extremely efficiently—and since anti-HIV medications are not readily available to most Africans, it follows that natural selection will favor the survival and differential reproduction of the rare AIDS-resistant Africans. The consequence will be an increase in the frequency of this particular membrane mutation, which is exactly evolution by natural selection.

The Designer Made a Mistake: Hot Flashes in Postmenopausal Women

HIV is a recent problem with which humans have had to contend. But there are many other, age-old problems with our physiology that cast considerable doubt upon the notion of ID. One such problem concerns hot flashes in postmenopausal women. When menstruation stops, a woman's hormonal balance changes, one result of this being hot flashes. After menopause, many women suffer from hot flashes, in some cases severely so. There are women who have hot flashes about every 15 minutes every single day, along with periods of severe sweating that interrupts sleep throughout the night. Hot flashes can be extremely uncomfortable, producing a strong sensation of overheating, flushing of the face, and sudden sweating. Not so many years ago, many *male* doctors told their menopausal women patients that they could expect "mild discomfort" from hot flashes "for a year or two." Not so. Hot flashes can continue for many years, beginning around the age of 50, continuing into a woman's 60s, 70s, 80s, and so on—in short, for life.

As an experiment, ask any woman who has suffered from severe hot flashes if this biological condition was put into women through ID. You are very likely to hear that if hot flashes are due to ID, the designer made a bad (and cruel) mistake. The Bible does have an account of why women suffer in childbirth—this is punishment for Eve's sin. But God said nothing about hot flashes! In fact, no one was saying much about hot flashes until relatively recently, and for a good reason: in the past, few women lived much beyond menopause. If, for example, we consider that average life expectancy in ancient Rome was 25 years, it is clear that postmenopausal hot flashes were not then, or earlier, a widespread health complaint.

Although no evolutionary scientists claim that hot flashes are in any way adaptive or useful for anyone, evolutionary theory does offer an explanation for why menopause (of which hot flashes are a by-product) exists at all. This is known as the Grandmother Hypothesis. According to this hypothesis, the reproductive success of females is actually facilitated by the timely cessation of a woman's fertility. This is because a woman's investment in her children (a long gestation, birth, nursing, and other infant care) is much higher than that of men, whose investment can be limited to impregnating a woman. If women, like men, could continue to reproduce into older ages, they could not care well for all the many children they could produce. Many of their children would die before reaching reproductive age; the women themselves would be worn out through reproduction, lowering further their capacity for adequate child care. It is far better for women to have children when young and healthy, cease reproduction afterward, and then invest in their needy biological descendants of the next generation, for example, their grandchildren. Helping to care for their grandchildren (to see that they reach reproductive age) increases women's fitness far beyond what their own continued reproduction would do.

Women's reproductive biology, with all its quirks and often painful consequences, came about through evolution and natural selection. But it is actually through human *cultural* evolution (discussed in detail in chapter 4) that hot flashes have come to plague so many women; advances in medicine have considerably lengthened women's (and men's) lives. But the capacity for hot flashes was with women all along. Does it make sense that an intelligent designer would design women this way, knowing full well that such problems would come about as medicine expanded the human life span? Finally, regarding postmenopausal problems, it is noteworthy that of the 41 fellows of the ID Center for Science and Culture in Seattle, only a single one is a woman.

As many people older than 50 know, there are other annoying "mistakes" in the "design" of human beings. Just to name two, consider the poor design of our spines and the sloppy engineering of our teeth. After a few decades of usage, our spinal column discs are prone to herniation and rupture, making life for many of us miserable at times. Clearly, our spines are not well adapted to a vertical posture, something a designer should have anticipated and corrected. Similarly, our teeth are not "designed" to last a lifetime, as proved by the constant professional care they require to stay in place. A designer should have anticipated and prevented periodontal disease and cavities, in which case root canals and dentures would be unnecessary. And the list goes on.

The Case of a Badly "Designed" Protein

The enzyme ribulose bisphosphate carboxylase/oxygenase (rubisco, in short) is in all likelihood the most prevalent protein on the planet. This is because it is present in all land plants, algae, and many photosynthetic bacteria. In land plants and algae, rubisco is located inside the chloroplasts, the cellular bodies where photosynthesis takes place. Rubisco represents 30% of the total protein in plant leaves, meaning that we ingest a lot of it every time we eat leafy vegetables, such as lettuce, spinach, and cabbage. The function of this enzyme is critical for all plant life because it catalyzes the fixation of atmospheric carbon dioxide and is the first step in producing sugars from carbon dioxide. This step is achieved by the carboxylase function of rubisco. But there is a problem with this enzyme: it is remarkably inefficient.

Given the importance of rubisco for life on Earth—remember that plants capture the energy of the sun to power their metabolism, that many animals eat plants, and that other animals eat animals that eat plants—one has to wonder why a designer would have so poorly designed this protein. Indeed, rubisco has a double function. One of these functions, as we said, is to fix carbon dioxide and produce sugar compounds necessary for the plants' metabolic pathways. But in addition, rubisco can also use oxygen as a substrate (this is its oxygenase function), and when it does so, it degrades some of the compounds that it just made through carbon dioxide fixation! In other words, this effect considerably lowers the photosynthetic potential of plants. What is more, when plant cells make rubisco, they use metabolic energy, as they do for the making of all other proteins. But since rubisco is so inefficient, much of that energy is wasted. If rubisco did not possess oxygenase activity, photosynthesis would be much more efficient, and plants could use the saved metabolic energy for other purposes, such as faster growth. Needless to say, a better rubisco enzyme would have dramatic effects on agricultural output and food production. Therefore, many plant biotechnologists—true intelligent designers—are busy trying to improve the functioning of this enzyme, one way being to reduce or eliminate its oxygenase activity.

In conclusion, one finds a number of examples of "bad design" in nature. Realizing this, some ID thinkers are now contending in yet another twist of logic that bad design is still design. Of course, this allows these thinkers to escape the accusation that ID is the same as Christian creationism: How could God possibly be equated with an incompetent designer? This new attitude is reminiscent of the story developed by the Canada-based Raelian cult. In it, human beings were created through cloning by extraterrestrials (called Elohim) who manufactured human DNA. The Raelians call themselves "scientific creationists" and have an exquisite explanation for the virgin birth of Jesus Christ: Mary was artificially inseminated by the Elohim aboard one of their spacecraft! Needless to say, the Raelians support the idea of Intelligent Design. It would be interesting to know what ID "theorists" think about the Raelian interpretation of the world.

Can a Mousetrap Evolve?

Michael Behe's most famous and iconic example of irreducible complexity is the familiar mousetrap, which we mentioned in chapter 1. Given that this metaphor has taken on a life of its own in the public imagination, it is important to discuss the possible origins and evolution of mousetraps. According to Behe, a mousetrap could not have evolved stepwise from simpler contraptions, thereby disproving evolution. In reality, nothing could be further from the truth, indicating again that simple metaphors can be false friends in the field of science. After Behe's publication of the mousetrap paradigm in his book, critical thinkers have analyzed his claim and come up with cogent rebuttals. As a result, several critiques have been devoted to the evolution of mousetraps, of which we mention only one that describes one mousetrap evolutionary path among many other possible ones. This critique goes as follows.

In early mousetrapping development, people could have used a big unstable rock that could topple easily and squash a passing mouse that would have disturbed it. This would have been a very unpredictable mousetrap because it relied on the facts that, first, the rock would not fall prematurely and, second, mice would be curious enough to take a close peek at the rock and nudge it. But next, in a further evolutionary step, the unstable rock could have been stabilized just a bit by a short twig that a mouse could displace by brushing against it, making the rock fall. But here again, there was still too much reliance on the curiosity of mice to trap them reliably. A third step would have been to attach bait to the twig with a thin thread. By attempting to run away with the bait, a mouse would have pulled the thread and hence displaced the twig, making the rock fall. This would have defeated slow mice, but not fast ones. Finally, to catch even the swiftest mice, a spring-like mechanism could have been affixed to the side of the rock opposite the bait and the twig. This would have accelerated the fall of the rock, leaving the mouse almost no chance of escape. Later, after further evolution, the rock could have been replaced by a snapping mechanism, still activated by a spring and bait, but no longer relying on gravity. At this point, the modern mousetrap would have been invented. Even though this evolutionary pathway is totally theoretical, it is certainly logical. Further, it is unlikely that humans came up with the idea of the modern mousetrap all at once, without episodes of trial and error. In other words, it was not impossible for mousetraps to evolve, and so Behe's metaphor of mousetrap irreducible complexity does not succeed.

After this foray into biology, medicine, and mousetraps, let us now see how creationism and neocreationist ID thinking and achievements are positioned in the field of general science.

Are ID and "Creation Science" Sciences?

It is true that controversy is the gist of science and that critical thinking is one of its key ingredients. Theories are established, revised, accepted, or rejected, always depending on the gathering of new observations or reinterpretation of old ones. What have been the contributions so far of "creation science" and ID? Both are critical of evolutionary theory and critical of the interpretation of many empirical facts that support it. So far, so good. But as we described in chapter 1, science can advance only by putting hypotheses to the test and by building theories that make predictions regarding future observations. In that sense, "creation science" and ID fail to contribute to scientific understanding. All we learn from them is that some theories are wrong, but all they offer in return are speculations as to why this is so. No experimental protocols to test the concept of a designer have been proposed, and certainly not carried out. Worse, ID supporters have been unable to define and explain "irreducible complexity" (as we just showed above in great detail) other than saying over and over that irreducible complexity is irreducibly complex, which is a circular argument.

As we explained in chapter 2, the accusation that evolution by natural selection is a tautology was resolved by making quantitative observations in natural populations. A saying in science is that if a perceived phenomenon is not quantitatively measurable, it might as well not exist. And so is irreducible complexity: it is not measurable, it is not quantifiable. Anyone can claim that anything, including a tornado or an earthquake, is irreducibly complex and hence always implies a designer. In brief, since irreducible complexity is an unquantifiable *subjective impression*, it has no scientific meaning.

Similarly, "creation science" and ID, based on what they call their "theories," have been unable to make verifiable predictions. To put it differently, where do creationists go now that they have vigorously tried to discredit aspects of science they do not like? In the absence of new facts, prediction of potential new facts, and no theoretical framework, there is nothing here that even remotely resembles science. Therefore, "creation science" and ID are not science; they are just negations, sweeping rejections of mainstream science based on theological or other beliefs. In a nutshell, "creation science" and ID have been unable to offer testable alternatives to solidly established— and tested—real scientific theories.

Has Research on ID Been Published in Scientific Journals?

First, no one can claim that there is such a thing as creationist or ID-inspired laboratory research, at least none that has ever been published. Neocreationists have composed slick Web sites, have published numerous books through their own channels, and have produced several DVDs with impressive special effects. None of that indicates any kind of recognition of ID or creationism by the scientific community, however. The normal publication process for scientists is to submit their results to peer-reviewed journals. These results are published only after rigorous screening by specialists, with many manuscripts rejected in the process. For example, the two most prestigious scientific journals, *Nature* and *Science*, reject up to 90% of the manuscripts submitted to them. This is because these manuscripts do not meet the quality standards of these two journals, sometimes because the submitted results are dubious, or the interpretation of the results is questionable, or simply because the manuscripts are of low interest. Of course, not all scientific journals have the same exacting standards, especially in terms of relevance or general interest. In brief, the process of publication in peer-reviewed journals *validates* scientific findings. In addition, scientific journals publish two broad types of articles: those containing new experimental evidence, and those reviewing progress or new debates in a given field. What, then, is the performance of ID believers and classical creationists in terms of published peer-reviewed articles?

At the time of this writing, the number of articles presenting new experimental results based on the ID and creationist approaches is exactly zero. However, ID proponents have published two review-style articles in legitimate journals. The first one, published in the little-known *Proceedings of the Biological Society of Washington*, is a long diatribe on all that is wrong—according to the author—with evolutionary theory. This article does not contain a shred of experimental evidence that could back up ID. It should also be noted that this paper was published under unusual circumstances, where the editor of the journal, who has since resigned, evaluated the article without consulting peer reviewers not affiliated with the journal. This former editor is also known for having signed a neocreationist document and for being a member of a study group that favorably investigates "creation biology." In other words, a cloud of uncertainty surrounds the publication of this ID article.

The other review article promulgating ID was published in a cryptic Italian journal called *Rivista di Biologia*. The Center for Science and Culture, the ID headquarters, announced in 2005 with great pride the publication of this article in a second peer-reviewed journal. But this journal only publishes articles on *theoretical biology* (as emphasized on the journal's Web page), and indeed, this second paper, again, contains no new experimental evidence whatsoever. Its topic is centrioles, little bodies found in animal cells that are involved in the movement of chromosomes. These centrioles, the author claims, could only have been "holistically designed." Thus, centrioles now join the ranks of the bacterial flagellum, the eye, blood clotting, and the immune system as structures and biochemical pathways that are "irreducibly complex." As we mentioned above, anything can be seen as irreducibly complex, including centrioles and countless other biological structures. However, making such a statement does not constitute truth, especially when experimental evidence is totally lacking.

In brief, the publication record of ID scientists is not impressive, and it is nil in the area of experimental science. Last but not least, in spite of optimistic predictions made back in 1998, ID research has never received funding from federal agencies such as the National Science Foundation and the

National Institutes of Health, both based on a peer-review mechanism for the allocation of research funds.

In view of this dismal record, it is very difficult to take any published ID claims seriously and think about ID as a new framework for the explanation of any scientific observation in the realm of evolution. Contrary to that, as we describe in chapter 4, evolutionary theory provides a consistent and logical explanation of a process of interest to us all: the origin of modern humans, the origin of their diversity, and the origin of culture. This explanation is abundantly supported by empirical facts. Since humans have designed science, it is indeed appropriate to take a look at how their own creation—science—views their origin and evolution.

Things to Think About

1. The description of so-called irreducible (or specified) complexity in living organisms by ID thinkers is incorrect. They sweep under the rug many scientific facts that go against their ideas.

2. Modern genetics strongly supports the concept that all extant life-forms descend from common ancestors that appeared billions of years ago and evolved by mutation, natural selection, and drift. Could it be that all of genetics is wrong?

3. If there is (was) a designer, this designer is (was) not very thoughtful and made innumerable mistakes in the design of life-forms, including humans. Can you think of truly "perfect" life-forms?

4. ID scientific research is nonexistent. How, then, can the ID viewpoint be defended as science?

4

The Origins and Evolution
of *Homo sapiens*

> What is clearly implied by the data . . . is that all modern human
> genetic diversity found around the world was in Africa around
> 60,000 years ago.
>
> —Spencer Wells, *The Journey of Man: A Genetic Odyssey*

Surveys consistently show that about 45% of the American public believes
that modern humans were created by God (the designer) some time between
6,000 and 10,000 years ago, in accordance with biblical precepts. The imprecision on this date is due to the difficulty of evaluating, based on biblical
information, the length of time that has elapsed since the creation of Adam
and Eve. This is because from the story recounted in *Genesis*, it is unclear at
which point humans stopped living for hundreds of years and assumed more
ordinary life spans, shortening generational times. Additionally, since creationists reject evolution, they also reject the notion that modern humans are
the result of a long evolutionary lineage that started millions of years ago. For
them, prehuman fossils are ape skeletons. Also, creationists claim that Neanderthal fossils are those of sick, deformed human beings who died in the
recent past and could not possibly be part of an evolutionary process that
eventually led to modern humans.

These types of beliefs baffle most educated people in the rest of the world.
This is because there is overwhelming scientific evidence that modern humans appeared much earlier than what is claimed by one sole document, the
Bible, which was at first orally transmitted for hundreds of years, and this
well before any type of serious scientific inquiry was possible. It is also known
that Neanderthals went extinct well more than 25,000 years ago and that they
were not deformed human beings.

In contrast to the recent dates offered by the Bible, genetic science based
on DNA shows that modern humans appeared approximately 160,000 years
ago. The imprecision here is due to the statistical error that invariably ac-
companies all scientific measurements. Genetics is not the only branch of science that supports this much earlier date for the appearance of anatomically
modern humans. Indeed, paleontological findings (fossil remains) agree very
well with genetic data and are presented first below.

As creationists and neocreationists have it, the fossil record is woefully
incomplete; they claim that it lacks evolutionarily intermediate forms

85

between species. This is actually untrue. For example, new discoveries in China clearly show that some dinosaur species had feathers, making them good candidates as precursors of birds. Similarly, new fossil finds in Arctic Canada strongly point in the direction of extinct fish on their way to becoming adapted to life on land. And finally, a recently discovered 100-million-year-old fossil bee clearly shows traits intermediate between those of modern bees and wasps, which today are fully differentiated, non-interbreeding species. But, of course, one must agree that the fossil record is not as complete as one would wish, because fossils are rare, and their discovery is mostly serendipitous. Interestingly, this cannot be said as forcefully of human and prehuman fossils. For obvious reasons, we humans are more excited about our own origins than we are about the origins of, say, flowering plants and aardvarks. It is then no surprise that the efforts of paleontologists have focused on the discovery of bipedal primates, our forebears.

Paleoanthropologists (paleontologists specializing in human evolution) have discovered that Africa occupies a special place in human origins because prehuman fossils are more abundant there than they are anywhere else in the world. What, then, does the fossil record tell us about the origins of humans? The following description is what some call a "streamlined" version of human evolution, that is, a simplified version accepted by most paleoanthropologists. Some scientists do not agree with this simplified version because some very rare and newly discovered fossils still await categorization. These are not discussed here. But we will show that, rather than lacking intermediate evolutionary forms, the human fossil record is rich and varied.

A Plethora of Intermediate Forms in the Human Fossil Record

Bipedalism, the ability to walk on two legs, is one of the major hallmarks of humanity. The other hallmark is a big brain relative to our body size. No other placental mammals can walk on two legs for significant periods of time, not even chimps. Further, even though elephants and whales have bigger brains, their brains are not as big as ours relative to their total size. Paleoanthropologists in search of human origins thus concentrate on these two factors, bipedalism and brain size. Brain size is very easy to determine once a fossil skull is discovered. All one has to do is to measure cranial capacity by estimating the volume of the brain case. Potential bipedalism is determined by studying the anatomy of pelvic and leg bones, the structure of the spinal column, and its abutting with the skull. Modern techniques, such as CAT scans, are routinely used by paleontologists to study fossils and analyze the structure of their bones. As for fossil dating, all dates reported below have been independently verified using several independent techniques.

The earliest prehuman bipedal fossil agreed upon by most paleoanthropologists is that of an animal discovered in Kenya called *Orrorin tugenensis*. Its fossil was dated at 5–6 million years ago, which puts it close to the generally accepted date for the pre-chimpanzee/prehuman split. Later came *Australopithecus afarensis*, a much better understood African primate because its fossil remains are more abundant. *Australopithecus* first appeared about 4.2 million years ago. Its most representative specimen, the famous "Lucy," lived in Ethiopia about 3.2 million years ago. Lucy was clearly bipedal, about 3 feet tall, and weighed about 55 pounds. Her cranial capacity was about that of a modern chimp. *Australopithecus* fossils have been found in multiple places in sub-Saharan Africa but not in the rest of the world. The genus *Australopithecus* became extinct about 1.5 million years ago.

However, about 2.5 million years ago, in Kenya and Ethiopia, some *Australopithecus* individuals evolved into the first representatives of our own genus: *Homo* (see figure 4.1). These first humans, called *Homo habilis*, developed stone tool technology, were taller, and had a bigger brain size than did *Australopithecus*. *H. habilis* became extinct about 1.5 million years ago, after some of them had evolved into more advanced *Homo erectus*, about 1.9 million years ago. *Homo erectus* also evolved in East Africa. The tool technology of *H. erectus* was much more sophisticated than that of *H. habilis*. *H. erectus* was also tall, measuring up to 6 feet, weighed up to 150 pounds, and had a brain size twice that of a modern chimp. There is good evidence that *H. erectus* had learned how to domesticate fire, perhaps as early as 800,000 years ago, and was probably able to build simple shelters.

But it is their travels that make *H. erectus* fascinating. There is excellent evidence that *H. erectus* traveled out of Africa to reach Europe (Georgia and elsewhere), Southeast Asia (Indonesia), and finally eastern China. Indeed, *H. erectus* fossils have been discovered in all these locations. All the non-African *H. erectus* fossils ever discovered are younger than their African counterparts, strongly indicating that *H. erectus* evolved in Africa and in Africa alone. This idea is, of course, consistent with *Australopithecus* and *H. habilis* also having evolved exclusively in Africa. *H. erectus* may have become extinct as late as 150,000 years ago, but not before differentiating about 1 million years ago into what is called *Homo antecessor* or *Homo heidelbergensis*, the presumed ancestor of both Neanderthals and anatomically modern humans.

Surprisingly, descendants of *H. erectus* may have survived until as recently as 18,000 years ago and may even have lived side by side with *H. sapiens* in

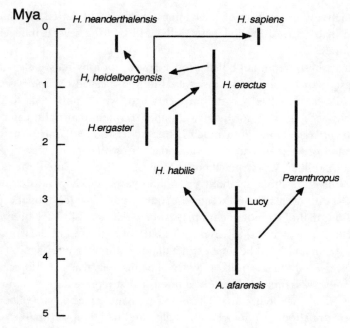

FIGURE 4.1
The ancestry of *Homo sapiens* as revealed by the fossil record. Vertical bars represent the longevity of each species as determined by fossil finds. "Lucy," the famous *A. afarensis* fossil found in Ethiopia, is indicated by a horizontal line. *H. ergaster* is the name sometimes given to African *H. erectus*. The genus *Paranthropus* is not in the human lineage. Mya, millions of years ago.

what is now eastern Indonesia. In 2004, a multidisciplinary group of paleoanthropologists reported the discovery on the small island of Flores of an apparently new species of humans, now extinct, which they named *Homo floresiensis*. These creatures were remarkably small, being about one meter tall (a little over three feet), and had a small brain size. For this reason, they were nicknamed "hobbits," in reference to the characters in J. R. R. Tolkien novels. The "hobbits" may have reached their island as early as 800,000 years ago, as indicated by the discovery on Flores of stone tools that old. *H. floresiensis* used stone weapons to hunt pygmy elephants (*Stegodon*, a species now extinct) also then living on Flores. Since *H. sapiens* arrived in the area at least 45,000 years ago, there exists the intriguing possibility that both species coexisted for tens of thousands of years.

The current interpretation for the existence of *H. floresiensis* is that these creatures were descendants of Asian *H. erectus*. But we also know that *H.*

erectus was tall, sometimes as tall as modern humans. What then accounts for the very short size of *H. floresiensis*? It turns out that size reduction (dwarfism) can take place when mammalian species find refuge on isolated islands, which also explains why elephants on Flores were so small. As we mentioned in chapter 2, this size reduction also happened to Nile hippopotamus that reached the island of Madagascar. This phenomenon is known as "island dwarfism." The same phenomenon would have been responsible for the evolution of the "hobbits." It should be noted, however, that not all paleoanthropologists agree that the "hobbits" are a new species of humans. A very few claim that these creatures may simply be pathologically deformed *H. sapiens*.

Another extinct species of humans, *Homo neanderthalensis*, lived in Europe and West Asia between about 300,000 and 28,000 years ago. Their fossils are numerous and well studied, and more than 300 Neanderthal sites have been discovered. Their average cranial capacity was slightly higher than that of modern humans, and they were more stocky and stronger than us. Given where they lived, and given the climate then prevalent in these places, the strong build of Neanderthals has been attributed to adaptation to a cold climate. Their stone technology was superior to that of *H. erectus*, and there is evidence that they had developed a culture involving art and jewelry. There is also evidence that Neanderthals cared for their injured or ill: many Neanderthal skeletons show healed fractures or healed stab wounds. Thus, the sufferers survived these injuries, most likely due to care and help from others. It is still unclear whether the Neanderthals could speak. Why they went extinct about 28,000 years ago is also a mystery. But certainly, they must have encountered *Homo sapiens*, ourselves, because by then we occupied all the places inhabited by the Neanderthals. Did *H. sapiens* commit genocide, were changing climatic conditions responsible for the demise of the Neanderthals, or was it something else? We simply do not know.

This very brief history of the premodern human fossil record shows that the tale of the "missing link," still held by some, is completely outdated. Many links leading from primates that lived several million years ago to our modern selves have been discovered. The appearance of bipedalism as early as 5–6 million years ago, the well-documented temporal sequence of increase in brain size, and the evolution of tool making all show that our ancestral lineage is very old, and by now the details of our evolution are well filled in.

As for "missing links" between the Neanderthals and *H. sapiens*, it is thought by many that none will be found. DNA evidence obtained so far argues against the idea that Neanderthals and *H. sapiens* interbred and left hybrid descendants.

Anatomically Modern Human Fossils

In 2003, a team of paleoanthropologists reported the discovery in Ethiopia of quasi-modern human fossils dated at 154,000 to 160,000 years ago. The use of the term "quasi-modern" refers to the fact that these humans showed a somewhat protruding brow ridge, which categorizes them as "archaic." Their brain size was as large as ours. The interpretation of these fossils, dubbed *Homo sapiens idaltu*, is that they were on the verge of becoming fully modern humans.

Fully anatomically modern human fossils, dated to about 130,000 years ago, have been found in Ethiopia and in Israel, while more recent human fossils have been discovered in South Africa (90,000–120,000 years old) and Australia (40,000–60,000 years old). This evidence strongly suggests that modern humans appeared in Africa, an interpretation supported also by Africa being the only place in the world where there is an uninterrupted line between the oldest bipedal fossils (*Orrorin*) and modern humans.

After about 25,000–40,000 years ago, fossils of anatomically modern humans are found practically all over the planet, with the exception of the Americas and Polynesia. The story, or rather theory, that emerges from the fossil record is thus that modern humans appeared in Africa from a long line of prehuman primates. From there, they migrated over time to the four corners of Earth.

We said above that, for reasons of simplicity, we would use the "streamlined" fossil lineage of *H. sapiens*. It turns out that many different bipedal primates lived in Africa between about 1.5 and 5 million years ago and thus coexisted with our direct ancestors *H. habilis* and *H. erectus*. These other primates went extinct and left no recognizable modern descendants. Just to name some, these were *Australopithecus africanus*, *Paranthropus boisei*, and *Paranthropus robustus* (who must have been a fearsome sight for other bipedal primates at the time because of their sheer size). Therefore, our forebears were part of a constellation of bipedal species that roamed the African savanna for a long period of time (see figure 4.1). Figure 4.2 shows fossil representatives of what some of our ancestors looked like.

How is it that our ancestors (starting with *Australopithecus*) left descendants while no other bipedal primate lineages did? Our best answer is that our ancestors' brains evolved toward a bigger size and greater complexity. We do not know exactly how this happened, although recent studies show that some genes involved in brain function are found exclusively in humans and not in chimpanzees and the other great apes. In all likelihood, these human genes evolved after the chimp/*Australopithecus* split, as revealed by DNA sequencing. In any event, bigger brains allowed the taming and use of

FIGURE 4.2
Fossil skulls of, from right to left, *Australopithecus afarensis*, *Homo erectus*, and *Homo sapiens*. Note the increase in brain case size.

fire, the steady improvement of stone technology, the appearance of symbolic language, and enhanced cooperation. In sum, a big brain size allowed the development of culture. Cultural evolution, as we describe at the end of this chapter, came to supplant biological evolution in humans because it is so much more flexible and is propagated so much faster than are biological adaptations. In the last 100,000 years or so, we became cultural animals, and culture became our primary means of adaptation to the environment.

Let us now turn to scientific studies that take us far away from fossils. To understand what follows, one must realize that scientists strive to corroborate theories by cross-checking them with data obtained independently, sometimes from studies undertaken in a totally different area of science. Fascinatingly, fossils are not the only source of information regarding human origins. DNA science is also a rich trove of information, and it fully confirms an ancient African origin of modern humans. Moreover, genetic science plots very well the early human diasporas that sent humans to colonize our whole planet.

However, DNA evidence has not been obtained from ancient human fossils. So far, it has not been possible to retrieve DNA from fossils older than about 30,000–40,000 years. This is because DNA is a rather fragile molecule that degrades over time. Rather, as explained in chapter 3, genealogies (phylogenetic trees) based on DNA can be obtained by looking at the types of DNA variants (evolved DNA sequences showing subtle base-pair differences) observed in organisms alive today. This principle applies equally well to human DNA sequences and human origins.

What DNA Says about the Origins of Modern Humans

Mitochondrial DNA Studies

DNA in human cells is separated into two subcellular compartments. The enormous majority of it (3.1 billion base pairs) is present in a structure called the nucleus, which contains the chromosomes. Chromosomes harbor roughly 25,000 different genes. However, a second category of structures, called the mitochondria, also contain DNA. Mitochondria are commonly dubbed the "energy factories" of cells because it is through mitochondria that the oxygen we breathe is metabolized to form energy-rich compounds that we use to power many of our metabolic activities. Contrary to chromosomal DNA, human mitochondrial DNA (mtDNA) is very short, only 16,600 base pairs long. Given its short size, our mtDNA only contains 37 genes.

The small size of mtDNA has one great advantage: it is easy and fast to sequence. Thus, information regarding the nature and number of mtDNA gene variants found among many individuals is easy to obtain. As we detailed in chapter 3, the existence of gene variants in living organisms informs us of their evolutionary past.

Another interesting characteristic of mtDNA is that it is passed down exclusively from mothers to their children. Children do not inherit mtDNA from their fathers. This is because the mother's egg contains many mitochondria, whereas the portion of the father's sperm cell that enters the egg to fertilize it contains none. This, then, means that mtDNA can be used to trace the genealogies of women but not those of men. Indeed, when a son inherits his mother's mtDNA, he cannot pass it down to his children: mtDNA always goes through women alone. But this also means that analyzing DNA from both sexes can help determine the evolutionary path of our mothers, grandmothers, great grandmothers, and so forth, deep into the past, until we reach the ancestress of us all. In effect, there is no reason to believe that mtDNA analysis cannot retrace the history of the entire human species through its women. To understand this, recall that those of us alive today come by definition from an uninterrupted line of ancestors.

Recall from chapters 2 and 3 that DNA always mutates over time; its base-pair sequence changes. Also recall the theory of neutral evolution by drift: under drift alone, evolution is proportional to the speed at which mutations accumulate over time. This is called the mutation *rate*. The mutation rate of human DNA has been determined by laboratory studies. Using the value of the mutation rate, it should then be possible to determine when individuals taken at random last shared a common ancestor, depending on how closely or distantly related their mtDNA sequences are. To do this accurately, scientists must take into account the effect of natural selection on mtDNA mutations. Indeed, natural selection, if acting on some mutations, would nullify the simple relationship between evolutionary distance and number of mutations that have accumulated. Therefore, scientists analyze portions of mtDNA that, to the best of their knowledge, are not influenced by natural selection.

Now, assuming a constant rate of mutation over time, and no effect of natural selection, what has mtDNA revealed about our ancestry? To date, mtDNA from thousands of individuals living in hundreds of different human populations, distributed all over the globe, have been studied. Phylogenies were then built based on the different variants of mtDNA found. All analyses made in many different laboratories agree: modern human females appeared in East Africa about 168,000 years ago, because this is where the most ancestral mtDNA is found. Therefore, as already suggested by paleontology, the cradle of *H. sapiens* is Africa, at least as far as women are concerned.

The mathematical equations of population genetics also allow us to determine the size of this original population of humans: between 1,000 and 10,000 individuals. Therefore, all humans on the planet are descended from one woman who was part of this relatively small East African population. Interestingly (and jokingly), our common ancestress was nicknamed "Eve" by the researchers who first discovered our African origins. But Eve was not the only woman on Earth at the time—she had between 500 and 5,000 female companions in her population. What happened to the mtDNA of all these other women? The answer is threefold: (1) some of these women did not reproduce, (2) others may have had boys only, or (3) their lineages stopped at a certain point in the past because their descendants failed to reproduce and hence their mtDNA lineages were lost.

Y Chromosome Studies

As one can well imagine, there must have been a genetic "Adam" as well as a genetic "Eve." Like Eve, we expect that Adam must have lived in the same East African population. Can science show that, indeed, there was an Adam and that this Adam lived at the same time as Eve? We cannot rely on mtDNA because it is transmitted solely through mothers. Fortunately for researchers, nature has equipped human males with a stretch of DNA that females do not possess: the Y chromosome. What is more, the Y chromosome, called a sex chromosome, is passed down exclusively from fathers to sons.

Sex chromosomes come in two types: the X chromosome and the Y chromosome. As described in chapter 2, women have an XX sex chromosome makeup, while men are XY. In other words, when couples reproduce, if the child receives one X chromosome from its mother and one X from its father, this child will be a girl. If, however, the father contributes a Y chromosome to the child, this child will be a boy. Thus, we can see that Y chromosome phylogenies trace the evolutionary history of human males. In that respect, the Y chromosome plays for male phylogenies the same role that mtDNA plays for female phylogenies.

But unlike mtDNA, the Y chromosome is large: it contains more than 60 million base pairs and is thus about 4,000 times bigger than mtDNA. This size makes sequencing this whole chromosome impractical on a routine basis. Rather, scientists sequence only portions of the Y chromosome to establish male phylogenies. But which portions? Fortunately again, it turns out that, aside from a number of male-determining genes whose location is known, the majority of the Y chromosome does not contain any genes. This is the part of the Y chromosome that phylogenists study because, not carrying any genes, the DNA on this part is not susceptible to natural selection; its variants found in populations are the result of genetic drift. This way, as in the case of mtDNA, the appearance of Y chromosome variants over time depends on known mutation rates and is proportional to time since separation of lineages.

In brief, the same reasoning and equations that are applied to mtDNA can also be applied to Y chromosome DNA in order to establish male phylogenies. All researchers agree that, like Eve, Adam was also an East African, because the oldest Y chromosome variants are found among East African populations. At what period of time did Adam live? By "Adam" we mean not the man who had children with "Eve," but the man who first passed on a distinctive Y chromosome variant to all subsequent human males on Earth. Intriguingly, and perhaps annoyingly, the age of Adam is presently set at 103,000 years, substantially less than Eve's age (168,000 years). Why this discrepancy? It may be simply that new results based on the testing of many more individuals will bring these two dates statistically closer together.

On the other hand, the reason for the age difference between Adam and Eve may be cultural rather than statistical. Today, most marriages around the world are monogamous, but several societies permit and practice polygyny, the marriage of one man to more than one woman at the same time. If this practice was more general a long time ago than it is today (which, of course, we do not know), this practice would have resulted in what is called in genetics a *bottleneck* (recall chapter 2). A genetic bottleneck is due to a reduction in population through events like famines or emigration of small groups. But another type of genetic bottleneck is possible: if only a few males reproduce because of a widespread practice of polygyny, many males will be left without descendants. This situation is equivalent to a bottleneck affecting males only. Population genetics equations indicate that, in the case of a male bottleneck, the result is an *apparent* age of the male population younger than it really is. Finally, Y chromosome data also agree with the fact that Adam lived in a population that numbered between 1,000 and 10,000 men and women. Thus, aside from an unanswered (or only partially answered) question regarding the age of Adam, genetic science demonstrates that modern humans appeared in East Africa.

Now that we understand our East African origins, how can we determine when and how our ancestors migrated out of Africa, and by which routes? After all, humans are found practically everywhere on the planet, and way back then they must have reached their distant destinations on foot.

Early Human Voyagers and Their Migration Routes

Fossil evidence shows that the oldest anatomically modern humans are found in East Africa, the next oldest ones are found in the Middle East, younger ones are found in Australia, and younger ones still are found in the rest of the world. Unfortunately, fossils are few and far between and are sometimes difficult to date precisely. Thus, fossil finds are not the best way to determine how early humans migrated out of Africa. This is where DNA studies of living humans come to the rescue.

Techniques to trace human diasporas are the same as those used in the discovery of human origins in East Africa. As in these previous studies, both mtDNA and Y chromosome analyses were used to determine how our ancestors moved on the planet by tracing the new gene variants that appeared over time as humans were migrating. Since humans originated in Africa, this is where one expects to find the most ancestral variants. As humans moved, mutations in the ancestral variants occurred, and by following these mutations, starting from the oldest ones to the most recent ones, it has been possible to retrace prehistoric human migrations. For example, we know that old gene variants are found in Australia (they are subsequent mutants of the ancestral African variants, however), but that much more recently acquired variants are found in the Americas. The conclusion is that populations of Australian aborigines are more ancient than Native American populations because the former are genetically closer to African populations than the latter. This view is supported by the fossil record.

This finding indicates that humans populated Australia before they populated the New World. Since the appearance of new variants can be dated based on mutation rates, we can also say at what point in time the occupation of new lands took place. To date, the age of gene variants found in many human populations distributed all over the world has been elucidated, which allows us to reconstruct human migration routes with great confidence. The story of our diasporas as established by genetic research goes as follows.

About 100,000 years ago, our ancestors spread out of East Africa to colonize the southern part of that continent. The direct descendants of these first migrants are still with us: they are the Khoisan (or San), who presently live in the Kalahari desert of Namibia, South Africa, and Botswana. They could rightfully claim the title of "First people." Interestingly, the Khoisan language is characterized by "clicks" that are not used in any other languages. This has led some linguists to think that the Khoisan language is as close to the primeval human language as any modern language could be. As is true of all extant human languages, the Khoisan tongue is as sophisticated as any language.

Following this African expansion, humans migrated out of Africa about 50,000 to 60,000 years ago, traveling toward South Asia. In all likelihood, this took place via a coastal route that took them first through the Middle East (thus first traveling in a north and then northeasterly direction) and subsequently moving southeastward to reach the Indian subcontinent. An alternative explanation is that early humans could have gone due east from their African location, crossed the Red Sea (but not under the leadership of Moses quite yet), and then traveled along the coast of the Arabian Peninsula until they reached and crossed the Strait of Hormuz. From there, they would have traveled east in the direction of India.

At about the same time that they reached northern India, several thousand years after leaving Africa, some subgroups split off from the main migrating group and moved northward, toward Central Asia. Other subgroups moved southeast and reached Borneo, New Guinea, and Australia. Later, starting about 40,000 years ago, as the human population was growing, migrants moved from Central Asia toward Europe and, in the other direction, toward eastern (China) and northeastern (Siberia) Asia. At this point in time, practically all of Eurasia (barring totally inhospitable areas) had been occupied by humans. Of course, one should not imagine millions of humans vying for territory; population density was quite low everywhere, including in ancestral Africa.

The Americas were colonized significantly later, not before 15,000–35,000 years ago, possibly through several waves of migrations, all originating in Asia. Finally, Polynesia was occupied very late, in historical times, only about 1,000 years ago, by skilled mariners who may have traveled from islands located southeast of New Guinea. These migrations (except the Polynesian migration) are summarized in figure 4.3.

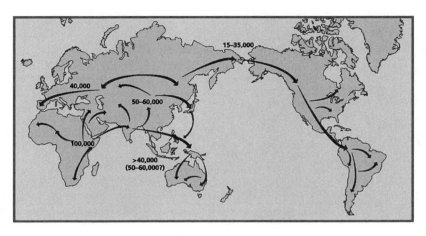

FIGURE 4.3
Timing of the migratory routes of *H. sapiens* in prehistory. Dates and routes are based on the measurements of thousands of gene frequencies in hundreds of human populations. From L. L. Cavalli-Sforza and M. W. Feldman, "The application of molecular genetic approaches to the study of human evolution," *Nature Genetics* 33(Suppl., 2003): 266–275, by permission of *Nature Genetics*.

This picture of early human migrations is corroborated by studies of Earth's past climate. Our planet started warming about 10,000 years ago, resulting in the relatively balmy climate we are experiencing today. But 100,000 years ago, Earth was cooler by 2–8°C than it is now. Additionally, between 70,000 and 55,000 years ago, our planet experienced a glacial maximum. These climatic conditions would not have been conducive to human migrations out of Africa until after 55,000 years ago or so because of the existence of extensive glaciers covering large areas and, of course, a cold climate. But about 55,000 years ago, a warmer interglacial period intervened that lasted until about 15,000 years ago. It is during this period that the migrations toward Australia, Eurasia, and the Americas took place.

Although the global climate had warmed starting about 55,000 year ago, it was not as warm as it is today. Cooler temperatures worldwide meant that more water was locked in glaciers. As a consequence, sea levels were lower than today, making New Guinea and Australia a single landmass separated from Southeast Asia by only fairly short stretches of open sea. Nevertheless, the migrants who traveled from Southeast Asia to Australia and New Guinea must have used some kind of floating devices to cross the water. No traces of such boats have been found, possibly because they rotted away a very long time ago.

Also, during the same interglacial period, the Sahara (including the Sinai Peninsula, which early humans would have had to cross) was not a desert, making the travel from East Africa to the Middle East much easier than it is today. However, the Sahara became a desert 40,000 years ago, which must have prevented or at least seriously hindered further expansions out of Africa. Finally, also thanks to lower sea levels, eastern Siberia was connected to Alaska by a wide isthmus called Beringia (which today is under water). Japan was similarly connected to Asia and could have been reached on foot. Thus, human expansions from Asia to the Americas and Japan did not require any type of sophisticated technology.

It is natural to wonder how long it took early humans to cross all these vast distances by traveling on foot. After all, it takes hours to go from, say, Nairobi in East Africa to Beijing, China, by jet airplane. Genetic data, based on somewhat shorter distances, show that it took humans only about 3,000 years to cross the distance separating India from Australia, which means a leisurely pace of 2.5 miles per year. Similarly, it took migrants from Asia to the Americas only a few thousand years to reach the tip of South America.

Genetic Drift and Natural Selection during the Early Human Migrations

Some people think of human variation in terms of "races." Africans are dark-skinned but Swedes are not—that much is obvious. But it takes only a few minutes of reflection to realize that not only Africans but also Australian aborigines, New Guineans, South Indians, and Ceylonese, for example, have relatively dark skin. Why is that so? The answer is natural selection.

As we were evolving in Africa, not far from the equator, our skin would have been dark because dark skin is selected wherever the sun shines brightly. Any person of white complexion who has experienced serious sunburn understands why. It also turns out that the dark-skinned non-African populations mentioned above also live in areas where sunshine is abundant. In fact, it is well known that skin color varies from north to south, from light to dark, in a gradual manner. Thus, the more sunshine, the darker the human skin.

Now, what about people with light skin color, such as the Europeans, the northern Chinese, and the Japanese, who live roughly at the same latitude? Why have they not kept the dark skin of their common ancestors? The answer is also natural selection. In northern climes, dark skin is not under strong selection pressure because sunshine is limited and severe sunburns are unlikely. On the other hand, sunshine is critically important for making vitamin D in the skin. Dark skin is not as efficient in making vitamin D as is white skin. But this does not matter in places where the sun shines practically every day because more sun compensates for lower efficiency. Therefore, keeping a dark skin near the equator prevents sunburns and allows production of enough vitamin D.

Where the sun shines more rarely, as in the north, humans evolved in a direction that maximized the efficiency of vitamin D synthesis in their skin while not having problems with sunburns. This meant evolving in the direction of less pigmented skin. Loss of pigmentation then occurred through a sequence of random mutations that decreased the production of skin pigments in some individuals. Gradually, the mutant individuals who made more vitamin D thanks to their light pigmentation—and were thus healthier—were favored over others for survival and longevity by natural selection. These better-adapted mutants were the ones who reproduced most and passed down their mutated genes, in typical Darwinian fashion.

To continue our analysis of human diversity, one might also say that, when one compares one extreme corner of Eurasia (such as Ireland, for example) with another extreme corner (such as Korea), one notices that human facial and body features change in a fairly obvious fashion. The Irish look different from Koreans, and vice versa. Why is this so? Since the Irish and the Koreans live at roughly the same latitude, climatic conditions cannot be invoked to explain the differences.

Our best answer here is genetic drift, that is, chance events (mutations) that determined stature and other physical traits in splinter groups as humans were on the move a long time ago. Let us remember that early migrations involved very small numbers of people. Thus, the migration of subgroups splitting off from small main groups could easily have led to population bottlenecks that resulted in the narrowing of an already narrow gene pool. These bottlenecks could have led to physical differentiation of human subpopulations. However, as all or most of the splinter groups grew in size over time, humans from different subgroups must have met one another where their territories overlapped. As it happens, humans from neighboring groups must have mated and so produced *genetic gradients* in an east–west fashion. The result of such genetic gradients is a smoothing out of the differences between adjacent groups, including their physical features. On the other hand, the ancient Irish and Koreans never had much of a chance to meet and mate, due to geographic distance, and thereby kept their differences intact. In other words, these two populations exist at the extreme poles of the genetic gradient and so are expected to show the greatest differences. These gradients are easily detectable at the DNA level, but they are also visible at a much cruder level: our external appearance.

Now that we understand gradients, we know why we cannot pinpoint a geographic line sharply separating the Irish from the Koreans (other than artificial political boundaries, of course). If we tried to do that, we would end up wondering whether the Central Asian Uzbeks, for example, should be clustered with the Irish or with the Koreans. This is a silly proposition, of course. The reason again is that facial and other features (including gene variants) change *gradually* from west to east, and not sharply. The take-home message and great spinoff of all this is simple: genetics does not recognize the antiquated notion of human "races" because gene gradients, not sharp boundaries, determine how we look. Thus, human "races" are totally undefinable scientifically, and hence they do not genetically exist. This is a great lesson that modern human genetics teaches us.

Controversy Is Grist for the Mill of Science, Including in the Realm of Human Evolution

Although the narrative of human diasporas given above is generally agreed upon by geneticists and anthropologists, not *everybody* agrees that it is entirely correct. Contrary to what some would say, this is not a sign of weakness. Instead, scientific controversy is healthy, because it forces the proponents of a theory to try to make it stronger by gathering more data or, sometimes, to revise or even abandon it. One such controversy in the field of human origins is the debate between the uniregional and multiregional models for the origin of humans.

As described above, *Homo erectus* evolved into an ancestor that would eventually generate two evolutionary branches: the Neanderthals and *Homo sapiens*. Also, *H. erectus* fossils were found in Africa, Europe, South Asia, and East Asia. These findings prompted some anthropologists to hypothesize that the African, European, and Asian lineages of *H. erectus* each evolved into their respective lineages of African, European, and Asian *H. sapiens*. This is what is meant by "multiregional": different lineages of modern humans evolved independently on different continents. The Americas are not included because the only human fossils ever found there are those of anatomically modern humans. The multiregional model also supports the idea that Neanderthals are direct precursors of *H. sapiens*. The uniregional model, on the contrary, supports the idea that modern humans appeared only once in the history of Earth: in Africa. From there, they expanded all over the world and differentiated into the populations we know today.

Which model is best supported by scientific evidence? So far, multiregionalists have based their model on the existence of very few fossils that seem to indicate the existence of intermediate forms between Neanderthals and *H. sapiens*. Most paleoanthropologists, however, do not agree that these fossils represent intermediate or hybrid forms.

On the other hand, genetic results strongly support the uniregional model. A Chinese American team has studied the Y chromosome DNA of 12,217 men from 163 populations across Asia. If the multiregional model is right, the variants of these men's Y chromosome should be as old as Asian *H. erectus*, about 1 million years old, because this is the species from which they should, in this model, be descended. Results showed that these variants are about 90,000 years old, consistent with the idea that Asians are not the direct descendants of an Asian *H. erectus*. In fact, the types of Y chromosome variants found in Asia are entirely consistent with an African origin of Asians.

Finally, mtDNA has been isolated with great effort from a few Neanderthal fossils. The gene variants found in these fossils show that Neanderthals and modern humans are not closely related. In fact, some scientists claim that Neanderthals should be considered a species distinct from *Homo sapiens*. More definitive results on the relatedness of Neanderthals and modern humans will depend on the future extraction and analysis of DNA from more Neanderthals, however. In summary, genetic evidence firmly supports the "out-of-Africa" or uniregional model of human evolution in the past 100,000 to 150,000 years or so, and it does not support the multiregional model.

As we just described, paleontology and genetics paint an interesting picture of human evolution and prehistoric human migrations. This picture is not without controversy, but it presently is the best one we have. Of course, human biological evolution explains only a few aspects of our modern human capacities, such as bipedalism, a big brain, and the ability to travel long distances. What else do we know about our big brains and their evolution?

The Human Brain May Still Be Evolving

It is tempting to believe that humans have reached such a high level of complexity, particularly in their brains, that they have stopped evolving. This is indeed a general belief among laypeople. But genetic science, which is advancing at a breakneck pace, actually suggests otherwise. Two studies published in *Science* magazine in September 2005 show that the human brain may still be evolving and that natural selection has played an important role in this evolution in the past several thousand years. Researchers at the University of Chicago have studied the distribution among human populations of two gene variants known to be involved in the determination of brain size. These gene variants are specific to humans and are not found in chimpanzees. Researchers then used the statistical equations of population genetics to estimate at which point in the past these gene variants appeared.

Their results were striking. First, they concluded that the very high frequencies of these variants could not be explained by genetic drift alone; natural selection must have played an important role in their spread among humans. Second, one of the gene variants was calculated to have appeared about 37,000 years ago. Remarkably, this is also the time when symbolic art exploded in Europe. Third, the second gene variant appeared about 5,800 years ago, at a time when humans started building the first cities in the Near East and invented writing. This time is late enough in our history to let us speculate that our brains may still be evolving.

The University of Chicago team interprets these findings as showing that the appearance of new gene variants involved in brain-related functions may have had an adaptive value in our species. This means that natural selection would have favored the spread of these variants because they were beneficial to our survival and proliferation. Certainly, newly acquired more flexible mental abilities would have been favorable to our fate as an intelligent species.

Now, whether these two variants are responsible for some aspects of cognition is presently unknown. In other words, scientists cannot yet claim that these gene variants *caused* (even if only partly) the appearance of symbolic thinking and later the ability to organize life around urban centers, as well as the invention of written language. All scientists agree that much work remains to be done to pinpoint the exact functions of these two gene variants. Nevertheless, this is an important first step in our attempts to determine what makes us human, at least as far as art (always a good thing) and city living (not necessarily a good thing) are concerned.

Finally, the sequence of the chimpanzee genome was published in 2005. Comparing the human and chimp genomes will reveal the similarities and differences between us and our closest cousins. For one thing, it now seems that both we and chimps evolved mostly by genetic drift (see chapter 2), with some influence of natural selection. There seems to be one exception: the rate of evolution of our respective brains. Preliminary data show that the human brain has evolved more rapidly than the chimp brain, possibly as a result of strong positive natural selection. These results are in agreement with those presented above. It should be understood that, at the time of this writing (winter 2006), these are cutting-edge results that are likely to be refined and expanded in the near future.

But evolution has more to say about modern humans and goes well beyond the origins of our physical and neurological features. To discover more about the nature of humans, let us now leave the realm of purely biological science and see how evolutionary thinking can help unravel perhaps the most significant attribute of humans: culture.

Cultural Evolution

Up to about 10,000 years ago, humans lived as hunter-gatherers, following animal prey for meat and gathering wild fruits, roots, and nuts for subsistence. By then they had already invented sophisticated symbolic art (as seen in the famous caves of Lascaux and Chauvet in France and Altamira in Spain) and made efficient weapons for hunting and possibly warfare. But by 10,000 years ago, a great transition in lifestyle took place roughly at the same time in West Asia, East Asia, and Mesoamerica. This major evolutionary change was the invention of agriculture, which developed in what is called the Neolithic (or New Stone Age) period. The Neolithic transition was accompanied by deep changes in the evolutionary rate of living species that humans were domesticating at that time. To show how quickly cultural evolution can influence biological evolution, we present a well-understood case of artificial selection, that is, an evolutionary process where humans, rather than natural phenomena, considerably modified the properties of a living organism.

Corn (maize) was first domesticated by humans in Mesoamerica starting about 7,500 years ago. This domestication process was very gradual. We know with great certainty that modern corn is derived from a wild plant called teosinte, which still grows in Mexico today. Teosinte is a spiky plant that does not even look like modern corn. However, prehistoric humans must have realized early on that the few kernels produced by teosinte had good nutritional value. Humans must also have observed that wild teosinte existed in the form of variants, much like Darwin's finches, and that some variants harbored more and bigger kernels than did others. They then selected these variants, sowed them, and continued to select further variants for the production of bigger ears harboring more and more kernels, until corn, as we know it today, finally appeared. The gradual transformation of teosinte into corn has been extremely well documented by archaeological findings and carbon-14 dating. We also know that modern corn, as we buy it in supermarkets, differs from original teosinte in the structure of at least 1,200 genes, a very large number.

The point here is that artificial selection by humans, exercised on a living organism that still exists today, allowed the fixation of an average of 16 different gene mutations every 100 years, the result of which was to produce an entirely different life-form: modern corn. Even assuming that natural selection is orders of magnitude slower than artificial selection (which we do not really know is true), just think about what *billions* of years of evolution (at least 100,000 times the number of years needed to go from teosinte to corn) did to naturally evolving life-forms.

Going back to the Neolithic transition and its impact on cultural evolution, both agriculture and, somewhat later, animal husbandry, led to the creation of the first cities, writing, taxation, and centralized governments in due time. These inventions and institutions relieved humans from the vagaries and risks of gathering fruits and roots and hunting large animals, but they also had downsides. These were epidemics due to the crowding of human beings in villages and towns, the appearance of social classes, and possibly, a decrease in the status of women. From then on, humans were on an evolutionary path where technology, medicine, and social structure would constantly interact with our biological makeup. We are the only animals on Earth to experience the effects of these interactions on a grand scale.

Of course, the invention of agriculture was not the result of gene mutations in humans. Rather, agriculture was a *cultural* innovation that spread to practically all societies on the planet. We describe below how cultural innovations can be construed as *cultural mutations* through which we became cultural animals, still subjected to natural selection and genetic drift, of course, but also influenced by cultural evolution.

An excellent example of the interplay between biological evolution and cultural evolution is the appearance of lactose tolerance in humans during the Neolithic. Lactose is a sugar found in milk. As infants, we are tolerant to the lactose present in our mother's milk. But as we grow up, some of us become unable to digest lactose and thus become lactose intolerant. This condition is not life-threatening, but it results in annoying bloating and diarrhea. When one studies lactose intolerance around the world, one notices that it is extremely common in East and Southeast Asia, reaching up to 99% in Thailand. One also notices that such countries as Thailand and China neither produce nor consume dairy products. If we turn our attention to countries that *do* produce and consume dairy products, such as Denmark, for example, one finds that, there, lactose intolerance is extremely rare. This is just the opposite of what is observed in East and Southeast Asia. How can this be explained?

It turns out that wherever dairy animals were domesticated, a cultural innovation occurring thousands of years ago, societies that started using milk for food were faced with a dilemma: lactose intolerance in adulthood was prevalent everywhere. On the other hand, milk is extremely nutritious and is an excellent source of protein. Then what happened? Well, those individuals (mutants, really) who were lactose tolerant in these societies benefited from the nutrition provided by milk and were not inconvenienced by lactose. These individuals' fitness was enhanced with milk as food, so they reproduced more than the lactose-intolerant ones, and little by little the frequency of lactose tolerance grew in these societies. This is what happened in Europe, where, as a whole, lactose intolerance is now infrequent.

In China and Thailand, cattle were also domesticated, but there, they were used as draught animals, not for their milk or meat. Also, in these countries, pigs are traditionally the main source of animal proteins. And pigs are not dairy animals. In East and Southeast Asia, lactose intolerance remains high because these societies never relied on milk as food. Individuals in China and Thailand who became lactose tolerant through mutation never experienced enhanced fitness and hence did not change the genetic balance of their populations. This example shows how biological natural selection in humans intersects harmoniously with cultural differentiation and evolution.

But, of course, there is much more to culture than subsistence mode and diet. Culture is also language, a worldview, social structure, religion and rituals, and a whole host of other things that we do not normally connect with biological changes like the increase in lactose tolerance. How does cultural evolution manifest itself? Can culture evolve, changing together with genes? The answer is yes, and the parallel evolution of human genes and human culture, called *co-evolution*, is the topic of this section. The theory of co-evolution was originally formulated by Marcus Feldman and Luca Cavalli-Sforza of Stanford University. Again, our aim is to show that evolutionary thinking pervades disciplines across the scientific spectrum and is by no means restricted just to biology. In the following, it is important to understand that we do *not* assume that genes determine culture—they do not.

There are many definitions of culture. Here, we use a standard definition: the total pattern of human behavior and its products embodied in thought, speech, action, and artifacts, and dependent on human capacity for learning and transmitting knowledge. Of particular importance is the word "transmitting," because it immediately suggests some analogy with genetic transmission, which is heredity. Of course, humans are not born with hereditarily infused knowledge. Instead, we learn. This learning is at first acquired from parents, and it can be shown that what we learn from our parents we also tend to transmit to our own children. This is a special form of "heredity" that, intriguingly, is passed from generation to generation in a Lamarckian fashion (recall chapter 2), so named because in this case *acquired* characteristics are indeed transmitted from parents to children. This type of cultural transmission is called *vertical transmission*.

A good example of vertical transmission is transmission of language, which often takes place mostly between mother and child (think about the expression "mother tongue"). Another good example is the transmission of religious beliefs from parents to their children, which tends to be stable over generations. Thus, like gene transmission, vertical cultural transmission is conservative and helps explain the stability and persistence of particular cultural formations in the world: changes are slow to come and may take several generations to be implemented.

But *horizontal transmission* also exists. Here, change—cultural mutation, if you will—can be very fast. Rather than dealing with the passage of cultural information from parents to children, horizontal transmission, as its name indicates, can take place within the same generation. Horizontal transmission comes in two varieties: the "one-to-many" type and the "many-to-one" type. In the one-to-many mode, a single person, often a charismatic leader, a monarch, or a respected scientist, such as, for example, Jesus Christ, Roman Emperor Constantine, or Darwin, can radically and quickly change the thinking of many. This is how Christianity first appeared, through the teachings of Jesus Christ (surely a type of cultural evolution), and then evolved further through the actions of among others, Emperor Constantine (who made Christianity the official religion of the Roman Empire), Martin Luther, and Henry VIII of England (the founder of Anglicanism), who can all be seen as innovators and modifiers of preestablished order. This is also how evolutionary theory first spread.

In the many-to-one mode, where several people are transmitting the same message to one individual, cultural innovations are rare because this type of transmission is akin to "social pressure" or "peer pressure." Thus, this type of cultural transmission is also conservative. Messages so transmitted by many sources are strongly reinforced and thus tend to be firmly held and to resist change.

But that is not all. There also exist the concepts of cultural selection and cultural drift. A good example of (negative) cultural selection is that of the Fore people in New Guinea. These people were nearly wiped out by the disease called *kuru*, which is very similar to "mad cow" disease. The culture of the Fores dictated that, to honor their dead close relatives, family members should eat a small piece of their brain. And this is how *kuru* nearly decimated the Fores: the brains of their dead relatives were infected with prions, the agents responsible for the disease. As soon as this cultural practice stopped, *kuru* disappeared. The story of this disease is a good example of the interplay between biology and culture.

As for cultural drift, first recall that genetic drift is caused by chance, especially when small populations or population bottlenecks (reductions in number of individuals) are involved. A good example of cultural drift is that of Puritanism and Puritanical culture in the United States. The Puritans who came on the Mayflower and other ships like it were few in numbers. In effect, they represented a religious (cultural) bottleneck because their denomination was *not* representative of European religious currents of the time.

Nonetheless, the Puritans were successful in America, so much so that many aspects of original Puritanism (such as work ethic and deep religiosity) still exist today in our society. And this happened in spite of the later immigration of millions of people who did not share the beliefs of the Puritans. Thus, America as a whole culturally drifted in the direction of a more fundamentalist interpretation of religion while Europe kept its more casual approach.

The theory of co-evolution is not based on anecdotal evidence alone, as presented here for reasons of simplicity. It has become very mathematical and oriented toward population genetics. It is a young theory that needs to be buttressed by a considerable amount of evidence.

In conclusion, paleontology and genetics strongly agree that modern humans appeared in East Africa more than 100,000 years ago and colonized Earth over tens of thousands of years. These dates, as well as the scenario of human migrations provided by science, are irreconcilable with literally interpreted biblical accounts in Genesis. Both views cannot be correct at the same time. Further, our genes and our cultures co-evolve in a constant interplay that can be studied naturalistically by social scientists. This means that there is no such thing as an immutable human essence (or absolute value) created once and for all, as implied by the Great Chain of Being and its theological underpinnings (described in chapter 2).

By definition, classical creationists and neocreationists must reject the theory of human evolution as presented above since natural selection and drift (chance) are involved. But then, rejecting these scientific findings and future analyses in a creationist or neocreationist fashion is equivalent to rejecting all of science, because both paleontology and genetics (and now even cultural anthropology) rely heavily on the sciences of chemistry, geology, physics, and their mutually supportive theories. Is rejecting the totality of science an option? Science—as long as it is not applied to questions of evolution, particularly human evolution—usually does not elicit much controversy among the public. And science works—without it, there would be no antibiotics, no television, no cars, no plastics, and no computers, just to name a few. Why, then, should science not work for investigating our human origins in a squarely evolutionary fashion? This attitude does not make sense.

To conclude this chapter, we would like to remind skeptical readers of the television show *Crime Scene Investigation* (*CSI*) and soap operas such as *One Life to Live*. In these entertaining series, the DNA technology used to catch criminals and determine fatherhood is the same as that used in real life, and what is more, it is the *exact same technology* used to study mtDNA and Y chromosome DNA to establish patterns of human evolution in particular, and all of evolution in general. If this DNA technology can be trusted well enough to convict dangerous criminals and specify whose father is who, it should be just as trustable when applied to evolution, should it not?

We describe in chapter 5 how evolutionary thinking does not stop at the study of human origins and the origin of species. Theories on the origins of the universe and life follow the exact same logic that is part of evolutionary reasoning. What is more, they provide us with elegant and intellectually stimulating models of where our entire wonderful and changing universe, including the life it harbors, came from.

Things to Think About

1. Science convincingly shows that human beings evolved, including by natural selection and drift.

2. The prevalent model for human evolution shows a single origin in Africa well more than 100,000 years ago. Humans subsequently migrated out of Africa to populate the whole world. This model is based on sophisticated molecular and population genetics.

3. Cultures also evolve, a phenomenon that presently has a significant effect on our future.

4. Can you provide a scientifically sound alternative to human origins?

5. Assuming that the human brain is still evolving, in what direction do you think it will evolve? To put this differently, what is it in our rapidly changing society that would favor some brain gene variants over others?

5

The Origins of Life and the Cosmos as Evolutionary Themes

> The indifferent chaos of equilibrium has given way to a fertile chaos from which different structures can emerge. (Translated by P.F.L.)
>
> —Ilya Prigogine and Isabelle Stengers, *La Nouvelle Alliance*

> It is no longer the rigorous [deterministic] physical law that represents the deep truth.... Rather, it is the statistical physical law [of elementary phenomena] that now serves as a basis for our [scientific] concepts, rigorous [deterministic] physical law being no more than a macroscopic appearance. (Translated by P.F.L.)
>
> —Louis de Broglie, *Savants et Découvertes*

In his famous *Foundation* series, the late Isaac Asimov, science fiction writer and biochemistry professor at Boston University, imagined that a new mathematical science called psychohistory, invented during the First Galactic Empire, allowed humans to predict the future and influence it. Scientist that he was, Asimov knew very well that psychohistory could not possibly be a deterministic science, a science that provided absolute certainty regarding the outcome of any events. He knew that psychohistory could only be *probabilistic*. In other words, this science provided only the *odds* that such or such an event (such as the fall of the Galactic Empire) would take place at a *statistically* estimated time in the future. Psychohistory could not guarantee if and when any specific event would take place; it could offer only probabilities. Unfortunately (or perhaps fortunately), psychohistory does not yet exist, because, as Asimov foresaw, the mathematics and computing time involved in compiling the trillions of actions taken daily by billions of humans, which all potentially determine the future, are utterly daunting and not within our present capabilities.

In Asimov's *Foundation* series, Hari Seldon, the mathematician from planet Helicon and inventor of psychohistory, had great difficulty convincing Galactic Emperor Cleon I that the world was essentially probabilistic. Cleon wanted certainty—determinism—that, he thought, only science could provide. And Cleon is not alone: many people believe that science *is* able to offer certainty because it is deterministic. But in actuality, nothing can be further from the truth, for several reasons.

The history of science has consistently shown that most theories formulated by scientists need to be refined as time passes. Some theories, such as the phlogiston theory of chemistry that posited the existence of negative mass, proved to be wrong and were thus rejected. Some other theories, such as evolution by natural selection, the Mendelian theory of the gene, and Einstein's relativity, have withstood the test of time. But even these "good" theories have been in need of adjustments. Such is the nature of science; it questions itself constantly and self-corrects when necessary. In that sense, science never offers certainty and itself evolves.

But there is much worse as far as determinism in science is concerned. Not only can we not be certain that scientific theories will remain accepted forever, but we now know also that the fabric of nature itself is probabilistic and not fully predictable. This is not to say that scientific theories can no longer explain nature and make *some* predictions regarding the universe and all it contains. Rather, we now know that the universe cannot be compared to a piece of clockwork that was wound up a long time ago and is running in an entirely predictable manner. This was the view held by science until the middle of the nineteenth century.

But today, we know that even planetary orbits are intrinsically unstable, although the exact extent of that instability cannot be pinpointed in time. As long as science was explaining the simplest of phenomena, such as apples falling to the ground, the world seemed deterministic. But today it is understood that natural phenomena can be deeply influenced by very small effects that had previously been ignored. This type of thinking is at the heart of chaos theory and what is colorfully called the "butterfly effect," referring to how a butterfly fluttering its wings somewhere in Australia could affect air currents in such a way to cause a cascade of atmospheric events resulting in a tornado in Kansas. The basic message here is that the world is much more complicated than previously thought. In short, modern science shows that our understanding of the universe can no longer be fully deterministic, contrary to what was thought until a little less than 100 years ago. Scientists have learned to appreciate the role of *chance* in natural events and know that science can offer only the most probable paths in its prediction of nature.

A good example of chance in physical phenomena is radioactive decay. Even though physicists can accurately measure—and predict—how long it will take the atoms in a radioactive sample to decay, it is impossible to predict *which* atoms in the sample are going to decay at any particular time. Ultimately, radioactive decay is a matter of probability, a concept introduced into atomic physics by Albert Einstein as long ago as 1916. In what follows, it is critical to remember that the word "probabilistic" is not at all the same as "arbitrary." Indeed, chance is governed by rules, the rules of statistical calculus.

This basic probabilistic view of science is discussed at some length in this chapter. As we will show, probabilistic science applies especially to the realm of atoms and molecules, both of which are relevant to the origin of the universe and life. A probabilistic universe is a difficult proposition for Intelligent Design (ID) and creationism. This is because teleology, embedded in creationism and ID, implies determinism, a set goal, and not chance. Thus, ID and creationism are, as we said before, basically at odds with all of science, not just evolution. Determinism and certainty are no longer part of science; they can be found only in religious faith and belief, not in scientific facts.

Let us now examine some scientific principles that underlie our understanding of life, the universe, and their appearance. In what follows, it will become clear that evolutionary thinking is not restricted to biology and human culture; it applies just as well to chemical evolution at the dawn of life and cosmic evolution at the dawn of the universe. We also demonstrate that introducing the notion of chance into science is not only intellectually stimulating; it is also an extraordinarily successful approach.

The Second Law of Thermodynamics Allows the Creation of Order Out of Disorder but Is Essentially Statistical

Some people claim that life could not possibly have appeared spontaneously, by chance, without the intervention of a designer because this would have violated the second law of thermodynamics. Their thinking is that life is a highly organized system (it is), too complex to have appeared from disorganized, random constituents. This, they say, is contrary to the second law. But these people do not really understand that law.

The second law states that the entropy of a system must ultimately increase or stay the same, but never decrease. What is a system, and what is entropy? First, the word "system" is confusing because it is so vague and so general. A system can be as simple as a cup of hot coffee or as complicated as the whole universe. But more than that, a *system* is a place where something is happening over time. For example, a cup of hot coffee—our "system" in this example—will always cool down when left alone; it will not get hotter. This means that the heat energy of the hot coffee will flow in only one direction— from the hot cup to the cooler world outside the cup—and not the other way around. What is the result of this process? The coffee will obviously get cool, *but* the air in the room will become just a little warmer. If the room is large, you will not be able to notice with an ordinary thermometer that it got warmer. So now, let us repeat the experiment by modifying the system.

This time, let us put the cup of hot coffee in a well-insulated small box and let us measure the temperature of both the coffee and the air in the box as time goes by. We will observe that, as the temperature of the coffee goes down over time, the temperature of the surrounding air goes up. After a certain time, the temperature of the coffee and that of the air will be the same, and both will remain constant, in principle forever if the box is perfectly insulated. What has happened in this system? Simply, the flow of heat energy from the coffee to the air has proceeded until both are at the same temperature, at which point the flow stopped. At this point, the system has reached temperature *equilibrium*.

Let us now turn to the meaning of entropy. One definition of *entropy* is that it is a quantity that measures order versus disorder. Let us go back to the hot coffee in the box. At the beginning of the experiment, the system, the box, is highly ordered (or highly structured) as regards heat distribution because it contains a cup of hot coffee on the one hand and air at room temperature on the other hand. By definition, we say that the entropy of this system is low (its order, or structure, is high). But as time goes by, the coffee gets cool and the air gets warm, until both are at the same temperature. This is a state of maximum disorder as far as heat is concerned. There is no longer a temperature distinction between the coffee and the air, and no further heat energy exchange can occur between the two components of the system. If you stuck a thermometer at random in the box you would not be able to tell the difference between the cup of coffee and the surrounding air because equilibrium has been reached; everything is at a standstill. Under those conditions, entropy is said to be at a maximum because order—the clear distinction between the hot coffee and the cool air—has disappeared. In other words, the entropy of the system has increased. This also means that, *left alone*, any system will tend toward maximum entropy. But this also suggests that life should not exist because it, too, should reach a state of maximum entropy at a certain point, which we know is not the case. We are here to prove it. The reason for life's continued existence is that it is in a state of thermodynamic *disequilibrium*, not equilibrium. What does this mean?

Going back to our experiment, let us assume that a thin electric heating coil is inserted through the wall of the box into the coffee. If the setting is just right, one should be able to maintain the temperature of the coffee because, even though the coffee continually transfers heat energy to the surrounding air, this heat loss is compensated for by the action of the heating coil. This way, you can continue to maintain a state of low entropy (high order) for the system for a certain period of time. But, of course, maintaining low entropy in this case depends on a source of added energy: the heating coil. Thus, a state of order (a state of disequilibrium) can be maintained (and even created, assuming the coffee in the box was cold before you inserted the coil), but at a price: the input of energy from an outside source.

How can this very simple experiment be linked with the idea of the spontaneous appearance of life on Earth and its continuation? Living organisms are obviously highly structured, highly ordered systems. As a result, they are in a high state of disequilibrium with their surroundings such as air, soil, water, and the whole planet, in fact. Thus, to appear spontaneously and create a state of disequilibrium, life needed a source of energy found outside of itself. Where could the needed energy have come from? There are two possibilities. One is the sun, which delivers tremendous amounts of energy to Earth in the form of heat and light. The other is heat that comes from Earth itself, through the decay of radioactive elements present in the crust and in the magma, as well as some residual heat that resulted from Earth's formation 4.5 billion years ago. Indeed, Earth was formed from colliding smaller bodies present in the young solar system. The kinetic energy of these colliding bodies was transformed into heat, which is still dissipating today.

As a matter of fact, the energy necessary to maintain life on Earth today is still ultimately provided by the sun in the form of visible light. Indeed, the energy of sunlight is massively converted into organic molecules thanks to plant photosynthesis mediated by chlorophyll. Almost all other life-forms on Earth are ultimately dependent on plants and their photosynthesis for survival and reproduction. The only exceptions are deep ocean communities of organisms that live in total darkness. Their source of energy is heat that comes from cracks in the ocean floor that puts their environment in close contact with the hot magma. In summary, neither a spontaneous appearance of life nor its continuation today is in contradiction with the second law of thermodynamics because our planet is an *open* system that receives large amounts of energy from our star, the sun.

You can see how order can appear out of disorder, given an outside source of energy, by conducting a simple experiment in your kitchen. Just pour a thin layer of cooking oil (a disordered system because all the oil molecules are distributed randomly) in a frying pan and heat it up on medium (this is the energy source). After a while, if you look at the oil from a shallow angle, you will see many highly structured—ordered—vortexes forming at the surface of the oil. These are called Bénard cells, after Henri Bénard, the French physicist who studied them (figure 5.1).

Of course, Bénard cells are a far cry from living cells and anyway, the term "cells" in this context is not meant to refer to living cells. But importantly, this simple experiment demonstrates the *principle* that making order out of disorder does not violate the second law as long as outside energy is fed into a system.

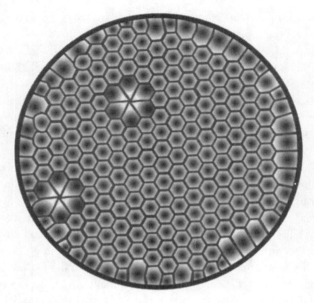

FIGURE 5.1
Bénard cells. From N. Shanks, *God, the Devil, and Darwin* (Oxford: Oxford University Press, 2004), by permission of Oxford University Press.

Bénard cells and other structures of similar nature are called *dissipative structures far from thermodynamic equilibrium*. Other examples are chemical "clocks," reactions that make a solution oscillate between different colors as a function of time and chemical reactions where rings of different colors appear spontaneously and alternate in a reaction vessel. The theory of dissipative structures and their appearance far from thermodynamic equilibrium was developed by 1977 Nobel Laureate for Chemistry Ilya Prigogine and his many students and associates (see appendix 1). They convincingly demonstrated that physical and chemical systems can be very sensitive to "butterfly effects" and can be "driven," in an unpredictable fashion and in an irreversible way, toward one kind of structure or another. Figure 5.2 shows that systems far from equilibrium can "jump" from one state to another through what are called "bifurcations," that is, branches "chosen" by a system made unstable by physical or chemical parameters (disturbances). Eventually, such disturbances can lead to an enormous spectrum, a wide pallet of chemical systems that may have been present at the origin of life and from which chemical evolution selected the most fit. Life today is still such an irreversible, far-from-equilibrium, dissipative system, albeit not

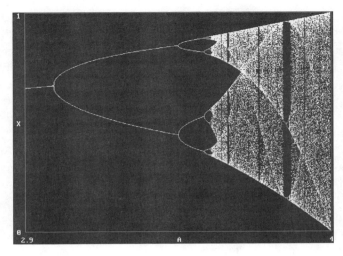

FIGURE 5.2
Bifurcations in unstable systems far from equilibrium. The vertical axis represents the various states that can be assumed by a system. The horizontal axis represents a disturbance that influences the number of states that a system can "choose" randomly. At the extreme left, the system is in a single state. As the disturbance increases, two states (two branches) are possible, then four, then eight, and so on. In this example, the system then starts behaving chaotically and the number of possible states becomes enormous.

quite as chaotic as suggested by figure 5.2 (see appendix 2 for where to find details on dissipative structures). Life is irreversible because, left alone (that is, barring events such as catastrophic asteroid impacts or a nuclear holocaust), it propagates itself and has done so for the last 3.5 billion years. Life is also far from thermodynamic equilibrium because there is no situation where living systems go back and forth between states of life and states of nonlife (or ordered life vs. unordered life). Finally, life is a dissipative system because it is order originating from nonorder and so it locally decreases entropy (increases order) where it appears.

To exist, ordered systems need a source of external energy in order to stay far from thermodynamic equilibrium. But also, since these systems *decrease* entropy locally by gaining order, for the second law to be obeyed, entropy must increase elsewhere. What, then, is the entropy "sink"? Ultimately, this sink is the whole universe. Thus, as life, or any kind of order, such as solar systems or new stars forming in galactic dust clouds, appears somewhere, the entropy of the whole universe increases. In effect, dissipative systems dump entropy into the universe and so maintain themselves.

Intriguingly, entropy is a statistical concept. Therefore, entropy itself joins the ranks of natural properties that are no longer seen as deterministic. This was demonstrated in the late 1800s by Ludwig Boltzmann (1844–1906), an Austrian mathematician and physicist who invented statistical thermodynamics. Statistical thermodynamics is extremely mathematical and difficult to simplify. Suffice it to say that the state of order or disorder of a system (its entropy) depends on the energy states of molecules that compose this system. It is impossible to predict and know at each moment the exact energy level of each of the billions of molecules or atoms that compose a system. Therefore, one can only describe and predict the behavior of a system within certain limits of probability, that is, in terms of statistics or chance.

This has important consequences for the formation and fate of dissipative structures (or systems). For dissipative systems, it can be demonstrated that even very subtle changes to their composition can swing them in a number of different states of disequilibrium, again in a probabilistic way that cannot be entirely predicted. This type of "butterfly effect" may have played a role in the origins of life when molecules, not yet cells, started self-organizing about 3.8 billion years ago, as we describe below.

Granted, the concepts of dissipative systems and statistical entropy are complex. But this also shows that crude metaphors such as watches, mouse-traps, and bicycles (as used by ID believers) are false friends. Everybody can understand them, but they are of no help because they are irrelevant to the questions raised. And besides, complex concepts, even though they may be hard to grasp, are not necessarily false!

In conclusion, the statistical notion of entropy and the existence of dissipative systems indicate that the appearance of life on Earth was not necessarily preordained; no deterministic principle had to be involved, nor was there a need for a probabilistic designer who cleverly manipulated the second law of thermodynamics. This is not to say that there *was* no such designer (science must be silent on that point), but only that it is not necessary to invoke a designer to explain the appearance of life on Earth.

After this broad conceptual framework, let us now consider some of the hypotheses put forth to explain the spontaneous appearance of life on Earth.

Building Blocks of Life Made in the Atmosphere

We do not know how life appeared on Earth, and perhaps we never will. However, scientists do develop hypotheses about how it may have happened. Multiple hypotheses now exist that attempt to explain the origins of life. We restrict ourselves here to just one combination of two hypotheses that, in our opinion, are best supported by experimental evidence so far. These are (1) the idea that the atmosphere of early Earth was rich in hydrogen gas (H_2), carbon dioxide (CO_2), nitrogen (N_2), and water vapor (H_2O), and (2) that ribonucleic acid (RNA) started the process of chemical evolution that eventually led to life as we know it. This model is called the "RNA world."

Other reasonable hypotheses for the origins of life invoke comets and meteorites delivering complex organic materials to Earth, or underwater volcanic activity driving complicated chemical reactions. These are also plausible scenarios, but at the risk of irritating some colleagues, we think they are less developed than the sequence we explain below.

Hydrogen is by far the most abundant element in the universe. It is present in its molecular form (H_2) in high concentrations in the atmospheres of the giant gas planets, notably Jupiter and Saturn. Thus, hydrogen is thought to have been part of the primeval atmosphere of all planets right after the formation of the solar system, about 4.5 billion years ago. Hydrogen is no longer found at significant concentrations in the atmospheres of rocky planets such as Venus, Earth, and Mars. This is because the low gravity of these planets—compared to that of the gas giants—could not prevent the escape of hydrogen into space. However, recent calculations have shown that hydrogen may have represented at least 30% of Earth's initial atmosphere. It is known that oxygen gas (O_2) was not present in the primeval atmosphere because Earth's oldest rocks are not oxidized.

It has been known since the 1950s that an atmosphere rich in hydrogen is capable of synthesizing a long catalog of organic compounds such as amino acids and nitrogenous bases, all used as building blocks by living cells. This was first shown by American chemist Stanley Miller in 1953, when he subjected a mixture of hydrogen, methane (CH_4), ammonia (NH_3), and water vapor to electric discharges that imitated lightning (figure 5.3). This experiment has been successfully repeated a number of times by others, using different conditions, such as ultraviolet light instead of electric discharges, and different gas compositions. Even though we now think that Earth's primitive atmosphere may not have contained high levels of methane and ammonia, it has been shown that carbon in the form of carbon dioxide (instead of methane) and nitrogen gas (instead of ammonia) also lead to the abundant formation of organics when sparked in the presence of high levels of hydrogen gas. In fact, the complexity of the mixtures of organics obtained in these experiments has earned these mixtures the name "soup" or, more precisely, "prebiotic soup," which means "before-life soup." This characterization is an exaggeration in terms of the thickness of an actual "soup," but nonetheless, it has been calculated that the rate of production of amino acids (a class of organic compounds) on early Earth may have been of the

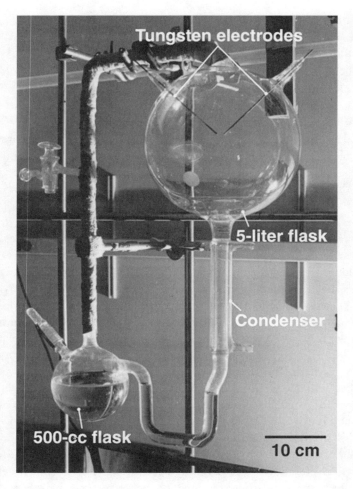

FIGURE 5.3
The apparatus used by Stanley Miller to synthesize organic compounds from a sparked mixture of methane, ammonia, water vapor, and hydrogen. The 500 cc flask contains water brought to the boiling point. The 5-liter flask is where the gas mixture is sparked. The refrigerated condenser (the vertical tube on the right) condenses water vapor into liquid water. The trap (the U-shaped tube at the bottom) is used to harvest samples for the analysis of dissolved organics. From J. L. Bada and A. Lazcano, 2003, "Prebiotic soup: Revisiting the Miller experiment," *Science* 300:745–746, by permission of the American Association for the Advancement of Science.

order of 10,000 metric tons per year. These amino acids and other organics then dissolved in the oceans.

Of course, there were no living cells before life appeared. But as mentioned, gas-sparking experiments have produced many of the key organic compounds that are characteristic of life today. Amino acids are required to make proteins, while special sugars (such as ribose) and nitrogenous bases (such as adenine) are required to make RNA. RNA is a close cousin of DNA, the genetic material, the blueprint of life, as we have described in previous chapters. RNA is in fact the genetic material of many viruses, indicating that on early Earth it could have started the process of genetic evolution—more about that later. For now, just remember that proteins and RNA are two types of large biological molecules without which life cannot exist.

To be sure, there are difficulties associated with gas-sparking experiments. First, there is the problem of the stability of organic compounds made in the atmosphere and raining down on the surface. Did they remain chemically stable long enough for them to react with one another and make the first large molecules necessary for life to get started? To answer this, we must consider that these organics were continuously produced for millions of years and must have accumulated to some extent. Next, it was recently discovered that a common mineral containing the element boron is able to stabilize the sugar ribose that is a critical component of RNA. In the absence of boron-containing minerals, ribose is quite unstable and would not have survived long enough to react with other organic molecules. The discovery of the stabilizing effect of boron-containing minerals was completely serendipitous. Earth's crust contains hundreds of different minerals that all have their own properties when they interact with organic compounds. We know very little about these properties, and checking these minerals one by one with all the organics made in the prebiotic "soup" will take time.

In fact, it may well be that surface chemistry (that is, chemical reactions taking place on the surface of minerals) played an important role in the prebiotic soup. To illustrate this, remember that the catalytic converters in our cars are based entirely on surface chemistry. Another example of a common reactive mineral is pyrite, a combination of iron and sulfur that makes beautiful crystals. Pyrite can bind all sorts of organic materials in very close proximity on its surface, thereby allowing them to react and make more complex compounds, as was shown in the laboratory. Pyrite is also a catalyst, that is, a substance that speeds up chemical reactions. Several organic compounds commonly found in living cells have been synthesized from carbon dioxide and hydrogen sulfide (H_2S) reacting with pyrite. We still have to discover what countless numbers of other naturally occurring minerals can do when reacted with organic compounds assembled in the prebiotic soup.

A second problem with gas-sparking experiments is the question of the chemical reactivity of organics made in the atmosphere. For example, simply mixing amino acids dissolved in water does not produce proteins, which are long chains of amino acids chemically linked together, and an absolute prerequisite for life as we know it today. This failure to make proteins in simple solutions is due to the fact that amino acids are unable to react with each other without the machinery afforded by living cells. In fact, the interactions between amino acids taking place in living cells are very complicated and could not have existed as such at the dawn of life.

But then, it has been shown in the laboratory that amino acids can react with certain sulfur-containing compounds that are produced by volcanoes and hydrothermal vents. These vents are Earth crust formations found at the bottom of the oceans, near tectonic plates, where water circulates and interacts at high temperature with the magma. When amino acids are reacted with these sulfur compounds, they form what are called thioesters, which, contrary to unmodified amino acids, *are* able to form chemical bonds *spontaneously* and produce "protein-like" molecules that we can call here "preproteins." These reactions could easily have occurred in the prebiotic world because there is no reason to believe that volcanoes and hydrothermal vents were fewer then than they are today. One can thus imagine the prebiotic oceans starting to accumulate molecules that were long chains of amino acids, perhaps the precursors of later proteins.

Last but not least, there is the question of the geometry of the molecules (amino acids and sugars) produced in gas-sparking experiments. Many complex organic molecules come in mirror images of themselves. Just imagine your left hand reflected in a mirror: both your actual hand and its image are exactly superimposable, which is not the case if you simply put your right hand over your left hand without rotating either. Molecules present in all living organisms come in only one geometric version, not both. It is as if the living world were only one-handed. Now, gas-sparking experiments make *both* types of molecules in the exact same amounts. How life came to have just one geometric form of these molecules, we simply do not know. Was surface chemistry involved, or did something else happen? We have no answer yet, but research continues.

The RNA World and the Appearance of Genetic Information

Most scientists do not think that the production of proteins in the primordial soup signaled the beginning of life. In good evolutionary fashion, they think that the molecules that really got life going must have been able to reproduce themselves, and mutate (and so create diversity), and then this led to natural (chemical) selection of the more fit molecules. Proteins, either in living cells or in the test tube, have never been observed to replicate, to copy themselves, and therefore they cannot multiply. The only biological molecules capable of replication are DNA and RNA. Even though DNA is by very far the major genetic material of the living world today (some viruses being exceptions), many scientists think that the first replicating molecules in the primeval soup were RNA molecules, not DNA molecules. This is because RNA is chemically much more reactive than DNA and thus lends itself more easily to synthesis, replication, and mutation in a putative prebiotic environment.

RNA molecules are chains of subunits chemically linked together. These subunits are the sugar ribose that we mentioned above, the four nitrogenous bases adenine, guanine, uracil, and cytosine, and a group of phosphorus-containing atoms called a phosphate group. All four bases and ribose can be made in the laboratory under plausible prebiotic conditions. Phosphate is abundant in Earth's crust and thus did not need to be synthesized before the dawn of life. However, linking two of these subunits together, the base and the ribose, has not been totally successful in the laboratory under plausible prebiotic conditions. Here again, mineral or perhaps even preprotein catalysts could have been involved in the actual linking of elements in the prebiotic world, but we have no information yet on what may have happened. On the other hand, tagging phosphate groups onto base-ribose combinations can be done easily under conditions that were prevalent before life appeared.

What has also been achieved in the laboratory is the linking together of RNA building blocks (combinations of bases, ribose, and phosphate groups called nucleotides) to form genuine chains of RNA. Interestingly, catalysts were also needed here. One of the most efficient catalysts was clay, a substance found abundantly on Earth, which happens to have complex surface properties.

At this point, and assuming that prebiotic chemistry worked the way we think it did, we can imagine the oceans, lakes, and ponds on prebiotic Earth not only containing the building blocks of proteins and RNA, but now also hosting a long list of dissolved, randomly made preproteins and RNA molecules. It would then have been necessary for these RNA molecules to copy and propagate themselves, as well as to start generating molecular diversity in order to get the process of organic evolution going.

Interestingly, some RNA molecules are capable of replicating themselves *without* help from external catalysts. In fact, these RNA molecules contain their own catalytic activity. For this reason, these RNA molecules are called *ribozymes*, a contraction of "ribonucleic acid" and "enzyme," where enzyme means a biological catalyst. It was also demonstrated in the lab that RNA replication through ribozyme activity is imperfect: its copying mechanism makes mistakes and incorporates "wrong" bases frequently. This is, of course, the equivalent of mutations. But this imperfect replication had the advantage of creating a large collection of different RNA molecules, all potentially possessing interesting and different properties.

Several types of ribozymes exist today in living cells, from simple fungal cells to human cells, where they may represent the "memory" of the prebiotic RNA world. Moreover, ribozymes, either natural or made in the laboratory, are also able to process themselves and non-ribozyme RNA molecules by, for example, stitching themselves and other RNA molecules together to make longer RNA chains. Some of these ribozymes can even bind and react with small organic molecules (including amino acids) that also existed in the prebiotic soup.

We can now see why one speaks of an RNA world: thanks to their catalytic activities, randomly made ribozymes replicated themselves and other RNA molecules, generated molecular diversity through copying errors, bound small molecules that they had the potential to modify chemically, and were able to stitch RNA molecules together to make longer chains and hence further increase molecular diversity. All these activities mimicked—in a very primitive way—the living world as it exists today. And all this occurred through random chemistry, without any preexisting living cells or, necessarily, a designer.

The RNA world hypothesis still needs substantial experimental confirmation. This type of research is being conducted in several labs, for example, at Harvard University and at the Scripps Institute near San Diego. But so far, the RNA world model already has made enormous progress, and one must admit that it is intellectually compelling, in that it gets life started with molecules that contain genetic information: the sequence of bases in RNA.

The Origins of Living Structures and First Effects of Natural Chemical Selection

How could natural selection act at the level of RNA molecules instead of cells and organisms as it does today? How could structures characteristic of living cells have appeared from simple mixtures of RNA molecules, perhaps preproteins, and other components of the primordial soup? The answers to these two questions are (1) hypercycles (a concept developed by 1967 Nobel Laureate for Chemistry Manfred Eigen) and (2) dissipative systems.

Let us imagine a pond somewhere on prebiotic Earth. This pond contains a large collection of RNA molecules, characterized by different lengths and base sequences, of which some possess ribozyme activity. This pond also contains a supply of nucleotides, the building blocks of RNA. How could this population of RNA molecules evolve? For simplicity, let us consider just two types of ribozyme activity possessed by two of these molecules: RNA 1 has the ability to replicate itself and can also replicate other RNA molecules, and RNA 2, is able to replicate itself and is also a facilitator, for example, an RNA molecule able to bind RNA building blocks. RNA 3 has no particular ribozyme activity and cannot replicate by itself. This collection of three interacting types of RNA molecules is called a hypercycle. In this example, the whole hypercycle (the whole collection of RNA molecules) will multiply and proliferate because one of its members, RNA 1, is "altruistic," in that it replicates not only itself but also other RNA molecules present in its vicinity. Type 2 RNA, a facilitator, is also "altruistic." An "altruistic" hypercycle containing these three types of RNA molecules is represented below:

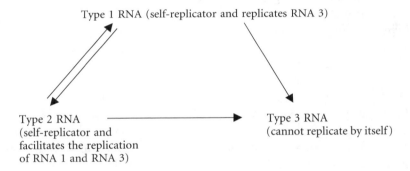

We can say that, because of its composition, this hypercycle possesses high fitness. The multiplication activity of this hypercycle could also perhaps have involved preproteins equipped with the proper catalytic activity.

Let us now imagine a second hypercycle coexisting with the first one, but this time consisting of a "selfish" ribozyme that can replicate itself but *inhibits* the replication of all other RNA molecules around it as shown below:

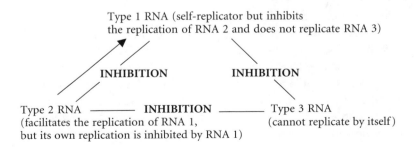

This second hypercycle cannot exist stably because only one of its members can replicate. Indeed, type 3 RNA cannot replicate, and type 2 RNA, even though it should be able to replicate, is inhibited by type 1 RNA. After a while, this second hypercycle will go extinct as an integrated system of several types of RNA molecules, in spite of the fact that type 2 RNA is a facilitator. In the end, only RNA 1 will be left. On the other hand, the first hypercycle will continue to thrive. In other words, the first hypercycle is more fit than the second one because of the different types of RNA molecules that compose each hypercycle. This is natural selection acting at the level of molecules rather than at the level of cells.

Are hypercycles purely theoretical models, or do they conform to reality? As all good scientific theories, the hypercycle model makes quantitative predictions that should be verifiable. And it turns out that, indeed, we know that hypercycles explain very well the infection cycles and evolution of viruses, including HIV, the virus that causes AIDS.

For natural selection to operate efficiently on a collection of coexisting hypercyles, the latter should be encapsulated, trapped in structures that resemble individual living cells. This is because RNA molecules floating freely in solution could make only temporary hypercycles, due to diffusion and dispersal processes, or simply wind blowing across the pond and making waves. Today, all living cells are bounded by membranes made of fatty acids. Interestingly, gas-sparking experiments abundantly produce molecules called carboxylic acids that resemble fatty acids. When dispersed in water, these carboxylic acids spontaneously form microscopic spherical vesicles, called liposomes. What is more, when these liposomes form in the presence of RNA in solution, this RNA becomes trapped, concentrated inside the liposomes. In this way, liposomes containing trapped hypercycles become bounded systems that contain genetic information in the form of RNA. These structures can be called pre-protocells because they imitate—very distantly so far—actual living cells. And these pre-protocells can evolve because they all potentially contain different hypercycles, some with "altruistic" ribozymes, and some with "selfish" ones. It has even been shown that liposomes can trap not only RNA molecules but also microscopic clay particles (figure 5.4), which can bind nucleotides and further facilitate RNA replication.

But then, for this RNA-world encapsulation in liposomes to be realistic, the formation of liposomes should be spontaneous. Furthermore, these liposomes should be able to engage in primitive division to imitate genuine cell division. Only under these circumstances can natural selection favor (or not) different liposomes containing different hypercycles. We know now that this can happen to some extent. First, countless types of fatty acids and carboxylic acids form liposomes when simply shaken in water. Second, some

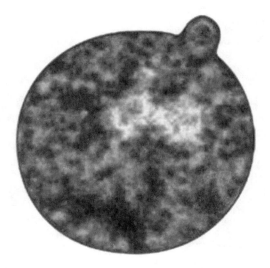

FIGURE 5.4
Photomicrograph of a single liposome containing several clay particles
to which RNA molecules are bound (these are the brightest areas inside
the liposome). The large liposome is several micrometers in diameter
(one micrometer equals one thousandth of a millimeter). The object at
1 o'clock is a much smaller liposome that contains no clay particles and
no RNA. The gray specks are clusters of dye molecules used to high-
light the lipid membrane of the liposomes. Adapted from S. Graham,
"Clay could have encouraged first cells to form," *Scientific American*,
News Section, October 24, 2003. (The original work was performed at
Harvard University in the laboratory of Jack W. Szostak.)

of these compounds can form liposomes in an autocatalytic fashion. This
means that these liposomes, when in the presence of their carboxylic acid
building blocks, induce the formation of more liposomes in a manner
reminiscent of dissipative structure formation described above: liposomes
simply make more of themselves once a particular chemical threshold is
reached. Recall that dissipative structures are chemical or physical systems
far from equilibrium that evolve in a particular direction once a certain
threshold is reached. And indeed, as has been well demonstrated in the
laboratory, spontaneous liposome formation, which occurs in the presence
of a simple heat source, is another example of order created out of disorder
(figure 5.5).

Once the RNA world in the form of hypercycles had been encapsulated
in liposomes to form pre-protocells, the RNA world could have spontaneously gained structure, order, without violating the second law of thermodynamics. In other words, the constituents of the RNA world could have

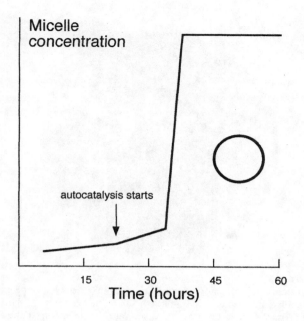

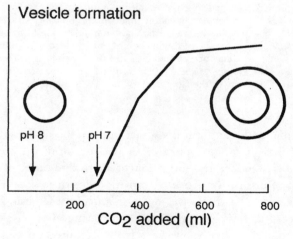

FIGURE 5.5
Spontaneous formation of liposomes from a carboxylic acid. Top: in this experiment, caprylic acid is gently stirred in hot water at a slightly alkaline pH. After about 20 hours, caprylic acid spontaneously starts forming micelles, vesicles consisting of a single layer of acid molecules. This process is autocatalytic, in that when micelles begin to form, they accelerate their own formation. After about 40 hours, all the caprylic acid is present in micelles. Bottom: When the suspension of micelles is made less alkaline by bubbling carbon dioxide in it, the micelles spontaneously form double-layered liposomes that imitate biological membranes.

self-organized, self-designed by chance alone. Here again, William Paley's watchmaker argument and Michael Behe's mousetrap argument do not apply (see chapter 1).

It is nevertheless dangerous to oversimplify. Modern cell membranes contain fatty acids that are highly impermeable to water and compounds dissolved in it. The role of transporting water-soluble compounds in and out of cells is played today by proteins embedded in the membranes. It is not known if laboratory-made pre-protocells containing preproteins in their membranes would be able to handle water exchange with the outside world because the relevant experiments have not yet been performed. On the other hand, if the membranes of pre-protocells were composed of fairly short fatty acids, water transport across these membranes would not have been a problem because short fatty acids are permeable to water. Another alternative yet is provided by the recent discovery that some short RNA molecules made in the laboratory *increase* the permeability of liposomes made from long-chain fatty acids. These RNA molecules are short enough that they could have been manufactured by random chemistry in the RNA world. Clearly, many questions regarding an RNA world encapsulated in liposomes remain to be solved, but work continues at a fast pace.

Steps Toward Protein Synthesis and the DNA World

Many types of viruses have a genome made of RNA surrounded by a simple protein coat. When viruses infect cells, the genetic message contained in their RNA is decoded by the infected cells' protein-making machinery, which then starts making copious amounts of new viral proteins. However, the protein-making machinery of modern cells is quite complicated and could not have existed in its present complexity in simple pre-protocells. This mechanism must have evolved from a simpler, more ancestral one.

As we mentioned above, traces—"memories"—of the RNA world exist in modern cells in the form of ribozymes. It turns out that the most critical step in protein synthesis, the chemical linking of amino acids, is also performed today in all living cells by a ribozyme. This type of catalytic activity could have appeared in the RNA world, which would explain why all life-forms share it today. But that is not all. Another critical step in protein synthesis is the precise positioning and lining up of amino acids, in the proper sequence, just before the chemical bonds between amino acids are made. Interestingly, this function is also performed today by short RNA molecules. In fact, laboratory experiments have demonstrated that such RNA molecules can be generated in the test tube by random chemistry. Thus, this other type yet of ribozyme could also have evolved in the RNA world.

Assuming this evolutionary scenario took place, we can imagine pre-protocells containing hypercycles that consist of up to five types of RNA: one population of RNA molecules contains a genetic message that encodes the instructions to line up amino acids in a certain order to make proteins. This population is equivalent to a first set of genes. A second population of RNA molecules is a group of ribozymes that can bind amino acids and bring them close together by interacting with RNA molecules from the first population. A third type of ribozyme chemically binds together the amino acids to form proteins. At this point, proteins would be formed inside pre-protocells in a directed manner, and no longer only outside of cells by random thioester chemistry. A fourth population of RNA molecules, consisting of "altruistic" ribozymes, helps all other RNA components of the hypercycle to replicate inside liposomes. And finally, a fifth category of ribozymes could have spliced together short RNAs to make longer genes and increase genetic diversity even further.

What would be the evolutionary advantage of pre-protocells that "learned" how to make proteins over those that did not? An example we gave above is the production of proteins that can lodge themselves inside the fatty acid membrane and favor the uptake of water-soluble compounds from the outside world, such as amino acids and nucleotides. A higher rate of uptake of these building blocks would have made pre-protocells containing the appropriate proteins more fit than their competitors. Another example is the appearance of proteins that accelerate all ribozyme functions and make their own synthesis, as well as RNA replication, more efficient. And finally, a great competitive advantage would have been the appearance of proteins able to actually *make* amino acids, nucleotides, and other cellular building blocks. These pre-protocells, thanks to their newly acquired metabolism, would have gained independence from the primeval soup and would have been the best competitors of all.

At this point, after the appearance of even primitive metabolism, one should consider that life had finally appeared. The structures equipped with evolved metabolism and ribozyme activity, enhanced by protein catalytic activity, should be called protocells instead of pre-protocells. What still differentiated these protocells from modern cells was their blueprint made of RNA, not yet DNA. These cells were *ribo-organisms*.

It should be pointed out that all five types of RNA populations mentioned above have been made and studied in the laboratory. What is still lacking, however, is the crucial demonstration that these five ribozyme activities can become integrated properly and truly function as coordinated hypercycles, particularly inside liposomes. This is a difficult problem, and—there is no denying it—it will take some time to solve it.

The RNA world is thought to have appeared about 3.8 billion years ago, soon after our planet stopped experiencing frequent bombardments by very large meteorites and comets left over from the formation of the solar system. But next, there is the question of the transition from an RNA world to a DNA world, which is the living world as we know it today. This transition, which is thought to have occurred at least as early as 3.5 billion years ago, may not have been as daunting a problem as one might think. Again, modern cells have retained a "memory" of the RNA world in that the building blocks of DNA are made through RNA building block intermediates. This strongly suggests that, indeed, RNA is ancestral to DNA. Some protein catalysts that today convert RNA building blocks into DNA building blocks may be mutant forms of protein catalysts that originally performed other functions.

Then, there is the issue of generating DNA genes from the RNA genes of the RNA world. Here again, this may not have been as problematic as one would think. It is well known that modern cells and viruses possess protein-mediated catalytic activities that can "read" RNA molecules and generate DNA copies of these molecules by a process called reverse transcription. These catalytic activities may be another "memory" of the RNA world yet, and this is possibly how DNA first appeared. The protein catalysts converting an RNA genetic message into a DNA genetic message could have evolved from the first proteins that simply helped RNA replication in protocells. But then, what was the evolutionary advantage of DNA over RNA? Why did the DNA world by and large replace the RNA world? Simply, DNA is chemically more stable than RNA, meaning that the cells that evolved a DNA blueprint were more stable than their ribo-organism counterparts.

A new hypothesis argues that DNA was actually "invented" by early viruses. Modern viruses are well known to develop mechanisms that allow them to evade the defenses of their hosts. This could have happened in the cellular RNA world, where ribo-organisms would have been unable to "recognize" and destroy the genomes of viruses made of DNA. Some of these DNA-containing viruses could have established themselves permanently inside RNA cells and progressively converted the latter's RNA genomes into DNA genomes through reverse transcription. The selective advantage for the cells whose genomes were converted into DNA was much greater genome stability, because DNA is chemically more stable than RNA. This hypothesis is supported by the existence of several DNA handling mechanisms (mediated by enzymes known as DNA polymerases and helicases) in existing domains of cellular life, some of which are more closely related to various viral functions than they are to each other. This also suggests that the DNA world may have evolved from the RNA world more than once in the distant

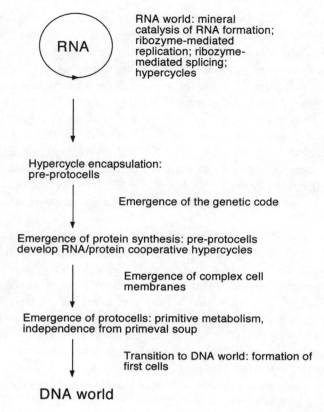

FIGURE 5.6
Evolution of the RNA world and its putative steps.

past. The sequence of events described above, the evolution of the RNA world, is summarized in figure 5.6.

Once simple DNA organisms appeared, life as we know it today was on its way. Evolution continued its course by acting through mutation, natural selection, and genetic drift to finally lead to the enormous genetic diversity of extant life. But this is a long story that unfolded in the past 3.5 billion years of the evolution of the DNA world on Earth. This is the story of the "tree of life" shown in chapter 3. What happened during the first billion years of existence of the tree of life, a time during which complex Eukarya appeared, is recounted in chapter 6.

To summarize, we have shown how random chemistry, coupled with natural selection, explains many aspects of the origin of life on Earth. Solid laboratory data support the scenario we describe above, but scientists agree that we are still far from a complete explanation. Finally, none of the pre-biotic events involved in this scenario requires more than the laws of physics and chemistry to have occurred: to account for the origin of life, science does not need to envision an intelligent designer who created life in a deterministic, teleological fashion.

False Statistics

People opposed to the spontaneous appearance of life often resort to simple statistics to try to show that this was an impossible event. For example, they claim that the odds of making from random events even a short protein that exists in cells today are astronomically low. But in fact, this type of reasoning would be correct only if someone *knew in advance* what type of result was to be achieved. In other words, this is teleological thinking all over again; this reasoning looks at the question in the wrong way.

Remember that evolution has no particular goal in mind. That a certain protein (and hence, gene) exists in organisms today means that it plays and played an important role in these organisms' continued existence and pro-liferation in the world. But at the dawn of life, there was no indication that *any* particular catalytic function would be more or less fit than any other function several billions of years later. Similarly, we cannot predict whether a certain protein (and gene) in an organism will have a positive or negative effect billions of years hence.

Nevertheless, assuming that RNA hypercycles played an important role in the origin of life, it is legitimate to wonder what the molecular heterogeneity of the emerging RNA world could have been. In a world where enormous numbers of purely random RNA molecules were formed, it is possible that the chances of several unique RNA species meeting each other to form hypercycles could have been vanishingly small. But in fact, since life appeared from chemical systems far from thermodynamic equilibrium, elementary statistical calculations are no longer adequate to estimate the chemical di-versity of the RNA world. Rather, one must use a mathematical technique of conditional probabilities called "Markov chains," in which the addition of an element to a chain is neither totally random nor totally determined. Each element thus has a given probability of being incorporated at a certain point in a chain. This statistical method applies well to RNA molecules that grow by incorporating one element (a nucleotide) at a time. A simple example from the English language illustrates Markov chains: there are more ways to complete a sentence that begins "The brown . . ." than there are ways to complete "The brown bear climbed the. . . ." In other words, the more complex the structure, the fewer the viable options to extend it.

Computer simulations have shown that, when several chemicals (such as RNA nucleotides) interact chemically with one another under conditions far from thermodynamic equilibrium, the diversity of possible RNA molecules so synthesized is *reduced by many orders of magnitude* compared to that of totally randomly made RNA molecules. This is because the outcomes of far-from-equilibrium reactions are strongly restricted by building block availability and reaction mechanisms. In this way, the chances of some given hypercycle formation with these "Markovian" RNA molecules would have been constrained. Physical conditions far from thermodynamic equilibrium existed and still exist in the vicinity of suboceanic hydrothermal vents, where temperature gradients are extremely steep.

Therefore, life originated by a process of trial and error, possibly according to a Markov chain mechanism, with the first most fit liposome-bounded hypercycles becoming able to multiply and overtake less fit hypercycles. This may have happened because, by pure chance, the fittest hypercycles happened to be more functional than others in the circumstances prevailing at the time. Doubtlessly, many mutant hypercycles appeared in the RNA world. But it is only the lineages of the most successful ones, including those that developed protein synthesis, which evolved into DNA-containing cells. From then on, through a similar process, some DNA genes mutated randomly and led to the demise of some lines, while other random mutations turned out to be beneficial. This process continues. Thus, rather than marveling at the incredible (and false) odds that allowed life to appear, we should marvel at the fact that all life-forms are the descendants of remarkably adaptive hypercycles that appeared eons ago, withstood natural selection, and evolved into beings adapted to the environment as it exists today.

Countless mutations must have taken place in the RNA world and subsequently in the DNA world to account for life's diversity as we see it now. In truth, we have very little understanding of all the mutations and selective factors involved in the evolution of early life-forms. Yet, scientists think that the RNA world was not irreducibly complex, as we discuss next.

A Good Example of Reducible Complexity Derived from the RNA World: The Ribosome

Ribosomes are small particles, present in the cell sap, on which the step of translation—protein synthesis—takes place in all living cells (see chapter 3). Life is impossible without ribosomes. Ribosomes are also very complex: they contain more than 50 different proteins and upward of 4,500 nucleotides' worth of RNA. This RNA possesses ribozyme activity. Yet, ID thinkers have never targeted ribosomes as candidates for their "irreducibly complex" structures, in spite of the fact that ribosomes are as, if not more, complex than bacterial flagella, one of their favorite examples. There is a good reason for this: the functioning of ribosomes is very well understood, and so are their detailed structure and evolutionary past. This is because the sequences of ribosomal RNA molecules from thousands of different and evolutionarily divergent organisms are known. In fact, these are the sequences that were first used (before DNA sequencing was available) to build the tree of life as described in chapter 3.

We know very well that these complicated ribosomal structures are not irreducibly complex because at least one-third of their proteins can be eliminated by mutation without causing any lethal harm to the mutant cells. This proves that ribosomes are not whole "modules" that were "holistically designed," in which case removing just one element would destroy the whole, as per ID reasoning. This is not at all what is happening. In fact, scientists now think that ribosomes may have started out as "naked" RNA molecules (not complexed with proteins) in the RNA world and then became associated, step by step, with a variety of proteins.

In the words of Harry Noller, the principal investigator in whose laboratory the fine structure of ribosomes was elucidated: "They [ribosomal proteins] are typically small and basic, representing a diverse collection of structural types . . . giving the impression that they were recruited to the ribosome in *many independent evolutionary events*" (Noller 2005, p. 1511, emphasis added). What Noller means is that, since many ribosomal proteins can be removed without destroying ribosomal activity, and since the structures of ribosomal proteins show no particular consensus, evolution can be seen as the reverse of step-by-step removal of ribosomal proteins as is done in the lab. Therefore, evolution *gradually* combined ribosomal proteins with ribosomal RNA over evolutionary time *in a piecemeal manner*. This is anathema to ID thinkers who claim that complex structures must have appeared as whole units right from the beginning.

In an interesting article (see the technical articles in Further Reading), Noller, an international leader of the field of ribosome structure and function, further makes a number of hypotheses regarding the evolution of translation, from naked RNA to ribosomes as we know them today. For him, primitive translation first developed by chance and was then naturally selected as soon as it produced simple proteins that assisted RNA in its ribozyme functions. Therefore, translation evolved not with a goal in mind—the synthesis of proteins as it exists today in living cells—but because a repertoire of simple proteins assisted (and made more efficient, more fit) the RNA world. Indeed, the structural and functional abilities of naked RNA

molecules—their fitness—are limited by the chemical bonds that exist between the atoms composing this RNA. These constraints ultimately restrict
the variety of shapes that RNA molecules can assume. In turn, the shapes of
RNA molecules define their function. Even small proteins bound to RNA
molecules considerably extend their catalytic (ribozyme) activities, meaning
that the RNA world could evolve more rapidly as soon as proteins appeared.
This evolution occurred in a stepwise fashion because the RNA world did not
"know" what its ultimate shape would be.

Readers are encouraged to consult Noller's article. It is not simple, but
anyone who has taken a college-level course in biochemistry and one in
genetics would benefit from it. This article and the elegant hypotheses described in it are in stark contrast with the crude and naive pronouncements
of ID biochemists. It is ironic that these latter biochemists are calling "irreducibly complex" a bacterial structure—the flagellum—that is in fact
dispensable for the bacteria. Indeed, most types of bacteria do not possess
a flagellum. On the other hand, *all* living cells *must* harbor ribosomes to be
alive. As we just described, ribosomes are *reducibly* complex. Should we
then assume that a "designer" wasted time designing irreducibly complex
but unnecessary bacterial flagella while ignoring reducibly complex cell
components—ribosomes—that are absolutely necessary for life? This makes
no sense at all.

The RNA world sits on firm theoretical and experimental ground and,
contrary to ID thinking, constitutes hypothesis-driven science. But as expected, not all scientists think that the RNA world appeared from organics
resulting from atmospheric chemistry. In other words, some scientists dis-
pute the origin of the RNA world, but not the previous existence of the RNA
world itself. We describe next what this alternative model has to propose.

Another Model for the Origin of Life

The other broad model, which we do not describe in detail, proposes that a
hydrogen-rich primeval atmosphere was not necessary for the synthesis of
the first organic compounds. These could have been made in the superheated
water of hydrothermal vents in the presence of iron and nickel catalysts or
even on Earth's surface. In both cases, sulfur-containing compounds are
involved. There is good laboratory evidence that some organic molecules,
including amino acids and even short proteins, can be made under these
circumstances. However, there is as yet no evidence that RNA can be made
this way. Thus, this model does not suggest how genetic information could
have appeared on prebiotic Earth. On the other hand, it is always possible
that organics made in hydrothermal vents could have cooperated with the

RNA world, perhaps playing a role similar to that of putative preproteins made through thioesters.

Hydrothermal vents provide a rich terrain for chemical reactions taking place far from thermodynamic equilibrium. We can thus imagine that building blocks of RNA, made through atmospheric chemistry and subsequently dissolved in the primordial soup, could easily have diffused to the vicinity of hydrothermal vents and their sharp temperature gradients. There, in the presence of mineral catalysts constantly spewed out by the vents, the formation of RNA molecules in a Markovian way could have taken place following the thermodynamics of dissipative structures. In this hypothesis, the RNA world would thus have been born from a combination of organic molecules made in the atmosphere that subsequently reacted chemically (perhaps with the help of preproteins made in the vents) to make RNA deep under the ocean surface. Or else some kind of primitive metabolism could have appeared in or near the vents, which would have led to the synthesis of RNA building blocks.

This scenario is amenable to experimentation in the laboratory. To do these experiments, one would have to construct a vessel in which superheated water at high pressure, containing suspended elements of the terrestrial magma, is shot continuously through a large column of cold water. The cold water should contain in a dissolved state all the organic compounds known to be made in a sparked hydrogen-rich atmosphere. To our knowledge, such experiments have not yet been performed.

The existence of two different models for the origin of life (which could actually be merged, as described above) means that research in this area is still very much in progress and that no definitive answers have been yet reached. This is not a vice; on the contrary, it is a sign that creative hypothesis formulation, in contrast to ID defenders' negativism and obstructionism, makes for original and exciting science.

We described how chance events played an important role in the formation and evolution of the putative RNA world. But the RNA world itself was one of the results of about 10 billion years of cosmic evolution. Does this mean that one can potentially imagine a correlation between cosmic evolution and the appearance of life in the universe? In the next section we examine this possibility in the light of another partly probabilistic branch of science: cosmology.

The Uncertainty Principle and the Universe

In many ways, cosmology, the science of the origin of the universe, is much more advanced than the science of the origin of life. The main reason for this is probably that cosmology is grounded in physics while the investigations into the origin of life are grounded in part in biology. Aside from the theories of Mendel and Darwin, biology has not yet developed the vast theoretical and mathematical framework that characterizes physics. Nonetheless, the twenty-first century has already been called the "century of biology" (the twentieth century was the century of physics), which promises great advances in the life sciences. For origins of life research, some type of merging between physical and biological thinking would be very helpful because, as is now thought, life in the universe is a direct consequence of the universe's formation. Let us now rewind the tape of the story of the universe and go back to its very beginning, 14 billion years ago.

Most people have heard about the Big Bang theory of the creation of the universe. What most people may not know, however, is that the appearance of life can be connected with the Big Bang in an uninterrupted sequence of events elegantly described by cosmology. The Big Bang is a respected theory that solidly rests on theoretical and experimental physics, including general relativity and quantum mechanics, the two most successful and most verified theories of physics. Let us first see very briefly what the Big Bang theory says about the origin of the universe.

There is abundant evidence that the universe is expanding, meaning that galaxies (huge collections of gravitationally bound stars) are receding from one another thanks to the stretching of space. This also means that at the beginning, as expansion started, at the moment of the Big Bang, the universe was an extremely small object containing a gigantic amount of energy at an unimaginably high temperature. Stable matter did not exist under these conditions, and the universe was for a very brief moment an object solely containing intense electromagnetic radiation composed of high-energy photons. As the universe expanded, its temperature cooled, allowing stable matter to exist. This initial matter consisted of about 75% hydrogen atoms and 25% helium atoms (plus very small traces of other light elements). This hydrogen:helium ratio was predicted by quantum mechanics and has been verified experimentally by telescopic observations, making this ratio between the two elements a fact.

Quantum mechanics is the theory that describes the behavior of atoms and their fundamental constituents (electrons and quarks) as well as the interactions between these particles and electromagnetic radiation. Its validity has been confirmed by 80 years of research and experimentation. Since the universe consists of both matter and electromagnetic radiation (visible light, in particular), it is reasonable to expect that the laws and equations of quantum mechanics apply to the creation of the universe. And this is where teleology, determinism, and a goal-oriented universe are unnecessary at the most basic level, the Big Bang.

Quantum mechanics is a statistical science, not a deterministic one. This means, among other things, that elementary particles such as electrons can no longer be regarded as tiny billiard balls zooming around atomic nuclei or traveling through space. According to quantum mechanics, elementary particles are "smeared out," "fuzzy" objects. In other words, it is impossible to pinpoint the location of an elementary particle with infinite precision; one can only estimate the *probability* that an electron is here or there. This has nothing to do with our instruments being imprecise: this "fuzziness" is part of the fabric of nature; it is, in fact, a law of nature. German physicist Werner Heisenberg (1901–1976) discovered and formulated this principle mathematically. It has been known since its discovery as the "uncertainty principle." This principle states that, at its most basic level, the world of atoms and subatomic particles, nature is indeterminate. Of course, the world at the human scale *seems* to be deterministic, but this is because at our scale, quantum effects are not discernible.

Quantum indeterminacy is completely counterintuitive and difficult for many people to grasp. But this aspect of the theory stopped bothering professional physicists a long time ago; they routinely apply the equations of quantum theory, and they know these will work to solve their research problems. This is why quantum mechanics is not "just a theory." One of its major offshoots is the electronics industry. To put it bluntly, without quantum mechanics, there would be no computers, no iPods, and no lasers that read and write our CDs and DVDs. In short, quantum mechanics works.

At the moment of the Big Bang, the universe was a very small quantum object and the uncertainty principle would have applied to it. This means that the universe could not have been designed in a deterministic way, as if someone were "pulling the trigger" at a predetermined time. At this point, it is important to qualify what is meant by the expression "the moment of the Big Bang." Intuitively, it is tempting to think of this event as taking place at time $t = 0$. But again, intuition and common sense are often false friends in science. It turns out that the timing of the Big Bang is also subject to Heisenberg's uncertainty principle, as is the size of the universe at its beginning. Quantum mechanics shows that both time and size become "fuzzy," impossible to determine exactly below certain values. For time, the earliest knowable moment in the origin of the universe is $t = 10^{-43}$ second (i.e., the number 1 preceded by a decimal and 43 zeros), not $t = 0$ second. As for size, the diameter of the nascent universe cannot be known below the value of 1.62×10^{-35} meter. These numbers are called the Planck time and the Planck length, respectively. They reflect the basic indeterminacy of nature, even at the level of the Big Bang. This also means that the Big Bang should be construed as an event marking the beginning *of* time, but it is an event that cannot be precisely located *in* time.

Thus, to create a universe of size zero at time $t = 0$, a deterministic designer (as per creationist thinking) would have had to violate a law of nature, the uncertainty principle, and then would have had to enforce it immediately thereafter for us humans to observe later. This type of action cannot be proved scientifically, and further, it cannot even be investigated by science because it is akin to a miracle.

Cosmology has provided a coherent picture, well grounded in experimental observation, of cosmic evolution, from the Big Bang until today. One cosmological model subdivides the history of the universe into three phases. To understand the first phase, it is important to know that, for many scientists, the net energy balance of the universe is zero. How is this possible? It is thought that the energy contained in both matter and radiation (represented by Einstein's famous equation $E = mc^2$) is the same amount of energy as the total gravitational energy of the universe (represented by the mutual attraction of all material objects in the cosmos). But since the universe is expanding, gravitational energy has a negative sign, balancing the positive energy in matter and radiation. In this way, the total energy of the universe is zero, and one does not need to invoke a special act that would have created energy from nothing. In fact, our material universe is energetically indistinguishable from a universe containing nothing at all, that is, a universe composed of a vacuum. But importantly, in quantum mechanics, a vacuum is not a void. In fact, a quantum vacuum is unstable and, within the limits of the Planck time, the Planck length, and the Planck mass, can actually create matter and energy through spontaneous (and probabilistic) *fluctuations* of the vacuum. The Planck mass is calculated to be 10^{-5} gram, as per Heisenberg's uncertainty principle. Small as it seems, the Planck mass equals the mass of 10^{18} protons, an immense number. One theory proposes that instead of protons, the Planck mass represented a collection of mini–black holes, very small bodies with gravity so high that even light cannot escape from them.

However, it has been shown by British physicist Stephen Hawking and others that black holes are not infinitely stable. They actually decay (or "evaporate," or "dissipate") by radiating electromagnetic energy through an experimentally verified quantum effect called the "tunnel effect." What is more, black holes are characterized by a temperature and a certain entropy content. Calculations also show that mini–black holes of the order of magnitude of the Planck mass have a life span of about 10^{-37} second.

What does this all mean? Phase 1 of the creation of the universe would have corresponded to an exponential burst of entropy taking place between the Planck time (10^{-43} second) and 10^{-37} second. Entropy was released at that time by the decay of the mini–black holes. Also, by tunneling through these mini–black holes, electromagnetic energy was released. After 10^{-37} second, all the entropy stored in the mini–black holes would have been dissipated, and the very young universe would have experienced a state of thermodynamic equilibrium where entropy (disorder) was maximized and structure could not have appeared. Phase 1 is also known as *inflation* because, during that time, the universe underwent a tremendous increase in diameter, from less than a size of a single proton to about 10 centimeters, roughly the size of a billiard ball.

The universe then experienced the beginning of phase 2. It is at the beginning of this phase that the universe assumed a slower rate of expansion that continues today. But it is also during this phase that particles of matter appeared, following Einstein's principle of equivalence between matter and energy. These particles are what compose all the matter present in the universe, initially in the form of hydrogen and helium. During phase 2, because of the expansion, the universe started to cool down significantly enough to allow stable atoms of hydrogen and helium to exist. Phase 2 lasted for about 400,000 years.

About 400,000 years after the Big Bang, the universe entered phase 3 of its existence. Once stabilized, hydrogen and helium atoms started concentrating in large clouds that began to shrink under their own gravity. As these clouds shrunk, their temperature increased, until it became high enough to start fusing hydrogen atoms to produce more helium atoms and large amounts of energy. It is this process of nuclear fusion (which can be replicated on Earth) that makes stars shine. The nuclear fusion process, under conditions that we do not describe here, leads to the formation of all chemical elements found in the universe, including in humans. This explains how some of the primeval 75% hydrogen : 25% helium ratio of the early universe generated all the dozens of other elements familiar today to chemists. Dramatic stellar explosions (called supernova events) dispersed these elements into space, where they were used to make new stars and their accompanying planets. Life then appeared on at least one of these planets. To use a well-known dictum, we are indeed made of stardust.

As we described above, the formation of structures that led to the evolution of life-forms does not violate the second law of thermodynamics. But what about gas cloud, star, and planet formation? Did these celestial objects also need a designer? After all, like living systems, they are also ordered structures relative to the space that surrounds them. Here again, the answer is that a designer is not needed—stars and planets could have easily formed spontaneously. How, in these cases, could energy be provided from the outside to allow the making of condensing gas clouds, stars, and planets? Recall that a source of external energy is necessary to create order from disorder. Also recall that during phase 2, the entropy of the universe was maximized, meaning that during this phase, order could not have appeared. Where could the energy needed for structure formation have come from? It could not have come from the stars themselves since they did not yet exist. It turns out that this source of energy is a direct consequence of the Big Bang itself, that is, a direct consequence of the expansion of the universe. This model, which describes phase 3, was developed by American astrophysicist Eric Chaisson and others and goes as follows.

Remember that after the Big Bang, the universe cooled down and allowed stable matter to exist. This drop in temperature was due to the expansion of the universe and its increasing volume. At a certain point in time, about 400,000 years after the Big Bang, matter and electromagnetic radiation (light, for example) are said to have *decoupled*, meaning that each went its separate way and stopped interacting strongly with each other. Of course, the universe contains today very large amounts of photons, particles of electromagnetic radiation, with wavelengths ranging to the very energetic (gamma rays, X-rays), to the moderately energetic (ultraviolet and visible light), to the very weak (microwaves). In addition, the universe also contains a lot of matter in the form of dispersed atoms as well as in the form of stars and planets.

What is fascinating is that it has been observed that, as the universe continued to expand, the temperature of radiation and that of matter *did not decrease at the same rate*. This process continues today. This means that right after decoupling, the whole universe started to be in a state of thermodynamic disequilibrium. This disequilibrium allows a flow of energy from radiation to matter, very much like in our simple example of the cup of hot coffee surrounded by cool air. Figure 5.7 shows that the decoupling of matter and radiation allows the whole universe to be in a lower state of entropy, and thus makes it able to generate information, that is, structure. Since the universe will continue to expand for many billions of years to come, thermodynamic equilibrium will not be reached anytime soon, which will allow the creation of even more structure without violating the second law. In brief, phase 3 in the evolution of the universe is a phase of structure formation. This is the phase in which we live.

Thus, much as life on Earth was ultimately made possible by the energy delivered by the sun, the whole universe can evolve because there is energy transfer between radiation and matter. In other words, cosmic evolution, including the appearance of life, is in the very end a consequence of the Big Bang. And let us remember that at the origin of it all lies the uncertainty principle, the law of physics that prevents determinism at its most fundamental level.

All physicists know that the uncertainty principle is a fact of nature. However, not all agree on its philosophical meaning and on how deeply it

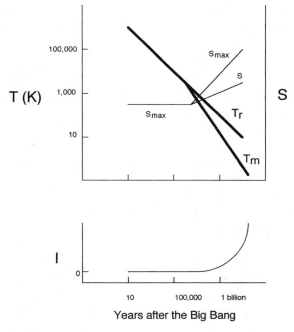

FIGURE 5.7
How the decoupling of matter and radiation in the young universe
allows the formation of structure. Top: the thick line shows the drop in
temperature (T, in kelvins) of the universe as it expands over time since
the Big Bang. After about 400,000 years, the temperature is low enough
to allow matter and radiation to decouple. Then, matter and radiation
cool down at different rates (T_r and T_m), meaning that entropy (S)
increased more slowly than it would have without decoupling (S_{max}).
Interestingly, the entropy of the universe was maximized between the
Big Bang and decoupling because matter and radiation still interacted
strongly. Bottom: it can be shown that information (I) and entropy
are two related quantities. Since S is lower than S_{max}, after 400,000 years
of expansion and beyond, information in the form of structure increases
in the expanding universe. Adapted from E. J. Chaisson, *Cosmic Evolution: The Rise of Complexity in Nature* (Cambridge, MA: Harvard
University Press, 2001).

represents the reality of nature. One of the doubters was Albert Einstein,
who, ironically, was one of the founding fathers of quantum mechanics.
Einstein is known to have said tersely, "God does not play dice." This does
not mean that Einstein was a creationist or even that he believed in God.
Einstein was born in a Jewish family, but he never practiced any religion and
never really revealed whether he had any religious faith or not. Be that as it
may, Einstein intended his metaphor to mean that he did not think that

nature was basically indeterministic. He thought that quantum mechanics was right, but that it represented only the surface of a more deeply hidden reality. However, it does not seem that Einstein got it right, at least for now. More than 50 years after his death, there is still no evidence against Heisenberg's uncertainty principle being the most fundamental law of nature at the submicroscopic level. And it is at this level that the universe was created.

To conclude this chapter, we have shown that evolution is a principle that can be applied to the whole universe, not just life. The universe is not static; it changes constantly—it also evolves. This blind evolutionary principle can be recognized in the indeterministic Big Bang, the expansion of the universe that allows formation of ordered structures thanks to a state of universal thermodynamic disequilibrium, and the existence of dissipative structures also formed under conditions that are far from equilibrium. In fact, life itself is in a situation of thermodynamic disequilibrium. This is what has allowed its appearance and evolution.

Going back to the phenomenon of life, chapter 6 describes what we think we know about the first steps in the evolution of the DNA world, which, as described above, is an evolutionary consequence of the primeval RNA world. We will show that science is far from having all the answers to this difficult question. However, scientists have built interesting evolutionary models that can be put to the test. Here again, unsurprisingly, science offers materialistic explanations for the events that led the first simple cells, Bacteria and Archaea, to produce much more complex Eukarya (a domain of life to which humans belong) through a series of evolutionary steps.

Things to Think About

1. Scientists have learned the important effect of chance in the unfolding of natural events. Just think how hard it is to predict the weather. Chaos theory shows how very small causes can have very large effects. Full determinism is no longer part of many scientific theories.

2. Cosmology, thermodynamics, quantum mechanics, and statistical mechanics show that the universe, from its largest structures to the world of the atom, is intrinsically probabilistic.

3. There exist sophisticated models for the origin of life. The RNA world with its ribozyme activities, RNA hypercycles, and liposome encapsulation of genetic information paints an exciting picture of what kinds of prebiotic events may have taken place. All scientists know, however, that an enormous amount of work remains to be done to

refine these models and resolve the great difficulties associated with this type of research.

4. The appearance of life can be seen as a direct consequence of the expansion of the universe and the universal thermodynamic disequilibrium it creates.

5. A creationist might say that nothing in this chapter makes any sense. But then, are there any other current explanations for the origin of life and the universe that rely on reason and scientific evidence?

6

Evolution of the DNA World and the Chance Events That Accompanied It
More about Complexity

> We know enough of the blueprint [of life] to validly attempt
> to reconstruct the manner in which it first materialized.
> —Christian de Duve, *Blueprint for a Cell*

We described in chapter 5 how the appearance of life on Earth 3.8 billion years ago, perhaps in the form of an RNA world, was a direct consequence of the expansion of the universe. The result of this ongoing expansion is the continuous production of energy that can be used to produce structure. We can thus surmise that the RNA world was not the end of the line in terms of the complexity of life-forms: we and other life-forms are here to prove it in the form of a rich, varied DNA world.

The first putative ribo-organisms (see chapter 5) must have been very simple indeed, barely more complex than membrane-bound hypercycles. But as far as we know, ribo-organisms no longer exist on Earth today; they seem to be extinct. All existing cellular life is based on a DNA blueprint that may have appeared as early as 3.5 billion years ago. DNA-containing cells evolved from ribo-organisms to produce the first genuine prokaryotic cells, Bacteria and Archaea, microorganisms that we would recognize today as bona fide modern life-forms, much more complex than primeval ribo-organisms. We described in chapter 5 how the DNA world may have originated from the RNA world. But then, how do we envision the evolutionary steps undergone by the first recognizable prokaryotes, which are microorganisms whose DNA is not enclosed in a nuclear membrane? After all, the prokaryotic world today is enormously varied, much more so than the macroscopic plant and animal worlds. Prokaryotes thrive everywhere on Earth, even in the most inhospitable environments, with some of them even able to metabolize arsenic, toxic mercury compounds, and oil spills. In reality, it is no wonder that prokaryotes are so fantastically diverse: they have had about 3.5 billion years to evolve and branch out in innumerable directions.

The Prokaryotic LUCA and Its Evolution

The last universal common ancestor of all life on Earth, or LUCA, should be thought of as a group of DNA-containing microorganisms that lived a little more than 3.5 billion years ago and from which all present-day life is derived (see the depiction of the "tree of life" in figure 3.3). We do not know with any kind of certainty what LUCA might have been like, other than it must have been single celled and have lived in the total absence of oxygen gas, which was not yet present in the atmosphere. Phylogenetic trees suggest that LUCA might have been a sulfur metabolizer. Although no microbial fossils that old have been discovered, some rock formations of that age have been found to contain organic compounds that bear the signature of life.

How genetically complex could LUCA have been? Research on existing simple prokaryotes shows that to be considered alive by today's standards, a cell should contain at least 180 genes, keeping in mind that cells with so few genes today can live only as parasites of eukaryotic cells. This seems to be the minimum number of genes that can provide enough genetic information for a cell's most basic metabolic functions. This is a very low number, considering that most modern prokaryotes contain thousands of genes. But, of course, the prokaryotes we observe today have had billions of years to evolve and to gain all sorts of secondary genetic functions that are in fact not all necessary for their life to continue. At any rate, LUCA, in order to be an independently living microorganism, must have possessed more than 180 genes.

After about 100 million years of evolution (this timing is quite uncertain), the descendants of LUCA split into two major groups: the Bacteria and the Archaea. Both types of microorganisms are prokaryotes, but they differ in a number of important characteristics. For example, some of their cell membrane components are different, and the genes that determine what biologists call "house-keeping functions"—that is, DNA and RNA synthesis—are different. Finally, the DNA of Archaea and Eukarya (also called eukaryotes) is associated with a class of proteins called histones that do not exist in Bacteria. Eukarya are the much more complex cousins of prokaryotes that split off from them after hundreds of millions of years of evolution. How histones appeared in the living world is not yet understood.

LUCA must have evolved by mutation and natural selection, as modern prokaryotes do. Indeed, laboratory experiments have shown that subpopulations of prokaryotes can adapt by mutation to very different environments in a relatively small number of generations. In addition to undergoing random mutations, many modern prokaryotes can achieve what is called *horizontal gene transfer*, a special way of exchanging DNA, which probably already existed a very long time ago. Horizontal gene transfer is different from the more familiar *vertical gene transfer*. In vertical gene transfer, DNA, in the form of genes, is transmitted from one generation of cells to the next by simple cell division or sexual reproduction. For example, when parents conceive a child, they are performing vertical gene transfer. In horizontal gene transfer, genes are transferred to individuals that can belong to the same generation. This type of heredity is not known to exist in humans, other animals, or plants, but it is common in the microbial world.

Three modes of horizontal gene transfer are recognized. The first is based on dead or dying bacteria releasing their DNA in the environment as a result of the rupture of their membranes. This free-floating DNA can then be picked up and incorporated by live bacteria that happen to be in the vicinity. Thus, these live bacteria acquire new genes that can code for new biological properties. The second type of horizontal gene transfer is achieved by viruses. Viruses are specific pieces of DNA or RNA wrapped in a protein coat. Some viruses, when they infect bacterial cells and multiply, can by chance wrap their protein coat around pieces of DNA that belong to the infected cell. Interestingly, such viruses can still infect other cells, but the genome they introduce into these other cells is bacterial DNA, not viral DNA. This bacterial DNA introduced by viral infection into recipient bacteria can, of course, contain new genes. Recent observations indicate that microscopic, eukaryotic phytoplanktonic (marine) organisms also evolve through virus-mediated gene transfer. This research is in its infancy, and we do not know whether other micro-eukaryotes evolve in the same fashion.

Third, some bacterial species have developed a type of primitive sexual reproduction. In this instance, two bacterial cells get in close physical contact and form a tubular structure through which DNA can travel from one cell to the other. Here again, genes are potentially exchanged. The result of horizontal gene transfer can be an extremely rapid evolution because the number of genes involved can be quite large, up to several thousands at one time.

Thus, in the case of the prokaryotic world, the beginning of the tree of life (where the prokaryotes are located) consists of diagonally oriented branches, just like the rest of the tree. But one should also think of some of these branches as being connected horizontally. These horizontal connections are usually not drawn because we still do not know enough about the extent of horizontal gene transfer among the many thousands of bacterial species alive today.

The Appearance of Photosynthesis
and the Oxygen Crisis

As the prokaryotic world was evolving, a new type of biological mechanism quickly appeared: photosynthesis. By definition, photosynthesis is the ability of some living cells to use the energy of sunlight to drive portions of their metabolism. A sugar, glucose, is also produced in the process and is metabolized to produce more cellular energy. Recall that there was no breathable oxygen gas in the atmosphere at the time. There exist today photosynthetic microbes that live in the absence of oxygen and metabolize hydrogen gas or even noxious hydrogen sulfide gas. The first photosynthetic microorganisms probably resembled these modern bacteria. Later, photosynthesis evolved into a mechanism called oxygenic photosynthesis, which is used by all modern plants and many microorganisms. It is based on the metabolism of water, which it decomposes into protons (hydrogen atoms devoid of their single electron) and oxygen, which escapes as gas into the atmosphere. Glucose is also produced in the process and is then metabolized. Intriguingly, some very ancient microorganisms, called cyanobacteria, that use this new type of photosynthesis still exist today. They live in thick mats called stromatolites. Fossil stromatolites dating back at least 3 billion years have been discovered and found to contain colonies of microorganisms whose structure strongly resembles modern cyanobacterial colonies.

Now, what was the result of oxygen release into Earth's atmosphere? It must have been catastrophic. Oxygen is in fact a dangerous gas. It is very reactive, and as its name implies, it oxidizes things, including organic compounds that make up cells. All life-forms that depend today on oxygen for survival (such as humans, fruit flies, and geraniums) are descended from early microbial life that had evolved mechanisms to detoxify oxygen. These mechanisms are catalyzed by protein enzymes, one of them called catalase, shared by humans, fruit flies, and geraniums. All life that had not evolved these mechanisms either perished or became confined to deep, oxygen-free, sediments at the bottom of lakes and oceans or deep inside Earth's crust.

Of course, oxygen accumulated only slowly in the atmosphere. At first it dissolved in the oceans, where it reacted with mineral compounds in the water. It is only when water was saturated and oxidation reactions had slowed down significantly in the ocean that oxygen started being released into the atmosphere. This took a very long time; we know that the present oxygen level of 21% was reached only about 400 million years ago; it is estimated that oxygen levels in the atmosphere were 1–10% of the present value between 2.4 billion years ago and 545 million years ago. It is also known that oxygen levels varied widely up until about 2 billion years ago, as revealed by the presence of *banded iron formations*, which are successive rock layers containing oxidized iron interspersed with rock layers not containing it. Iron salts dissolved in water came out of solution after contact with oxygen and formed the bands containing oxidized iron. The existence of banded iron formations then shows that oxygen concentrations went up and down. The exact reason why this phenomenon took place is not well understood. Some think that banded iron formations were paralleled by cycles of active and then less active proliferation of photosynthetic microorganisms.

Then, as oxygen was appearing in the atmosphere, some microbes evolved a new metabolic pathway called *respiration*. This pathway actually metabolizes oxygen to produce cellular energy. Each time we breathe in some air, our cells are using respiration to power other metabolic reactions. The end products of respiration are water vapor and carbon dioxide, which we exhale. Many types of prokaryotes also use the respiration pathway. Interestingly, photosynthesis and respiration both depend on the existence of a class of organic molecules called *porphyrins* that may have been present in the primeval soup, because they are made in gas-sparking experiments. Even hemoglobin, the protein that ferries oxygen to the cells of our body, contains a porphyrin molecule associated with an iron atom. Chlorophyll, which is necessary to perform photosynthesis, also contains a porphyrin molecule, in this case associated with a magnesium atom.

The appearance of oxygen in the atmosphere had another consequence that is still with us today: the formation of an ozone layer around the planet. The ozone molecule contains three oxygen atoms, contrary to breathable oxygen, which contains only two. The presence of the ozone layer is critical; without it, the unabsorbed ultraviolet light emitted by the sun would wipe out all life on Earth, except that which dwells in water about 50 feet below the surface (at which point ultraviolet light is completely blocked out) or underground.

In the absence of oxygen, there was, of course, no ozone layer. As far as early life was concerned, this was a give-and-take situation. On the one hand, the lethal effects of ultraviolet radiation killed some cells (the ones close to the surface), but on the other hand, cells that were only marginally exposed to it could mutate—and so evolve—at high rates. This is happening less frequently today, but we must remember that the ozone layer is not completely impermeable to ultraviolet light, meaning that mutations induced by it are still possible, including those that cause skin cancer. Based on geochemical data, it is estimated that, by about 2.2 billion years ago, there was enough oxygen in the atmosphere to permit an ozone layer to form.

In summary, from about 3.5 billion years ago until about 2 billion years ago, prokaryotes reigned supreme on Earth. As a matter of fact, they still do.

In sheer diversity and biomass, bacteria vastly outperform all other life-forms put together.

At this point, we should stop for a moment and take a critical look at the scenario described above. How do we know that any of this is true? In chapter 5, we described many laboratory experiments that prove the reality of organic molecules made in gas-sparking experiments, the reality of ribozymes, the reality of hypercycles that explain the life cycles of viruses, and the reality of liposomes that can self-organize. But what about the evolution of the first DNA-containing cells, the appearance of cyanobacteria, horizontal gene transfer, and the evolution of oxygenic photosynthesis? Have any laboratory experiments shown that these evolutionary steps actually occurred?

The answer is no in most cases (except regarding horizontal gene transfer, which is very well understood in a number of microbial species). There is one good reason for this lack of direct demonstration: the time spans involved—many hundreds of millions of years—preclude ordinary laboratory experiments. For example, it would be futile to grow existing sulfur metabolizers in the lab and wait for a few million years to see if they develop photosynthesis. Similarly, no one has ever seen a fish sprouting legs to become a salamander.

One could extend the same criticism to the RNA world and its evolution. After all, the RNA world may have existed for as long as 300 million years before the DNA world appeared. How, then, can scientists hope to reproduce within their lifetimes what may have happened in this RNA world? The situation here is very different because the RNA world was initially composed of RNA *molecules*, not living cells. A set of techniques called *in vitro* evolution (meaning evolution in the test tube) allows scientists to generate millions of different RNA molecules in a semirandom fashion in matter of a few hours. Carrying out these experiments over a few months generates a fantastically high number of different RNA molecules, all potentially equipped with different properties.

In other words, by using modern techniques, scientist can "shrink" evolutionary time down to days or months. Other specific techniques allow researchers to identify the special properties of RNA molecules made in these *in vitro* evolution experiments. Just to mention three examples, scientists have generated RNA molecules that spontaneously bind amino acids, a step in protein synthesis, as explained in chapter 5. Further, some RNA molecules have their ribozyme activity enhanced or changed by binding small molecules that may have been present in the primordial soup. Such RNA molecules are called "riboswitches." And finally, a short RNA molecule made in the laboratory has been shown to catalyze the universal "aldol" reaction, involved in the metabolism of sugars, which is shared by all life-forms.

Thus, we see that sophisticated laboratory experiments can imitate the evolution of the RNA world. However, these types of experiments cannot be conducted easily with living cells and organisms because these cannot be forced to multiply any faster than they do naturally; no matter what one does, fruit flies reproduce no faster than every 20 days, and elephants take two years. Some rare bacteria divide every 30 minutes, but others take days or weeks. It should be noted, however, that experiments with bacteria are in progress at Michigan State University, in particular. There, starting in 1988, researchers have grown fast-multiplying bacteria for more than 20,000 generations. After subjecting bacteria to different regimens of sugars, a process that applies selective pressure on the cells, they observed significant changes in the bacteria. The cells had doubled in size, some grew better (had acquired greater fitness) in the presence of a specific sugar, and other cells had increased their mutation rate. These experiments show that it is possible to observe evolution at work in the laboratory. Nevertheless, much work remains to be done to fully understand the evolutionary mechanisms operating in these long-term experiments with bacteria. Also, the bacteria used in these experiments harbor more than 4,000 genes, each and every one a potential target for evolutionary events. Obviously, it will take time to sort out what happens to all these genes, taking into account that many of them do not even have a known metabolic function.

How, then, can scientists have confidence in evolutionary models dealing with DNA-containing cells and organisms? The answer is twofold: phylogenies based on DNA, and the fossil record. Let us start with the fossil record, which is easier to understand. We described in earlier chapters how fossil dating techniques are generally reliable. It turns out that the oldest rocks contain the fossils of microorganisms, but no human fossils or even fossils of worms. This means that a long time ago life started in a very simple form (prokaryotes), with more complex life-forms (the first eukaryotes, for example) appearing later, and very complex life-forms such as worms appearing much later. Thus, the fossil record gives us the order in which different species appeared and when.

Then, there are DNA-based phylogenies that can tell us which genes—and hence which organisms that carry them—are ancestral to others. These phylogenies tell us that, for example, photosynthesis using hydrogen sulfide (and the genes coding for it) preceded photosynthesis that uses the splitting of water. By doing this type of comparison at the DNA level, we can reconstruct the tree of life (see chapter 3), from the most ancestral genes still in existence today to the most recent ones. This type of analysis has shown that the human species is a young one, which is confirmed by the existence of young fossils (see chapter 4), and that cyanobacteria are a very old species, as confirmed by the very old fossils of stromatolites where these bacteria proliferated.

Detractors of these methods—one based on paleontology and the other one based on genetics—have been remarkably silent, other than saying that all of this is impossible or wrong, and that the Creator (or the Intelligent Designer) just made everything look that way.

The Structure and Origin of Eukaryotes

Let us now turn our attention to newcomers: the complex cells and organisms called eukaryotes. In addition to prokaryotes, the living world is also composed of eukaryotes, a category of organisms that includes amoebas, sponges, ferns, oak trees, zebras, and humans. These organisms range from single celled (amoebas) to billions of cells (humans, oak trees, whales, and zebras), depending on the species. Regardless of the number of cells that compose them, eukaryotes are structurally more complex than prokaryotes.

What events could have led to the evolution of some branches of the prokaryotes into more complicated eukaryotes? According to the fossil record, the first simple Eukarya appeared about 2 billion years ago. However, chemical fossils, that is, organic compounds found in rocks, put the appearance of Eukarya at about 2.7 billion years ago. Let us now consider which observations warrant the categorization of some organisms under the name "Eukarya" or "eukaryotes."

Even though all living cells use the same biological principles to maintain and reproduce themselves, there are major differences between prokaryotes and eukaryotes. We have a good understanding of some of these differences, but we are quite ignorant of the origin of many others. But, of course, this does not mean that we will *never* understand eukaryotic evolution.

For a long time, it was thought that cell size was the simplest way to distinguish prokaryotes from eukaryotes, with prokaryotic cells being very small and eukaryotic cells much larger. This is no longer true; some recently discovered marine bacteria are as large as some eukaryotic cells. What most distinguishes Eukarya and prokaryotic cells is their *internal* structure and/or the number of genes they harbor. For example, baker's yeast, a very simple, unicellular eukaryote, carries 6,000 genes. This number is not much higher than the number of genes carried by some prokaryotes, but nonetheless, its structure makes yeast a true eukaryote. More complex, multicellular eukaryotes have more genes. For example, fruit flies carry 16,000 genes, while humans have 25,000. Recall the Great Chain of Being described in chapter 2—if numbers of genes were an indication of where a being should be listed, corn would rank higher than humans! This is because corn has a whopping 59,000 genes, more than twice as many as humans.

A look at figure 6.1 reveals some of the major differences that distinguish prokaryotes from eukaryotes. Immediately obvious features include a

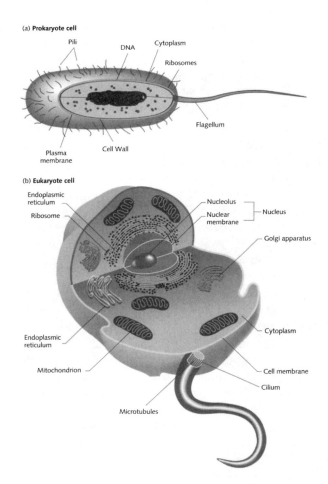

(a) **Prokaryote cell**

Pili
DNA
Cytoplasm
Ribosomes
Flagellum
Plasma membrane
Cell Wall

(b) **Eukaryote cell**

Endoplasmic reticulum
Ribosome
Nucleolus
Nuclear membrane
Nucleus
Golgi apparatus
Cytoplasm
Cell membrane
Cilium
Endoplasmic reticulum
Mitochondrion
Microtubules

FIGURE 6.1

A typical prokaryotic cell (top) compared with an animal cell. Ribosomes are small bodies where proteins are synthesized. In the animal cell, the nucleus is the cellular compartment where most of the cell's DNA is present in the form of chromosomes. The nucleolus is the part of the nucleus where ribosomes are assembled. The endoplasmic reticulum and the Golgi apparatus are membrane systems. From J. Maynard Smith and E. Szathmáry, *The Origins of Life: From the Birth of Life to the Origins of Language* (New York: Oxford University Press, 1999), by permission of Oxford University Press.

complex membrane system (the Golgi apparatus and the endoplasmic reticulum), the existence of a membranous nucleus where eukaryotic DNA is confined, and the existence of small membrane-bound bodies, such as mitochondria. Not shown are chromosomes, the complex rodlike structures that contain eukaryotic DNA and histone proteins mentioned above, and chloroplasts, which exist only in plant cells. The same figure shows that a prokaryotic cell has none of this complicated internal structure. Let us analyze this eukaryotic internal structure component by component.

The Golgi apparatus, the nuclear envelope (which houses the cell's DNA in the form of chromosomes), and the endoplasmic reticulum are part of a vast internal membrane system involved in the trafficking of metabolites, the export of RNA molecules out of the nucleus, and protein synthesis. The origin, as well as the genetics, of this membrane system and its evolution are not understood but are being investigated. Nonetheless, scientists recognize their ignorance in this area and make few claims regarding the evolution of the eukaryotic membrane system.

The cytoskeleton is an internal protein scaffold that gives cells their shape and allows crawling movements on solid surfaces. For a long time it was thought that prokaryotes contained nothing coming close to a cytoskeleton. However, recent discoveries show that prokaryotes contain genes that are homologous to eukaryotic cytoskeleton genes. The function of these genes in prokaryotes is to produce proteins that also maintain cell shape, as in eukaryotes. In addition, these proteins also play a role in the equal distribution of DNA into daughter cells during cell division.

For a long time, too, it was believed that complex chromosomes were a unique feature of eukaryotes. Chromosomes contain the cell's DNA and a whole host of proteins, including those called histones. DNA is an extremely long molecule, much longer than the size of any cell containing it. For example, if the DNA of a single human cell were to be stretched out, it would be six feet long! To be accommodated in microscopic cells, DNA must thus be enormously compacted. This compaction is achieved in part by histones that coil the DNA tightly. Histones were thought not to exist in prokaryotes. However, a close study of Archaea demonstrated that they—but not Bacteria—contain a primitive chromosomal structure also mediated by histones. This, then, suggests that eukaryotes must somehow be descended from prokaryotic Archaea.

As for the origins of mitochondria, chloroplasts, and peroxisomes (vesicles involved in detoxification processes), these deserve special coverage and are explained in detail further below.

Eukaryotes May Be Derived from the Fusion
of an Archaeal Cell with a Bacterial Cell

As described above, Archaea, like eukaryotes, contain histones. What is more, DNA homology studies have revealed that the eukaryotic genes involved in DNA, RNA, and protein synthesis are close to their archaeal cousins. This supports even further a model in which eukaryotes are descended from Archaea. But then, homology studies also show that eukaryotes contain a vast collection of genes derived from the other branch of prokaryotes, the Bacteria. This suggests that Bacteria *also* played a role in the evolution of the Eukarya. How is this possible?

A clever model, not accepted by everyone, proposes that the first eukaryotic cells appeared as a result of the *fusion* between an archaeal cell and a bacterial cell. Fusing two cells means merging them into a single structure through the melding of their outer membranes. This can be done easily in the laboratory, but it also seems to occur in nature, especially under the influence of certain viruses. Here is what the fusion model has to say. First, let us imagine a member of the Bacteria able to metabolize oxygen and produce carbon dioxide, which is released. This organism is thus able to perform respiration. Then, let us also imagine that this same cell possesses a metabolic pathway that allows it to produce and release hydrogen gas. This type of metabolism actually exists today in several types of cells. Next, imagine a member of the Archaea that is unable to metabolize oxygen but *uses* carbon dioxide and hydrogen for its own metabolism. Such organisms also exist today. If these two cells were to fuse, they would now possess a mixed metabolism where carbon dioxide and hydrogen would no longer be waste products; these two products would be used immediately by the metabolic machinery of the archaeal part of the partnership. What is more, this fused cell would now be able to live with or without oxygen, giving it great flexibility, great fitness, regarding the types of ecological niches where it could survive and multiply (figure 6.2).

As evolutionary time passed, the ability to produce hydrogen would have become a cellular compartment called the *hydrogenosome*. This evolutionary step would have taken place in early eukaryotes occupying niches devoid of oxygen. On the other hand, for early eukaryotes that occupied oxygen-rich niches, the ability of the bacterial partner to metabolize oxygen would have become a *mitochondrion*, a cellular compartment where oxygen metabolism takes place today. Under all circumstances, the archaeal partner would have contributed genes coding for histones, the proteins that compact DNA and still exist today in all eukaryotes. It would also have contributed the genes and enzymes involved in DNA, RNA, and protein manufacturing.

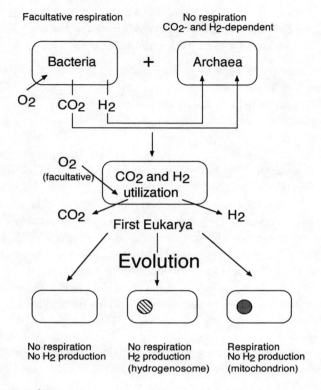

FIGURE 6.2
A possible origin of eukaryotic cells. Rounded rectangles represent individual cells. The "+" sign indicates a fusion event between a bacterial cell and an archaeal cell. The diagonally hatched circle at the bottom is a hydrogenosome, and the vertically hatched circle is a mitochondrion.

We are all familiar with eukaryotes that can live in the presence or absence of oxygen: we call them yeasts. Now, known yeast species do not harbor a hydrogenosome, but other eukaryotes do. Were some primitive yeasts or other early eukaryotes once equipped with a hydrogenosome, as well as a mitochondrion and then lost the hydrogenosome during the course of evolution? We do not know. We do know, however, that some types of eukaryotes are unable to perform respiration but do produce hydrogen via their hydrogenosome. Did these organisms lose the respiration function provided by the bacterial partner of the fused organism but kept a hydrogenosome? Here again, we do not know.

How can we find out? Even when metabolic functions are lost, some of the genes coding for these functions are left behind in the genomes of organisms. In a sense, these genes are "ghosts" from the past that can be detected by DNA sequencing. We do not yet have answers to all our questions because the strange and rare eukaryotes that produce hydrogen and/or cannot survive in the presence of oxygen have not yet had their genomes sequenced. Indeed, full genome sequencing is expensive and takes time. But, of course, time will invariably tell. And indeed, researchers reported in 2005 that hydrogenosomes isolated from the microscopic eukaryote *Nyctotherus ovalis*, which lives in the hindgut of termites, contain DNA that exhibits the hallmarks of genuine mitochondrial DNA. This shows that hydrogenosomes and mitochondria are phylogenetically related, adding credence to the archaeal-bacterial fusion model. Further research will show whether DNA-less hydrogenosomes from other species have transferred this DNA to their main chromosomes.

If the first eukaryotes truly appeared this way, this means that yet another chance event, the random fusion of Archaea and Bacteria, was at the origin of a major evolutionary step. What allowed these hybrid cells to proliferate was their higher fitness in a particular environment relative to archaeal and bacterial cells that did not fuse. This does not mean that Archaea and Bacteria went extinct, of course. They continued their own way of life, and so did the first eukaryotes, which were soon to acquire more complexity and sophistication, as we describe below.

The Endosymbiont Hypothesis for the Existence of Mitochondria and Chloroplasts

The bacterial-archaeal fusion hypothesis for the origin of eukaryotes coexists with an older model called the endosymbiont hypothesis. Apart from rare exceptions, all eukaryotes possess mitochondria, with or without chloroplasts, collectively called "organelles." Animal cells contain mitochondria only, whereas plant cells contain both mitochondria and chloroplasts. No known plants contain only chloroplasts. Chloroplasts are the sites where the first steps of photosynthesis, the splitting of water and production of oxygen and chemical energy take place. Mitochondria are the sites of oxygen metabolism, which also results in the production of chemical energy. Already by the 1910s, some scientists were struck by the size and shape of mitochondria seen under the microscope: they look like bacteria trapped inside a large cell. It took several decades to obtain strong evidence that, indeed, mitochondria once may have been *free-living bacteria*. And so, it turns out, were chloroplasts.

The endosymbiont hypothesis explains the origin of both mitochondria and chloroplasts. The word "symbiosis" applies to two types of organisms living in very close proximity and benefiting from their interactions. Familiar examples are lichens, formed from the symbiotic association of certain algae and fungi that live in harsh environments, such as the surface of rocks.

Another example is the symbiotic association between humans and the bacterial flora that live in their guts. In the 1970s, Lynn Margulis of Boston University developed her hypothesis that mitochondria and chloroplasts are symbionts that exist *inside* eukaryotic cells. What is more, she proposed that in the distant past mitochondria and chloroplasts were free, independent prokaryotes. Her model was not well received, one criticism being that isolated mitochondria and chloroplasts cannot divide, something pro-karyotes should be able to do.

But as time went by, it was convincingly demonstrated that mitochondria and chloroplasts contain their own DNA, RNA, and protein-synthesizing machinery. What is more, antibiotics known to kill bacteria, when fed to some eukaryotes, also interfered deeply with the functions carried out by these organelles. And finally, when chloroplast and mitochondrial DNAs were sequenced, no doubt was left that their genes were prokaryotic in their structure and phylogeny. We now see mitochondria as once free-living prokaryotes able to perform respiration, while chloroplasts were once free-living prokaryotes much resembling the cyanobacteria described above.

The scenario, then, is that primeval eukaryotic cells, which harbored neither chloroplasts nor mitochondria, engulfed *whole* respiring (that is, able to metabolize oxygen) and photosynthesizing prokaryotes. Those eukaryotic cells that only picked up respiring prokaryotes became mitochondria-harboring animal cells, whereas the eukaryotic cells that picked up both respiring and photosynthesizing prokaryotes became plant cells. Isolated mitochondria and chloroplasts can no longer divide because the genes con-trolling this activity were transferred from the originally engulfed pro-karyotes to the main genome of the eukaryotic host.

The success of these first animal and plant cells—as proven by their many descendants—is again due to natural selection: animal cells gained a superior ability to use oxygen thanks to their mitochondria, while plant cells, thanks to both mitochondria and chloroplasts, could now rely on both enhanced respiration and the ability to use sunlight to produce energy and catalyze many metabolic reactions. How (or whether) the fusion hypothesis and the endosymbiont hypothesis can be unified for a full explanation of the origin of the Eukarya is not yet known. The endosymbiont hypothesis assumes that an organelle-less primitive eukaryotic cell appeared, but it does not explain how. This primitive eukaryote then engulfed preexisting photosynthetic and/ or respiring prokaryotes.

Some researchers consider the fusion hypothesis not to be sufficiently supported by DNA sequence data. For these researchers, primitive, organ-elleless ancestors of eukaryotes coexisted with the ancestors of Bacteria and Archaea. In such a scenario, LUCA would have been a community of cells in which the precursors of eukaryotes already possessed a number of complex features (such as a developed membrane system) owing nothing to ancestral prokaryotes. These cells then engulfed respiring bacteria that were to become mitochondria. On the other hand, the fusion hypothesis proposes that the bacterial member of the fusion partnership became either a mitochondrion or a hydrogenosome. This evolution would then have taken place *inside* the primitive eukaryotic cell. One event that the fusion hypothesis does not explain is the appearance of chloroplasts. One can still imagine a fusion-derived first eukaryote engulfing photosynthetic bacteria, as in the endosymbiont hypothesis.

The last category of organelles we will mention are called peroxisomes. They are the sites of oxygen and oxygen by-product detoxification in eukaryotes; whether or not they were once free-living prokaryotes is unknown, although preliminary evidence indicates that they are of eukaryotic origin. Peroxisomes contain no DNA.

Up to this point, the evolving DNA world we have described was composed entirely of single-celled organisms: already well-diversified prokaryotes, and emerging eukaryotes, perhaps evolving by engulfing existing prokaryotes and exchanging genes by horizontal gene transfer. This state of affairs did, of course, change later in time after hundreds of millions of years of evolution that saw the birth of multicellular organisms.

The Triumphant DNA World: The Generation of Diversity and Complexity

Describing the evolution of life after the appearance of the first eukaryotes would easily fill an entire book, and several fine books on the subject have been published. Therefore, we restrict ourselves to a very brief account of what happened between 2 billion years ago and the present and focus particularly on the appearance of sex. It can be said that the "invention" of sexual reproduction by eukaryotic cells was an extremely important milestone in evolution. One basic question about sex is what does it actually achieve? The answer is simple: when two organisms engage in sexual reproduction, their mixed genomes end up in their progenies. In other words, an organism resulting from sexual reproduction, such as a human being and countless others, contains two copies of each gene. What is the importance of having duplicate genomes? First, remember that random mutations are a fact of life. If an organism has only one genome, such as all prokaryotes have, a deleterious mutation potentially signifies the death of the organism. Consider now life-forms that contain two genomes as a result of sexual reproduction. A mutation, even a lethal one, taking place in one of their genomes is extremely unlikely to take place at the same location in their other genome. Thus, even if one gene is knocked out by mutation, the second copy of that gene will remain functional. In a sense, and to use a metaphor (a relevant one, however), having two genomes is an "insurance policy" against mutation, or, if you will, a plane equipped with two engines is safer than a plane equipped with only one.

Sexual reproduction is not restricted to complex animals and plants, however. Even the simple photosynthetic unicellular eukaryote *Chlamydomonas reinhardii* engages in sexual reproduction when conditions warrant it. This suggests that sexual reproduction appeared before multicellular organisms did. The cells of *Chlamydomonas* come in two varieties: male and female. But since these cells are completely indistinguishable under the microscope, the preferred designations for the two sexes are mating-type plus and mating-type minus. When nutrients in the environment where *Chlamydomonas* lives become depleted, the two mating types mate by fusing their cells and melding their genomes. The result is the formation of a tough structure called a zygospore, which not only contains two genomes but also is dormant and resistant to adverse conditions such as absence of nutrients and drought. As better environmental conditions reoccur, the zygospore germinates and liberates regular cells. In this case, the advantage of sexual reproduction, zygospore formation, is to ensure survival under adverse conditions. But contrary to complex eukaryotes, *Chlamydomonas* cells originating from germinating zygospores contain only a single genome, not two. Thus, for most of its life cycle, *Chlamydomonas*, like many lower eukaryotes (yeast is another example), contains only one genome.

Of course, complex eukaryotes do not form zygospores, but they have kept the ability to mix two parental genomes when producing their offspring. What is more, these offspring retain two genomes throughout their entire life cycles. Also remember that the genomes of the parents are not necessarily identical; they are likely to contain genes that are slight variants of one another, thereby allowing higher genetic diversity in their offspring and enhancing their ability to react to the environment, that is, to react to the force of natural selection, in a more flexible fashion. This was recently demonstrated in *Daphnia pulex*, a type of water flea. Intriguingly, some populations of this flea reproduce sexually while others reproduce asexually, that is, without the intervention of male fleas. Researchers have shown that asexual reproduction leads to an accumulation of deleterious mutations, reinforcing the idea that the blending of two different genomes (one from the father and one from the mother) is advantageous from an evolutionary viewpoint. Nonetheless, the origin and evolution of sex remain fundamental and difficult problems in biology.

It seems that the first multicellular eukaryotic organisms appeared about 650 million years ago, that is, almost 1.4 billion years after the appearance of the first eukaryotes. These may have been wormlike and jellyfish-like creatures, although their physical shape is debated because these creatures did not fossilize well. About 100 million years later, our planet experienced what is sometimes called the "Cambrian explosion." The word "Cambrian" refers to a geological period in the history of Earth, and "explosion" refers to an abundance of fossils in the corresponding rock layers. This time, the fossil remains of the fauna that lived and evolved back then are plentiful. This is also the time when the first hard body parts (shells) appeared. The Cambrian fauna was composed of marine animals that are the recognizable ancestors of those that exist today but also contained bizarre animal forms that went extinct without leaving any descendants, possibly as a part of the great extinction of many species that followed about 40 million years later. One explanation for the extinction of these animals is that they were poor competitors under changing ecological circumstances.

What triggered the Cambrian explosion is not known, although some think that rising oxygen levels may have played an important role. Additionally, scientists are not sure at all that the term "explosion" is really warranted. Indeed, it seems that life diversified significantly before the Cambrian but that these earlier life-forms were too fragile to fossilize. In this case, the Cambrian "explosion" would simply be the continuation of a steadier evolutionary phenomenon. In fact, there is evidence that 100 million years, hardly a short period, separate simple multicellular organisms such as sponges from the more complex Cambrian fauna. Therefore, scientists now prefer to use the word "radiation" of species rather than "explosion."

It is unclear what types of genetic mechanisms were responsible for the appearance of so many different life-forms before and during the Cambrian. But now that we understand that some genes can act as "master switches," called *hox* genes, which control many other genes (recall the example of extra eyes on flies described in chapter 3), it may well be that Cambrian genetic diversity was produced through a relatively small number of mutations in these "master" genes.

From then on, life continued to diversify at a rapid rate. To appreciate this, recall that the first eukaryotes appeared about 1.8 billion years after the formation of our planet. It took about half as much more time for simple multicellular life to evolve, and about half as much as that time for life to become almost as diversified as it is today.

A point of discussion among evolutionary biologists is the type of mechanism through which evolution proceeded. Was new species formation gradual, or did new species appear in bursts? The first model favors slow but steady changes over long periods of time, whereas the second model hypothesizes long periods of stasis, during which no new species appear, followed by relatively fast speciation. The second model is usually known as evolution by "punctuated equilibria." Punctuated equilibria explain why there exist fewer intermediate fossil forms than expected, but other biologists think that, since the soft parts of life-forms do not fossilize well, we know very little about potentially major evolutionary changes that took place in soft tissues. This is another area of evolutionary science where the jury is still out. But contrary to what creationists claim, this is not evidence that discord reigns in the ranks of evolutionary biologists. Rather, this shows that the *process*, not the reality, of evolution is still debated in the scientific community. Again, this is a sign of health, not one of sickness.

One question on people's minds surely is how the enormous diversification of life could have taken place. Or, to put it differently, how did the genes of evolving organisms lead to the formation of differentiated organs (liver, heart, and so on) and other morphological characters (limbs, heads, tails, and so on)? The fossil record allows us to picture *when* bony structures (but usually not soft tissues) in animals appeared but not *how* this happened. The same holds true for plant fossils. The science of genetics, by studying the genes of existing species with known ancient genealogies, is coming to the rescue, although, without a doubt, an enormous amount of work still needs to be done.

One genetic mechanism that has certainly played a role in evolution is gene duplication. When DNA replicates, mistakes in the copying mechanism of base pairs are made that result in mutations. But sometimes the replication mechanism makes much bigger errors. As a result, occasionally, long stretches of DNA are present in multiple copies in the genome. What happens then? Let us assume that only one copy of a gene is necessary for the survival of an organism. Adverse mutations occurring in that single copy will be eliminated by natural selection because the affected organism will not reproduce. But let us now assume that this particular gene is present in multiple copies due to a DNA replication error; mutations taking place in these extra copies will have no influence on the fitness of an organism as long as one copy of the gene remains intact. This means that extra copies of that gene are "free" to mutate and hence diversify. Over many generations, the mutated copies can assume new functions and confer new biological properties on their hosts.

This is how scientists think the genes belonging to the hemoglobin family were generated. Humans possess nine different genes coding for hemoglobin and one gene coding for myoglobin, a related protein found in muscle that also plays the role of ferrying oxygen in this tissue. The phylogenetic analysis of these genes in many vertebrates has shown that 600–800 million years ago, an ancestral gene evolved into a myoglobin gene, on the one hand, and a hemoglobin gene, on the other hand. Later, the hemoglobin gene family

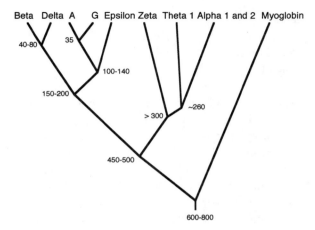

FIGURE 6.3

The evolution of human globin genes. The precursor of both myoglobin and hemoglobin existed as early as 600–800 million years ago. It then split into two branches, one leading to myoglobin and one leading to the various hemoglobins. The numbers indicated at the branching points are millions of years ago. Alpha 1 and alpha 2 hemoglobins are clustered because they evolved too recently to show as a split on this scale.

diversified further by gene duplication. These different hemoglobins play different roles today; for example, embryonic hemoglobin (epsilon) has higher affinity for oxygen than does adult hemoglobin because an embryo receives oxygen from its mother's blood, not from the air (figure 6.3).

Most people probably do not know that plants of the legume family (peas and beans, for example) have genes that code for proteins similar to hemoglobin. Therefore, "hemoglobin-like" genes must have existed in ancient eukaryotes that lived before the plant/animal evolutionary split.

To close this section on the evolution of the DNA world, we now present a simplified timeline of the major evolutionary events that took place since the birth of the universe. In the following, BYA means billions of years ago and MYA means millions of years ago.

Big Bang	14 BYA
Formation of Earth	4.5 BYA
Origin of life	3.8 BYA (?)
Eukaryotes	2.7 BYA
Multicellular eukaryotes	650 MYA
First animals	600 MYA
First land plants	400 MYA

First vertebrates	400 MYA
First flowering plants	150 MYA
First modern humans	160,000 YA
First recorded history	5,000 YA

As we can see, the time span involved in the history of the universe and that of life is gigantic and practically impossible to grasp. To use a good analogy that makes it easier to understand this time scale, if the age of the universe were concentrated into one single calendar year, with the Big Bang taking place on January 1, Earth would have formed on September 14. The oldest bacterial fossils would have been alive on October 9 and the first worms would have appeared on December 16. The first dinosaurs came into existence on December 24 and the first humans on December 31 at 10:30 P.M. The Roman Empire was flourishing on December 31 at 11:59:56 P.M., and the Renaissance in Europe took place on December 31 at 11:59:59 P.M. The last second of the year represents the last five centuries that saw the Industrial Revolution, the appearance of modern democracy, and space exploration. It is only with a good appreciation of the time elapsed since the birth of the universe that one can come to accept that chance events, as pointed out in this book, certainly could have had a major influence on the evolution of life.

Microevolution Versus Macroevolution

Some creationists and neocreationists accept the concept of microevolution—evolution by mutation *within* a species—presumably because this concept does not violate the notion of biblical "kinds." Some creationists even consider microevolution trivial because, they say, mutated variants appearing in populations are not fundamentally different from their nonmutant counterparts. But in our opinion, insects becoming resistant to pesticides, bacteria becoming resistant to multiple antibiotics and heavy metals, and soil bacteria becoming able to metabolize human-made chemicals *are* very significantly different from their nonmutant counterparts. Not only that, but these variants proliferate and occupy niches exactly as predicted by evolutionary science.

Incidentally, some creationists, including ID proponents dismiss microevolution as representing "mere adaptation" to new environments. But this is a very misleading way to account for this evolutionary phenomenon. Indeed, it has been known since 1943 (and confirmed in 1952 and 1956) that living cells *do not* adapt to new environments as is commonly construed. Rather, random mutations take place in cells all the time, and it so happens that some of these preexisting mutants acquire by chance the ability to survive in a new environment *without prior exposure to the new environment.* In other words, a new environment does not drive mutations in any particular direction; adaptive mutations occur *before* the new environment is present. These mutations are then *selected* for survival and proliferation. This is exactly how Darwin envisioned evolution by natural selection. And as we showed, his vision was confirmed in the above case well over six decades ago.

What all creationists and neocreationists reject, however, is the notion of macroevolution, the appearance of new species from old ones. This concept, unlike microevolution, clearly violates the precepts of the Old Testament that stipulate that "kinds" were fixed by God once and for all. In other words, species cannot evolve into other species, such as amphibians evolving from fishes and *H. sapiens* evolving from *Australopithecus.* They claim, with some degree of justification, that no one has seen a mouse sprouting wings in order to become a bat. But evolutionary biology never claimed that such deep transformations should be detectable overnight; rather, very long periods of time are of the essence. Also, evolutionary biology does not affirm that there are major differences between microevolution and macroevolution: both follow the same processes of random mutation followed by natural selection and drift. In addition, creationists have never been able to tell us where—in their view—microevolution stops and macroevolution starts.

Gene duplication and mutations in "master" genes have the potential to create entirely new functions and produce dramatic morphological changes. Granted, an enormous amount of work remains to be done to understand the effects of these mutations on evolutionary processes, particularly their effects on the development of organisms—such as organ formation in developing embryos. This is a very active field of research, often referred to as evolution and development or simply evo-devo. Work in this area has already shown that animal body plans (and body parts) are controlled by large numbers of genes called *gene regulatory networks.* Genes in these networks operate in a hierarchical manner, meaning that some genes determine which cells are going to be involved in a particular body part formation, whereas other genes, under the control of the first ones, determine the morphology of the body part in question. A third category of genes controls the fine physiological details of the body part. Gene regulatory networks involved in the gut, eye, heart, and nervous system formation, as well as the development of immune systems, are being investigated in several species. DNA homology studies will soon tell us to what extent the three gene categories are similar or different across species. This, in turn, will tell us what types of past mutational events were responsible for the appearance in the course of evolution of species with different body plans.

A good example of the use of evo-devo thinking in evolutionary studies is our present understanding of the evolution of the heart. The heart is a pump whose functioning depends on the presence of contractile proteins. Phylogenies indicate that such proteins existed in animals that were the precursors of organisms such as hydras and jellyfish that first appeared at least 700 million years ago. These organisms had no hearts, however, and probably used contractile proteins to regulate fluid movement during feeding, much like modern hydras and jellyfish do.

The first heartlike organ is thought to have appeared at least 500 million years ago. It may have been a simple contractile tube without chambers or valves, as currently exists in tunicates (of which the sea squirt is an example). The insect (fruit fly) heart is slightly more complex in that it contains a single valve and is connected to a primitive aorta. The next level of complexity is found in fish, whose heart has a single atrium and a single ventricle. All other vertebrates possess hearts with two atria and a single ventricle (amphibians) or two atria and two ventricles (reptiles, birds, mammals). The questions then is: How did the heart gain complexity during evolution? We currently have a partial answer to this question.

As we showed, the contractile proteins found in the heart are of very ancient origin. We also know that heart development in all studied species is under the control of five evolutionarily conserved core transcription factors operating as a network. These factors regulate the timing and level of transcription (RNA synthesis, see chapter 3) of, among others, the genes coding for contractile proteins. Further, we know that duplication of the genes that code for these transcription factors has occurred over the course of evolution. For example, hydras and jellyfish contain only one copy of the factor called *Tbx*, insects have three, fish have at least four, amphibians have at least five, and reptiles, birds, and mammals have at least seven.

Thus, one can see that the increase in morphological complexity of the heart is accompanied by an increase in complexity of a regulatory gene network. In addition, we also know that other, ancient gene networks control the activity of the five core transcription factors mentioned above. Therefore, the development and evolution of the heart is an excellent example of a genetic "cascade" involving many genes, each of which is potentially able to mutate, be duplicated, and thereby create complexity from simplicity.

The evolution of genetic networks does not explain everything, however. In addition to mutation, natural selection, and drift, the formation of new species from old ones must be accompanied by *reproductive isolation*. In other words, two populations in the process of branching away from one another and in the process of forming two potentially different species must stop mating with each other. This actually has been observed in nature. One example is that of the cichlid fish that live in Lakes Victoria and Tanganyika in Africa. There exist several populations of these fish, some dwelling near the surface and some living on the bottom. These fish have developed different feeding habits as well as some different morphological characteristics. Interestingly, these fish populations are sexually compatible and do mate under aquarium conditions. However, they are not seen to mate in nature. There, these populations are reproductively isolated and are presumably undergoing a process of speciation. The same phenomenon of reproductive isolation has been observed with subpopulations of Hawaiian fruit flies and crickets, as well as European corn borers (also insects) and even European birds called blackcaps. It will be interesting to find out which changes at the DNA level are correlated with these cases of reproductive isolation. And as in the case of marsupials and placental mammals described in chapter 2, geographic isolation facilitates even further the differentiation of species by physically separating them.

Reproductive isolation, following the appearance of new species, has been well documented in plants. Hybrid formation between related (but not identical) species is not unusual in the plant kingdom. When this happens, two different genomes are united in one plant. A hybrid plant is often sterile because the chromosomes from the two parental species do not match and fertile germ cells (pollen and egg) cannot form. However, accidental chromosome doubling (a type of massive mutation) can occur in hybrids during germ cell formation, a phenomenon that restores fertility. For example, bread wheat, leaf mustard, and oil seed rape are the results of hybrid formation between known ancestors. It has been shown that these fertile new hybrids can no longer mate with their ancestral species because their chromosome numbers do not match. Thus, the hybrids are reproductively isolated from their progenitors, although they are fertile among themselves. For example, *Brassica napus* (oil seed rape), which results from the hybridization of *Brassica campestris* (turnip) and *Brassica oleracea* (cabbage), is no longer sexually compatible with the latter two. In fact, it is estimated that up to 70–80% of flowering plants, including many crop plants, originated through a process of hybridization. These are typical cases of macroevolution that cannot be easily dismissed.

Finally, even simple bacteria still have much to tell us about the complexity of evolutionary pathways. For example, *Pseudomonas fluorescens*, a soil bacterium, can evolve under laboratory conditions from free-floating cells in liquid medium to mat-forming communities that concentrate at the interface between liquid broth and air. This new trait is due to the mutation of a single base pair in a gene responsible for the control of several other genes. The result of the mutation of this single gene is what is called a *pleiotropic effect*, an effect that modifies the expression of several genes. In the case of mat-forming *P. fluorescens*, the expression of up to 52 genes is affected by the single mutation in the control gene. Remarkably, none of these 52 genes is required for mat formation. In other words, a single adaptive mutation can "rewire" a whole genetic network in a completely unexpected way, reminiscent of a "macromutation."

All in all, then, we do not think that there should be a distinction between microevolution and macroevolution because attributing different names to phenomena that might, in the end, be the same only adds to confusion among the lay public. Ironically, it is scientists themselves who came up with these two designations. If only they had known where this would lead them!

If Life Is "Irreducibly Complex," Is There Any Hope That It Can Ever Be Created in the Test Tube?

One Intelligent Design (ID) web site, called the Access Research Network, claims that the role of life scientists is to "dissect" (i.e., analyze) the molecular mechanisms that make living cells and organisms function the way they do. Presumably, these scientists can then wonder at the complexity of life and the existence of a designer who made it all possible. But, in fact, life scientists go well beyond these analytical procedures. Yes, biochemists traditionally grind up living cells and try to identify the many chemical reactions that take place in them. But, on the other hand, geneticists, a class of scientists largely ignored by creationists, work on whole, living systems. They do not normally grind up living organisms; they add, subtract, and replace genes in these organisms while focusing on the new properties of the organisms so manipulated. Therefore, geneticists, contrary to biochemists, have a more holistic view of life and, unsurprisingly, are quite unimpressed by ID claims of irreducible or specified complexity. Interestingly, it does not seem that any professional geneticists currently enrich the ranks of ID defenders. To exemplify the difference between a biochemical (analytical) and a genetic (synthetic) approach to the study of life, we describe some cutting-edge genetic research in the next sections.

According to creationists and ID believers, creating life in the test tube should be impossible because life is irreducibly complex and cannot be built piece by piece. Yet, most scientists (particularly geneticists) disagree with this position. In fact, science is taking giant steps in that direction. In 2002, researchers at the State University of New York at Stony Brook completely reconstituted, or synthesized, the RNA genome of poliovirus from commercially available reagents. The synthesized virus was completely infectious and indistinguishable from its natural counterpart. These researchers selected poliovirus because its genome is particularly small and hence easier to synthesize. Granted, viruses are not truly alive in a classical sense because they can only replicate inside a host cell. Nevertheless, viruses are very much part of the living world, and it is now clear that humans can reconstruct at least one of them. This means that the scientific understanding of viruses— notwithstanding irreducible complexity—is so good that building one in the test tube has become possible.

Other research groups are attempting to go further and are currently trying to create artificial bacterial life in the laboratory. As we noted above, simple prokaryotes may need no more than 180 genes to be truly alive. With our existing laboratory techniques for the synthesis of DNA, making a genome this size in the test tube is within our capabilities. Creating prokaryotic life in the laboratory will be a stepwise process, very much like evolution. As we envision it, the process could go as follows.

Some bacterial mutants created in the lab are incapable of normal cell division. Instead of each cell dividing into two full-sized daughter cells, these mutants generate one full-sized daughter cell and one small one called a "minicell." It turns out that these minicells contain no DNA, no genes, and hence are incapable of dividing any further because they lack the genetic instructions to do so. But these minicells still contain all the "hardware," protein enzymes and other ingredients, to perform all other metabolic functions. Now, there exist techniques to introduce DNA into minicells from the outside. One possible experiment would then be to build a completely artificial genome in the test tube, insert it into minicells, and see whether the manipulated minicells can carry out the instructions coded for by the introduced DNA, including cell division. Doing these experiments will take time, because we do not know in advance exactly which genes and which minicell system will work. However, there is little doubt that researchers will be successful, given the results of the first step with viruses.

Another approach, called the "bottom-up approach," consists in trying to make completely synthetic cell membranes and thus avoid the use of minicells. These experiments involve the formation of liposomes from phospholipids. These liposomes would trap DNA and the ingredients necessary for DNA transcription and RNA translation, as well as factors enabling the liposomes to import RNA and protein building blocks from the outside (figure 6.4). These experiments have been successful in that these artificial cells can make proteins for a period of at least four days. Division of these artificial cells has not yet been observed; however, these experiments are just a first step in the creation of life in the test tube.

Finally, a third approach consists in progressively removing non-essential genes from bacterial cells. This can be done by using standard genetic

FIGURE 6.4
Liposomes containing trapped DNA made brightly fluorescent with a
dye. From Paul F. Lurquin, *The Green Phoenix: A History of Genetically Modified Plants* (New York: Columbia University Press, 2001),
reproduced by permission.

engineering techniques. Once this work is completed, we will have a good
idea as to which genetic functions are necessary for bacterial life. Scientists
will then have produced "bare-bones" bacterial cells, cells that will allow us
better to define what simple life is. At the time of this writing, researchers
have removed 15% (743 genes representing 708,627 base pairs) of the genome
of the bacterium *Escherichia coli* (a common inhabitant of the human gut)
without any adverse effect on its physiology.

We now finish this chapter with some considerations of what biological
science has achieved (and will discover sooner than later) and how these
advances further contradict creationism and ID.

The Production of Transgenic Species by Gene Cloning
Already Shows That Irreducible Complexity Is a Myth

Some say that the invention of genetic engineering has allowed humans to
play God. Others wonder whether we should play God at all and oppose
genetic engineering, not because it has taken on a religious meaning, but
because it could lead humans in the wrong direction regarding their tam-
pering with nature. Of course, scientists are not actually trying to play God;
they are just following their curiosity.

It is now possible to isolate specific genes from one organism and shuttle
them into any other organism. The step of isolating specific genes is called

gene cloning. Organisms receiving new, foreign cloned genes are called *transgenic*. Examples of transgenic organisms are pest-resistant corn and herbicide-resistant soybeans that we eat on a routine basis. These two crops were engineered with bacterial genes. Animals have been engineered with foreign genes, as well. For example, there exist sheep that produce spider silk in their milk after being engineered with a spider gene. Other transgenic animals have been engineered to produce human blood clotting factors, and bacteria have been engineered with human genes to produce insulin and growth hormone. Transgenic trout have been engineered with a growth hormone gene to make them grow faster and larger. The bacterium *Escherichia coli*, a normal inhabitant of the human intestine, has been engineered with a photosynthetic gene that allows this non-photosynthetic bacterium to "see light." This list is potentially limitless.

But our ability to genetically engineer any creature poses an interesting question: if all life-forms did not basically use the same blueprint for life, could we do this at all? The answer is, of course, no: if all life-forms did not basically use the same blueprint for life, we could not produce transgenic organisms because there would be basic incompatibilities between genetic systems. The follow-up of this is that the very basic mechanisms that determine life have been conserved by evolution, reinforcing the idea that all life-forms today are derived from a single root a long time ago. In addition, if organisms were irreducibly complex, would adding, subtracting, and replacing genes not be so deleterious as to make the existence of transgenics impossible? Yet, even without simplifying too much, creating new gene combinations in living creatures in the laboratory is now almost routine work. In conclusion, it is possible to add piecemeal new biological functions to existing organisms without disturbing their so-called irreducible complexity, an achievement in full opposition to ID thinking.

An Interesting Conundrum

For millennia, our Earth was seen as the only heavenly body where life, and particularly sentient life, existed. Our centrality was assured by the old (and wrong) Ptolemaic system in which our planet occupied the center of the universe. As we know, this view was endorsed by the Catholic Church for many centuries and was officially rescinded only recently in an official, and much belated, apology to Galileo.

In the meantime, modern astronomy has shown that nearby stars also have planetary companions; our sun's planetary system is no longer unique in the universe. In fact, it now seems that planetary systems analogous to our solar system are common in our stellar neighborhood. These systems seem to be a direct consequence of star formation, with primeval circumstellar dust disks coalescing into planets, given enough time. Moreover, recent observations suggest that some stars are orbited by rocky planets just like our own. Although our telescopic techniques are not quite sophisticated enough to study small extrasolar planets, we already know that some of the large ones (Jupiter sized or bigger) contain water in their atmosphere. This is not all that surprising; water is one of the most common compounds in the universe. But then, the presence of water, one of the prerequisites of life as we know it, on extrasolar planets suggests that life may also have appeared elsewhere in the universe.

An inescapable signature of life would be the presence of oxygen gas in the atmosphere of these extrasolar planets, because this would be a strong indication of the existence of photosynthesis. But, of course, our own Earth's atmosphere became significantly oxygenated only hundreds of millions of years after life appeared. Thus, the age of extrasolar planets is of the essence. We do not know yet whether any extrasolar planets have oxygenated atmospheres, nor do we know when these planets formed. It is only a matter of time for these questions to be answered, however.

In truth, search for life on Mars, much closer to home, has so far yielded negative results, even though Mars harbors very large quantities of water ice (and perhaps transiently liquid water) in its polar regions. On the other hand, methane gas was recently discovered in the atmosphere of Mars, which could be a sign of bacterial life there. The search continues.

A little less close to home, one of the large satellites of Jupiter, Europa, is thought to have a large ocean of liquid water under its outer ice crust. Space probes are being designed to penetrate the icy surface of Europa and search for life in its putative ocean. Even farther away from Earth is Titan, the largest satellite of Saturn. The *Huygens* probe launched by NASA and the European Space Agency soft-landed there in 2005. The probe revealed the existence on Titan of a brew of carbon-containing molecules and riverlike structures where liquid methane perhaps flows. Even though Titan is unlikely to harbor life because it is so cold, it may well be that it is a "frozen" example of what prebiotic Earth may have looked like, with all sorts of organics raining down on the planet's surface. Furthermore, in 2006, the spacecraft *Cassini*, which is currently exploring the Saturn system, discovered liquid water geysers on Saturn's small satellite Enceladus. What is more, Enceladus was also shown to harbor organic compounds, such as methane and propane. The existence of geysers suggests the presence of liquid water under Enceladus's water ice crust. Presently, we do not understand how liquid water can exist in the frigid environment of the Saturnian system, but here also, it may be that Enceladus is a "laboratory" where prebiotic (or perhaps more advanced) chemistry is taking place.

In brief, to the extent of our present knowledge, there is no indication that life exists elsewhere in the universe. On the other hand, many scientists are driven by this prospect, and so must be some of the politicians who hold the strings of the purse of NASA.

Now, let us assume for a moment that life *is* discovered elsewhere in the universe. How will this affect creationism and ID thinking? Both approaches are highly teleological and believe in a creator (designer) with a purpose. Does this mean that putative prokaryotic (or even more complex) life on Europa or putative life in the Gliese 876 star system (Gliese has planetary companions and is located only 19 light-years away from Earth) also has a purpose? What could this purpose possibly be? Would life there also be seen by some as irreducibly complex? These are, of course, speculative questions, but they are not completely out of line. Indeed, some scientists think that the appearance of life in the universe is a direct and inescapable—but still statistical—consequence of cosmic evolution. Given our technological advances in remote observation of extrasolar planetary systems, we will soon have some answers regarding the existence of life elsewhere in the universe. If the answer is positive, many philosophical and theological issues will have to be revisited, inasmuch as humans have never really considered so far the full implications of extraterrestrial life.

Expectedly, ID enthusiasts and creationists usually rail against scientists' efforts to find life—particularly intelligent life—elsewhere in the cosmos. This is in line with their idea that our planet, and our planet alone, was singled out by a designer. In truth, there is as yet no evidence for extraterrestrial life, past or present. But then, these astrobiology research programs are in their infancy. For example, the SETI (Search for Extraterrestrial Intelligence) programs use radio telescopes to detect artificial radio signals sent by putative advanced civilizations that may exist outside our solar system. So far, none has been found. But then, SETI programs have barely scratched the surface in terms of the number of star systems (a total of about 100 billion in our galaxy alone), as well as the enormous range of possible radio frequencies, they have listened to. If a nascent research effort has not yet yielded positive results, should we abandon it? We think not.

Chance and Necessity

This chapter concludes the scientific part of this book. As we have demonstrated over and over, chance, unguided events are at the root of many natural phenomena. These phenomena range from the birth of the universe, to self-organizing structures that dissipate entropy, to the RNA world, to mutations in DNA genes, to fusion events between cells, to the origin of organelles, and to the evolution of modern human beings mostly through drift. As far as the origin of life is concerned, chemical selection (which is also a type of natural selection) first favored better fit ribozymes and hypercycles. Once life became cellular, natural selection favored those first organisms that had become better adapted to their early ecological niches. Evolution proceeded (and still proceeds) in a blind manner because it is a non-teleological force.

The great French geneticist and Nobel Laureate Jacques Monod (1910–1976) published a book titled *Chance and Necessity: An Essay on the Natural Philosophy of Modern Biology* (1971). This title echoes a motto attributed to Democritus of Abdera (460–370 B.C.E.), the ancient Greek philosopher-scientist and author of the first atomic theory of matter: "Everything in the universe is the result of chance and necessity." In his book, Monod clearly abides by this statement. For Monod, as for so many other scientists today, the universe and life both may have happened by chance. But then, having appeared, both the universe and life evolved, changed, and continue to do so by necessity. The inanimate universe evolves because the laws of physics so dictate. In biology, where the laws of physics also apply, an added note of necessity determines the fate of life-forms: evolution by mutation, natural selection, and drift. Our world and humankind are not at the pinnacle of any preordained set of categories; we will continue to evolve by necessity, whether we like it or not.

A question that may arise in one's mind is at what point in the history of life did chance (probability) give rise to necessity (a form of determinism, although far from an absolute one)? Indeed, it is undeniable that causality exists in our living world; for example, some mutations (the cause) can have an effect on the fitness of organisms. At this point, it is necessary to distinguish between *intrinsic* probabilistic events and *extrinsic* probabilistic events (or chance) that influenced the path taken by life. Intrinsic probability deals with the quantum world of atoms and molecules. There, as described in chapter 5, Heisenberg's probabilistic uncertainty principle restricts what is predictable about the properties of matter. Interestingly, some types of DNA mutations are due entirely to quantum effects. These types of mutations (said to be due to tautomeric shifts) occur when DNA bases experience spontaneous—and unpredictable—modifications of their electronic structure. These modifications lead to base mispairings (see chapter 2) and, ultimately, base pair substitutions that, by definition, are mutations. Such mutations are "intrinsic" chance events because they depend on the probabilistic quantum nature of molecules, even those that compose DNA.

However, such mutations may or may not be acted upon by natural selection. Natural selection is the interplay between mutations and environmental circumstances. Some mutations are neutral, others are detrimental, and others yet are favorable, depending on the environment in which they take place. Whether natural selection will act upon certain mutations is thus also a question of probability. We can call this type of probability "extrinsic" because it is imposed by external circumstances and no longer depends on the properties inherent to the atoms that compose DNA. Another word for extrinsic probability in this context is "contingency," or what we can also call "necessity" for our purpose. Quantum properties of matter (including DNA) are not contingent, but the way that changes in the structure of DNA (mutations) interact with the environment are. These interactions define "necessity." Can these two types of probabilities, intrinsic and extrinsic, be connected in a scenario where first chance and then necessity cooperated, making life possible?

In the early prebiotic world, quantum probability (which underlies the laws of chemistry) must have reigned supreme because only isolated biomolecules existed. The prebiotic world was thus governed by quantum properties alone. But then, what was at the origin of the transition between chance (intrinsic probability) and necessity (extrinsic probability) when life, or its simple precursor, the RNA world, first appeared? Our answer is the self-organizing structures, generators of complexity, that were produced in the primeval soup.

The synthesis of the first biomolecules in the atmosphere and/or in hydrothermal vents was a chance event dictated by chemical reactions taking place far from thermodynamic equilibrium. Next, as these molecules started to self-organize, possibly as entropy-dissipating structures, necessity took over in the form of a competition between, for example, subsets of cooperating RNA molecules able to replicate faster than other subsets. The self-organization of successful RNA molecule subsets was itself a chance event. But as soon as these successful subsets appeared, they would have outcompeted other, less efficient subsets under the conditions prevailing at the time. From then on, protolife would have continued on the same path, as an event constrained by the necessities imposed by physical and chemical conditions acting on the most efficiently organized protolife structures. This starting point would have led to the production of a continuum of life-forms on Earth, with adaptation, evolution, and selection of living species taking place as environmental situations specified (determined) these events.

It will not be easy to put to the test the hypothesis that the appearance of structure in the prebiotic world signaled a transition between chance and necessity. However, initial experiments could be conducted *in silico*: computer simulations of self-organizing dissipative structures are available on the Internet (see Further Reading). But as far as we know, no simulations involving linked, competing dissipative structures have been done (or at least published) to see whether, and under which initial parameters, spontaneously forming structures can overtake others or perhaps lead to entirely new ones by interacting with each other. This would be a very nice project for a computer-savvy person.

Finally, the boundary, the transition, between the quantum world and the macroscopic world in which we live remains a challenge for twenty-first-century physics. Viruses, bacteria, and liposomes are not quantum objects, even though they are very small. At which increasing size and structure does the world cease to be dictated entirely by the rules of quantum mechanics? We do not know. But here again, only science, not creationism or ID, will eventually provide some answers.

We are aware that the science explained in this book is complex. Researching the origins of the cosmos, life, and human beings involves many facets of scientific knowledge. Probing our origins must be done today in a multidisciplinary fashion, preferably by multidisciplinary teams. This type of approach is still in its infancy. On the other hand, given the complexity of the questions asked, one could understand that laypeople would throw their arms up in discouragement. After all, it takes only faith to believe in a supernatural creator or a designer, whereas it takes considerable intellectual efforts to understand dissipative structures and the RNA world, not to mention quantum indeterminacy (see chapter 5). Does this mean that the situation is hopeless? We think not. An easy remedy would be to expose children to solid science and logical reasoning as soon as possible during their schooling. To be interested in science, one must be curious about the world. And who is more curious than a child?

Things to Think About

1. A combination of genetics, paleontology, and geology provides a credible model for the evolution of life on Earth, from prokaryotes, to simple eukaryotes, and then to humans.

2. The evolution of life over the past 3.8 billion years has indeed resulted in increased complexity. But this complexity is not irreducible. If this were the case, many biological elements would be "designed modules" that would show no phylogenetic relationship with one another. We know this is not the case.

3. Many uncertainties remain associated with the evolutionary model presented here, a fact of which scientists are very much aware. But

scientists also know that future work should clarify the problems raised by this evolutionary scenario. That the model is currently incomplete does not make it wrong, and surely does not mean that alternative metaphysical explanations (such as ID) must be right. Further, scientists *do* agree on the basics of the evolutionary sequence presented in this chapter, even though they may disagree on many details. This is perfectly normal in science, and it is a sign of health.

4. The achievements of genetic engineering run counter to the notion of irreducible complexity. If irreducible complexity were a reality, introducing genes into a foreign background would not be compatible with the continuation of life, and hence genetic engineering would be impossible.

7

The Dangers of Creationism

Human values remain a human matter, for which human beings, not nature, must provide justification and ultimately accept responsibility.

—Kathryn Dooley, spring 2005 term paper

People need purpose and values in their lives. But as eloquently stated above by one of our students, values (which in many ways define purpose) should not be rooted in and justified by the physical world; they must come from within our moral selves. Traditionally, human beings have found purpose and values, as well as morality, in religions. But religions are not the only way to a moral, purposeful life. Over the centuries, secular moral philosophies have been developed and adopted by many all over the world. Great figures such as Einstein, Linus Pauling, and Mahatma Gandhi, who based his fight for dignity and freedom on both secular and religious ideas, have taught us that the search for peace, freedom, and tolerance need not be based only on the principles of one particular religion. And so it should be for the search for truth in science, which absolutely requires free thinking, independent from—but not necessarily antagonistic to—a religious framework.

Free thinking and religion have not meshed very well in the past. Things got particularly bad when religion and state cooperated in matters of deciding which kind of thinking was orthodox and which was not. Socrates in ancient Greece and Galileo in Renaissance Italy learned this to their detriment. And then there is the twentieth-century Scopes trial in the United States. Could this process repeat itself today in this country? We see and hear many activists trying to censor the teaching of evolution in public schools based on their religious beliefs. But, and this has never happened in history anywhere, we do not see scientists claiming that creationism and Intelligent Design (ID) should not be taught in faith-based institutions or that science should be taught in church! Why then do creationists and ID believers think they are entitled to exercise censorship in the science classroom? And what are the potential consequences of this attitude? We address these questions in what follows, in the form of a few vignettes.

Political Ramifications

> President Bush invigorated proponents of teaching alternatives
> to evolution in public schools with remarks saying school-
> children should be taught about "intelligent design."
> —*LA Times–Washington Post* Service, 2005 Press Release

August 3, 2005, will be seen by future generations as a landmark date because
on that day, the U.S. leader and most influential politician, announced that
ID and standard evolutionary theory have equal scientific value. By that, he
seems to have also implied that politics, science, and religion are somehow
linked in a grand scheme of things. Also, perhaps, his announcement suggested that the teaching of ID could be in line with a particular political
agenda—his own and that of his allies. About three weeks later, Senate
majority leader Bill Frist (R) also announced publicly that he endorsed the
teaching of ID in public schools. In his words, "I think today a pluralistic
society should have access to a broad range of fact [*sic*] . . . including faith."
At least Bill Frist admits that ID and faith are linked. What is one to make of
these remarks made by prominent politicians?

It is all too easy to build "conspiracy theories" (or what scientists would call
"conspiracy hypotheses") to explain almost anything. That some degree of
actual collusion exists among creationism, neocreationism, ID, and politicians
may or may not be true. But this is not entirely the point because, after all,
elected officials come and go. The point is more about whether creationists are
objective allies of those who promote particular societal and political trends in
the United States, trends that run the risk of swaying our country in an
antiscientific, theocratic direction for the long run. This indeed seems to be the
happening with the U.S. government of the early twenty-first century.

Many of our elected officials depend (or think they depend) on the votes
of their right-wing, Christian fundamentalist constituencies. Further, when
the federal government makes decisions based on the tenets of a particular
religious faith, there is always the danger that the examples of these decisions
will trickle down to the level of state governments. And states determine
what will be taught in public schools and how. It is therefore not surprising
that, in this political climate, interest groups in several states are now advocating equal time for the teaching of faith-based creationism and/or ID.
This raises two important questions: do these interest groups base their
position on solid scientific evidence, and do they represent the views of a
majority of people with or without religious faith? The answers to both
questions are a definite no.

As we described in the preceding chapters, creationism and ID have no scientific basis. Furthermore, creationist activists do not represent the positions taken by mainstream religious denominations; they are religious fundamentalists. For example, the Roman Catholic Church is *not* opposed to the theory of evolution by natural selection, nor is it opposed to the Big Bang theory. Church officials learned much from the Galileo affair more than 350 years ago and are no longer intent on mixing the doctrine of the faith with scientific matters. Much has been made about the communication of Cardinal Christoph Schönborn, archbishop of Vienna, to the *New York Times* on July 7, 2005. In it, the cardinal said that the Catholic Church does not accept neo-Darwinism. It now seems that the cardinal may have overstepped his authority to speak in the name of the Church. In fact, Pope John Paul II declared in 1996 that evolutionary theory *is* compatible with Catholic doctrine. This position was reiterated in 2004 by Cardinal Ratzinger, who is now Pope Benedict XVI. At the time of this writing, nothing indicates that the Catholic Church will reverse its position on evolution.

Journalist and author Thomas Frank offers an interesting interpretation of the American anti-evolution forces and their political agenda. In his book *What's the Matter with Kansas? How Conservatives Won the Heart of America* (2004), he proposes that the religious right wing of the Republican Party, which hosts many Protestant evangelicals, is in fact engaged in a fight against intellectuals. These, says Frank, are seen by the religious right as a left-leaning, arrogant elite responsible for America's moral and social decay. Thus, they believe, this haughty elite—which endorses evolution—is the enemy of the plain people who truly represent American ideals and the American way. In other words, Republican fundamentalists have started a culture war against evolution, which, for them, is equivalent to a pagan religion that lures young people into unbridled sex, the use of drugs, abortion, violence, and suicide. In short, as Frank reports, "Evolution, one of them [the Christian conservatives] claims, is nothing less than a part of a sinister war against God" (p. 168).

But Frank thinks that Christian conservative politicians cannot ultimately prevail scientifically in the evolution controversy, and they know it. Rather, for Frank, their goal is to get themselves reelected by appealing to the anti-intellectualism of their constituents. This, says Frank, is sure to happen once the science establishment reacts with its usual arrogance and put-down-the-ignorant-little-people attitude. Thus, according to Frank, the evolution war is simply a populist strategy to ensure Republican political victories. Intriguing, and quite Machiavellian if true.

Author and journalist Chris Mooney presents a somewhat similar opinion in his book *The Republican War on Science* (2005). For him, the Republican Party, particularly its growing fundamentalist right wing, has been meddling with science for many years. The Republicans do this by distorting and abusing the scientific process in order to politicize science. By putting appropriate "spins" on scientific findings, from acid rain, to embryonic stem cell research, to global climate change, to creationism, the Republicans placate their pro-industry and religious fundamentalist allies. To quote Mooney, "Science politicization succeeds, at least in part, because it confuses the public and policymakers, leading them to believe that a scientific 'controversy' exists where one actually does not, or that widely discredited claims are still given serious consideration in the world of science" (p. 252).

As we have described in many places in this book, this is indeed the tactic used by the ID movement. For Mooney, the attacks against evolution for political reasons parallel the surge of the religious right under Ronald Reagan's presidency. Already back then, organizations such as the Moral Majority advocated incorporating teaching "creation science" (ID did not yet exist) in schools alongside evolution. According to Mooney, President Reagan himself pronounced evolution to be just a theory that in recent years has been challenged in the world of science, which is totally untrue. The main difference between "classical" creationism of the 1980s and modern neocreationism is that neocreationists try to recruit individuals who hold academic degrees rather than evangelical preachers. Other than that, says Mooney, their goal is the same: introduce theology into science for political gains. But, of course, hiring people with academic credentials, as well as widely advertising creationist thinking in the form of books, Web sites, and CDs, requires significant funding.

The Money Trail

The Seattle-based Discovery Institute (the umbrella organization that houses the neocreationist Center for Science and Culture), the think tank where much of the ID program is being concocted, opened an office in Washington, D.C., in 2005. Presumably, this will allow ID thinkers to have easier access to our lawmakers. Adding to that the fast pace at which the Discovery Institute publishes its materials and updates its Web page, it is legitimate to wonder where the funding for all these activities is coming from.

According to the *New York Times* (August 21, 2005), a major benefactor of the Discovery Institute is Richard Mellon Scaife, a conservative American billionaire. Among others, Scaife is a trustee of the right-wing Heritage Foundation, and his own Scaife Foundations are known to have donated hundreds of millions of dollars to conservative causes. Scaife was a well-known opponent of President Bill Clinton. Other supporters of the Discovery Institute are the Ahmansons (California banking tycoons) and Philip F. Anschutz—all well-known Christian conservatives—who have donated millions of dollars through their foundations. And so have the Verizon and Bill and Melinda Gates Foundations. Millions of dollars have been spent by these benefactors on salaries and fellowships allocated to members of the Discovery Institute, as well as on the publications put out by this institute. In 2003, the most recent year for which data are available, the Discovery Institute took in $4.1 million in gifts and grants.

When asked, prominent figures of the Discovery Institute do not hesitate to proclaim their conservative Christian beliefs. One of these individuals is actually a "Moonie" who once wrote, "My prayers convinced me that I should devote my life to destroying Darwinism" (quoted in the *New York Times*, August 21, 2005). In spite of claims that ID endorsers come from a variety of religious backgrounds, in reality members of the Discovery Institute are Christian fundamentalists. Amusingly, some ID defenders have gone so far as to claim that an intelligent designer should not necessarily be construed as a monotheistic divinity: a polytheistic god would also do. But as we described in chapter 1, Hinduism, a polytheistic religion par excellence, has so far shown no interest in ID. Be that as it may, it will be interesting to continue to follow the money trail that connects big donors and ID-based institutions. To our knowledge, no billionaire has yet announced that he or she intends to support the teaching of evolution in this country.

The Strange Conflation of Postmodernism and Creationism/ID

Postmodernism (PoMo) is a secular intellectual movement popular among some sections of liberal arts academics and even a few scientists. PoMo advocates that all knowledge is biased, conditioned by the cultural background, social class, and so on, of those constructing it. There can be no objective truth, but only alternative modes of thought, none having higher truth value over others. Extreme PoMo takes the position that all knowledge is relative, including scientific knowledge. For postmodernists, everything we explain about nature, from human cultures, to Einstein's theories, to molecular biology, is a "text," that is, a story very much like one recounted in a novel. And novels can always be interpreted in different ways.

This is where, strangely, a "secular humanist" doctrine, PoMo, joins hands with creationism. For some postmodernists, the fact that our genes are 98% similar to chimpanzee genes and 30% similar to daffodil genes is totally meaningless—it is just a story. This is exactly what Christian fundamentalists also proclaim! For sure, PoMo and Christian fundamentalism are extraordinary bedfellows. But if both adopt the idea that science is in the end something that resides entirely in the eye of the beholder, then Christian fundamentalism should also consider relativity in religious matters. This means that, to be logically consistent, Christian fundamentalists should advocate equal time for the teaching of Christian, Hindu, Muslim, Buddhist, Native American, and so on, stories of creation. In fact, this would not be such a bad idea, as long as these stories were told in a course on comparative religions, for example, but not in science courses.

Creationism and Science Education

Questioning and requestioning empirical observations and the theories that explain them are at the core of the scientific process. Of course, new analyses should follow the scientific method and not be based on principles that are not part of it. In the words of student Kathryn Dooley, "evolutionary theory, like all science, is a collection of methodical observations and inferences about the natural world, nothing more and nothing less." We have described in this book how creationism and ID do not see evolutionary science in that way and use unscientific methods to try to discredit it.

But what is more, creationists and their allies often subtly suggest that what science does not understand *now*, science will *never* understand. In other words, they insinuate that incomplete scientific theories (in fact, many of them are), since they are incomplete, must be wrong. Adding to this a twist of byzantine reasoning, these people then imply that their alternative explanations (ID or old-style creationism) must be right! This is a losing proposition, because the advancement of science is unpredictable and sometimes lightning fast. For example, before the invention of antibiotics, pneumonia was almost always fatal. As soon as penicillin was produced commercially, pneumonia became, literally overnight, a treatable disease. Right now, we do not know how to treat cancer without using techniques that are invasive physically (surgery) or physiologically (chemotherapy and radiation therapy). This does not mean that we will never discover much gentler "magic bullets" to cure cancer. But for creationists, it seems that time has stood still; in effect, their rigid views cannot adapt to the fast pace of scientific progress.

We described in preceding chapters how much we now know about the evolutionary history of the eye and the evolution of modern humans. Similarly, the old creationist argument of the absence of intermediate fossil forms between dinosaurs and birds (which has to do with appearance of feathered wings) is now over: several such intermediate forms have been discovered and are well documented. As a result of the progress in science, creationism and ID are forced to continually adapt their claims and counterclaims. In other words, creationists are forced to make frequent recourse to what is sometimes called the "God of the gaps." This expression means that when scientists do not understand a particular phenomenon, this phenomenon must have a supernatural origin. But when scientists finally do understand this phenomenon, the gap is filled and a supernatural explanation is no longer necessary, forcing creationists constantly to identify new targets for criticism in the life sciences. This frequent switching from one temporarily unexplained phenomenon to the next is advertised by creationists as critical thinking, something they say is important for students' education.

Indeed, critical thinking must definitely be taught to our students. But critical thinking cannot be based on any dogma of any kind, for example, the postulated existence of an omnipotent intelligent designer able to govern the natural world through a series of miracles. Many people would scoff at the idea of alchemy, astrology, and magic being taught in schools, other than in history or anthropology classes. We know why: in spite of what some enthusiasts might say, alchemy, astrology, and magic are not scientifically verifiable. Why, then, try to introduce miracles in science classrooms? And besides, the teaching of ID would take about five minutes and would have a scientific informational content of zero.

The absurdity of this situation is well illustrated by the cartoon in figure 7.1. Assuming that both physics and magic, for example, are taught in schools, how can the students possibly decide which one is right? They could only do this by comparing the results obtained in a physics lab with those obtained in a magic lab. For example, they could do experiments with electronic circuits and see that physics works. In the magic lab, they could learn incantations, practice them, and see that they do not work. But what a ridiculous waste of time and money this would be!

A 2005 Gallup poll showed that American teenagers (13–17 years of age) are divided on the issue of evolution. For 37% of them, the theory of evolution is well supported by empirical evidence. Another 33% have no opinion on the subject, whereas the remaining 30% affirm that the theory of evolution is not well supported by evidence. The same poll also showed that 43% of the teenagers think that human beings have developed over millions of years and that God guided this process. Eighteen percent think that human evolution also took place over millions of years but that God played no part. Finally, 38% think that human beings did not evolve and appeared in their present form about 10,000 years ago. This is a question for educators to resolve. On the other hand, the support for evolution increases dramatically with education, with 65% of the people with postgraduate training thinking that evolution is a firmly based theory. This value drops to 20% among those with a high school education or less.

Most of us are well aware that science and mathematics education in primary and secondary schools leaves much to be desired in the United

FIGURE 7.1
Is this where our schools are headed? By Tony Auth, *Philadelphia Inquirer*, copyright 2005, reproduced by permission.

States. International tests consistently show our country ranking not far from the bottom of the pile. Things are not much better at the college level; the percentage of American undergraduates majoring in science, mathematics, and engineering is low, which does not bode well for the future of a highly technological society like ours. Something similar is happening in our graduate schools of science and engineering.

Creationism and Scientific Research

The United States, starting shortly before World War II and continuing today, has attracted countless scientists from around the world. This is because the modern American university system was outstanding already in the late 1930s, and became even more so thanks to a significant influx of international scholars and students. Many of these international scientists were escaping pernicious totalitarian European ideologies—Nazism and fascism—or their aftermath, the destruction of European cities by war. These scientists may or may not have been religious; this did not matter at the time. Much more recently, as another example of scientific transfusion, thousands of science graduate students and postdoctoral students, mainly from Asia, are presently occupying the slots left vacant by American students. These students do much more than just study here; they produce an immense amount of new data without which American science would not be what it is today.

Let us now assume for a minute that our country veers more toward Christian fundamentalism and its natural ally, creationism. Combine this with the much longer screening process for issuing U.S. visas—a result of the 9/11 catastrophe—and the perception of the United States now being a belligerent nation trying to force its values on other nations. What do you think will be the effect of this on international students and scientists? They may no longer be too interested in coming over and might opt for Europe, Canada, or Australia instead. The negative consequences of this would be incalculable; the United States might see its prominence in science wane away.

Are Neocreationists Modern Galileos?

The Access Research Network, a Web site that posts neocreationist propaganda, has likened some ID proponents to modern Galileos. Galileo (1564–1642), the Renaissance Italian physicist and mathematician, is well known for having been condemned for heresy by the Catholic Inquisition in 1633. Galileo's mistake at the time had been to oppose a geocentric interpretation of the solar system, whereby planet Earth was at the center of the universe and did not move relative to other celestial bodies. Of course, Galileo was right, and the Catholic Church was wrong. Later, Galileo rightfully became an icon for thinkers opposed to established dogma, scientific ignorance, and intolerant worldviews.

Does this mean that anyone opposing a consensus view of nature must by definition be a scientific hero or a misunderstood genius? Not at all. The history of science abounds with false claims, flawed observations, and unsustainable theories. Even today, there are still some who pretend they have manufactured a perpetual motion machine (and try to patent it), can change lead into gold, have proved Einstein wrong, and routinely photograph the "aura" surrounding human beings. These are all pseudoscientific claims that have never withstood the scrutiny of sound science. The difference between Galileo and these "scientific mavericks" is that Galileo actually performed reproducible experiments that shattered the view held in his time by religious and other authorities. These experiments dealt with the motion of accelerated bodies, the results of which were in agreement with a rotating Earth but could not be reconciled with universally accepted ancient Greek Aristotelian physics and its reinvigoration by religious, Scholastic medieval thinking.

The key term here is thus "reproducible experiments." In other words, Galileo was not an armchair philosopher-scientist who merely thought up alternatives to "old science." Contrary to Aristotle and his medieval followers, Galileo put nature to the test. Do neocreationists, who, superficially, emulate some of the bold thinking of Galileo and his demise at the hands of the establishment, merit the title of scientific victims of pervasive Darwinism? The answer must be no. For one thing, what they call the establishment is no longer a powerful Church—it is a world community of independent scientists whose yardsticks are logic and fact-based science, not faith. Next, neocreationists have never produced even a semblance of experimental evidence that evolution by natural selection is wrong. They are at best armchair philosophers who think things up and have never proposed how to put their own ideas to the test. In fact, their only response to the many rebuttals from genuine scientists is that ID "theory" is misunderstood by scientists or that the rebuttals do not address the true nature of irreducible complexity. These are poor, vague, slippery, and self-defeating arguments. If scientists cannot correctly understand ID and irreducible complexity, there may be something deeply wrong with these concepts. Modern Galileos neocreationists are not.

Teleology, Purpose, and Free Will

It is a sobering fact that among industrialized nations, the U.S. public ranks low in terms of the understanding of basic scientific facts. For example, a significant proportion of Harvard graduates could not answer the question, "How long does it take planet Earth to make one revolution around the sun?" Many similarly simple questions went unanswered or were answered the wrong way by many Harvard graduates and many others. For example, a significant fraction of the American public believes that the sun revolves around Earth. That the opposite actually occurs has been known for 500 years! This means that the American public has a fragile grasp of basic scientific knowledge, probably for lack of proper exposure to it. This makes the public fertile terrain for the acceptance of pseudoscientific pronouncements, especially those with religious connotations and biblical authority. This fragility allows sectarian thinkers to con the public into seeing acceptance of their unscientific views as simply an exercise of a democratic "freedom of choice." But that is not all.

Freedom of choice is a tenet of American society, but so are free will and purpose in life. Creationists and ID believers are wont to demonstrate that the theory of evolution is in opposition to both free will and purpose, because, they proclaim, undirected evolution is incompatible with both. To rebut this, and to show that these people lack understanding of modern science, we again draw on the cogent student writings of Kathryn Dooley. To understand her argument, remember the medieval "Great Chain of Being" and its ranking of the "progress" of things from rocks to God described in chapter 2. Now contrast this view with Dooley's description of evolution by natural selection:

> Natural selection invokes neither progress nor purpose, and rejects the idea of perfection as either a state of the natural world or an evolutionary goal. Evolution by natural selection is neither progressive, nor teleological, nor in any way intelligent or purposeful or externally directed. It is simply a consequence of the fact that, in a naturally variable population, certain types of individuals will tend to survive and reproduce more frequently than others. Unlike previous speculations on the origins and development of life, Darwinian evolution offered a purely naturalistic explanation for the mechanism of adaptation and diversification, appealing to no vague or mysterious forces, whether vitalism or progress or divine intervention.

There we have it. Evolution by natural selection could not in Darwin's days and still cannot today be accepted, let alone understood, by some because it dethroned the concept of progress toward perfection in nature and did not make recourse to a perfect designer. This also explains why the enemies of evolutionary theory call it an ideology. In Dooley's words again:

> A more bewildering and disturbing trend, however, is the tendency of evolution's opponents to attack Darwinism as an ideology rather than a scientific theory, and one that is simultaneously ruthlessly amoral and that worships progress. [One notices here an internal contradiction regarding "progress."] In his book *Defeating Darwinism by Opening Minds*, Phillip E. Johnson [law professor at the University of California–Berkeley] insists that Darwinism is antithetical to Christianity because it teaches that "human beings did not fall from perfection to sin but evolved from savagery to civilization." The vision of progress he asserts, and even the language of "savagery" and "civilization" he uses, originate directly from the 19th century evolutionary concept that Darwin's mechanistic theory opposed and refuted. Far from acting as a cornerstone of a "modernist" materialist philosophy, as Johnson supposes, Darwinian evolution has, over the years, steadily divorced itself from ideology and claims to moral significance. The extent to which Darwinism continues to slip into public discourse as

an ideological or moral principle is, perhaps, the extent to which the Darwinian revolution is not yet complete.

In addition to misrepresenting evolution by natural selection, Johnson—a neocreationist and opponent of evolution—bases his reasoning on antiquated anthropological notions ("savagery" and "civilization") and openly religious, teleological principles. This is not science.

As for free will, a very important human value, nothing in evolutionary science makes it nonexistent or limited in spite of the undirected character of evolution. It so happens that the time when human brains experienced their biggest size increase, starting with *Homo erectus* approximately 2 million years ago, is also the time when culture started developing. Since free will is a philosophical concept, it must automatically be seen as part and parcel of our complicated brains and not something bestowed upon us from "outside." It remains, however, that the evolution of the human brain is not yet well understood, nor is the extraordinary complexity of its neuronal circuitry. Be assured, however, that research in this area continues actively.

Our grand conclusion for this section is that evolutionary biology is solidly buttressed by observational facts. It is the best biological theory we have. Undoubtedly, it will be modified in the years ahead, as practically all scientific theories have been. But these modifications will not come from creationism and ID. Indeed, these ideologies do not ask any scientifically answerable questions and, in fact, do not ask any questions at all. The claim that creationism and ID are an expression of critical thinking is unfounded.

Why Do Scientists Have Such a Difficult Time Communicating with the General Public?

Many people see scientists as individuals isolated in their ivory towers and interacting only with their peers, using a jargon that nobody else understands. Unfortunately, this image is largely true. To add insult to injury, many scientists think poorly of their colleagues who attempt—through trade book publishing, for example—to communicate with the general public. In fact, the situation in universities is so bad that it is often *detrimental* to someone's academic career to engage in popularizing science. One sad example is that of Carl Sagan (1934–1996), astronomer, best-selling author, and director of the TV series *Cosmos*. In spite of being an innovative and successful scientist, Sagan was repeatedly barred from becoming a member of the U.S. National Academy of Sciences, reportedly because he was too well known outside academia. Of course, there are exceptions, such as evolutionary biologist Stephen J. Gould (1941–2002). But still, a few exceptions do not change the general rule. The take-home message is that, by and large, scientists expect science to eventually explain itself correctly to the public, which of course never happens.

An added difficulty associated with the proper communication of science to the lay public is the amount of mathematics now used in all fields of science, including biology. It is not difficult to translate into common English the meaning of Heisenberg's uncertainty principle and the quantum "fuzziness" of electrons. Neither is it difficult to explain dissipative structures, especially with the aid of visual examples such as Bénard cells. But unfortunately, it is much more complicated and challenging to describe *how* these explanations and interpretations are *derived* from empirical and thought experiments. This is because arcane mathematical equations are often involved. However, math is a formalism that in fact considerably simplifies the communication and teaching of quantitative scientific principles. The problem, of course, is that many people have a deeply felt aversion to math. This means that, in the absence of the crisp language of mathematics, many ambiguities in the exposition of science cannot be avoided. In the end, this also means that the public is asked to *trust* the conclusions of science without the benefit of demonstrations. Needless to say, this opens the door to dogmatic, miraculous, or poor metaphorical explanations of natural phenomena, all under the guise of critical thinking.

What is to be done? Surely, the teaching of math could be vastly improved. In addition to "consumers' math," which teaches students how to calculate and handle change, simple statistical principles could be taught by using tossed coins. Further, the study of a few differential equations would go a long way in helping the public understand how the natural world undergoes changes over time and space, from atoms, to the universe, to life itself. In fact, P.F.L.'s students are consistently flabbergasted when they see how simple the equations of Einstein's special relativity truly are. Once they are exposed to these equations, students understand (and accept) much more easily counterintuitive facts such as time elapsing more slowly at very high velocities and the shrinking of spaceships (as well as that of subatomic particles) traveling near the speed of light. As this example shows, and as always, rigorous education is a great eye-opener, and the key to distinguishing sense from nonsense.

To conclude this section, we quote the American physicist and 1965 Nobel Laureate Richard Feynman (1918–1988): "I think that a scientist looking at nonscientific problems is just as dumb as the next guy." We interpret this quote as also meaning that just as theology is for theologians, so too science is for scientists. Or, to quote the Bible, "Render unto Caesar the things that are Caesar's and to God the things that are God's."

Conclusions

We hope that we have presented to readers interesting and persuasive arguments demonstrating the usefulness of evolutionary thinking in science and in the humanities. In their opposition to evolution, creationists and ID proponents are a threat to more than just biology. It is, however, in the latter area that they have inserted what they call their first "wedge," a term that suggests that their true intentions are much wider. As the Wedge Document of the Discovery Institute states, the aim is "to replace materialistic explanations with the theistic understanding that nature and human beings are created by God." Those of us who are convinced that science cannot and should not suffer interference from politics and religion must act now.

The creationists' attempts to warn high school students that evolution is "just a theory" have been defeated in court and in other venues in Pennsylvania, Kansas, and Ohio. But some members of the Discovery Institute are reported to have claimed that the "wedge" policy will shift its emphasis from the courtroom to individual biology teachers. Therefore, we are far from having seen the end of the battle between evolution and creationism.

Let us repeat that evolution is *not* against religion and that it is *not* a question of fair play and objectivity to allow the teaching of unscientific concepts in science classrooms. Many evolutionary scientists believe in various religious precepts, but then, many others do not. This is the way it should be because science knows no political, religious, and philosophical boundaries. No single country, no single faith can lay claim to any part of science, nor should any faith try to sway science in one direction or another. In fact, some of the greatest thinkers mentioned in this book, Mendel, Darwin, and Einstein, were not against religion.

As is often the case, history repeats itself or, in this case, may be in the process of repeating itself. It is perhaps time to learn from previous mistakes regarding evolution. One country in the recent past successfully curtailed the teaching of genetics and evolution for several decades because, so thought its leaders, this branch of science was contrary to its political philosophy. This country was the USSR. In the case of genetics, Trofim Lysenko, Stalin's science advisor, convinced his boss that Mendel was wrong, and so genetics became an unacceptable "bourgeois" science. The stance of the USSR against evolutionary theory is more difficult to understand. Marxism is not intrinsically anti-evolution or antiscience. After all, Marxism calls for deep changes in society. But more subtly, Marxism predicts that humans are socially perfectible, particularly under the aegis of the Communist Party, not God. On the other hand, evolution by natural selection is blind and undirected and does not necessarily lead to perfection. This idea was not quite in accordance with the policies implemented in the Soviet Union, hence the dismissal of evolutionary theory there. The result was an enormous setback for biology in the USSR. In fact, Russian biology is still suffering from the aftermath of these old political decisions. We cannot allow this to happen again anywhere.

Unfortunately, a rigorous statistical study performed in 2002–2003 in the United States, Japan, Turkey, and 31 European countries shows that the U.S. population ranks very low (immediately above Turkey) in its acceptance of evolution. To wit, 78% or more of adults in Iceland, Denmark, Sweden, and France think that evolution is a correct theory. In the United States, this figure is 38%. Turkey ranks at the bottom, with only 25% of adults who think that evolution is a valid theory. The authors of the study (J. D. Miller, E. C. Scott, and O. Okamoto) blame Protestant fundamentalism and the politicization of science for the poor showing of the United States. As for Turkey, it is likely that Islamic fundamentalism is responsible for its score. Thus, in both countries, one witnesses the negative impact of religious thinking on science.

What, then, can we do to counter creationism? Interestingly, Eugenie Scott of the National Center for Science Education reminds us that the creationist movement is highly factionalized. Among several other factions, one distinguishes what we call "classical" creationists, who believe in a young Earth and the full fixity of species. These people reject all scientific evidence supporting a very old age for Earth and the evolution of species. Other creationists accept the findings of physical science pointing to an old Earth but argue that the Creator made a young Earth look old. And finally, some ID supporters—those we call neocreationists—accept the scientific fact that Earth is old but reject evolution, save some minor evolutionary changes that they wrongly qualify as "mere" adaptation.

Modern creationism might, then, eventually self-destruct thanks to its internal tensions. But this is not something we should count on. Rather, the cure is education provided within the tried and true framework of solid science. Several Web sites listed in Further Readings give good advice on how evolutionary thinking can be taught in the classroom. The scientific method has worked very successfully for many decades and has resulted in countless groundbreaking scientific and technical innovations. There is presently no reason to turn it upside down.

Unfortunately, Scott also notes that many biology teachers are now deemphasizing evolution "because it's just too much trouble." Although this position is understandable, it is discouraging that psychological factors complicate the evolution versus creationism issue even further. Surely, this is the "wedge" at work. To combat this trend, we strongly encourage parents to become vocal, serve on school boards, and provide encouragement to teachers and principals who want to maintain sanity in the science classroom.

We must maintain the technological prominence of our country alive and well, and we can do so by preventing the introduction of theology and miracles into science courses. If we fail to discard this ideology, the world will watch, ponder, . . . and suddenly burst out laughing.

Appendix 1
The Brusselator

The Brusselator is the first computer-generated dissipative structure developed by Ilya Prigogine and colleagues at the University of Brussels, Belgium, in the early 1970s. It is based on hypothetical coupled chemical reactions, some of which are autocatalytic. These reactions involve four compounds, A, B, D, and E, and two intermediate compounds, X and Y, which do not accumulate in the reaction vessel because they are converted into E and D as the reactions progress. Compounds A and B are fed into the system in a continuous manner. The reactions are written

$A \rightarrow X$

$B + X \rightarrow Y + D$

$2X + Y \rightarrow 3X$

$X \rightarrow E$

and can be graphed as follows:

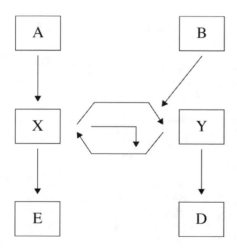

The two loops connecting compounds X and Y represent the autocatalytic portion of the reaction. Using conditions far from thermodynamic equilibrium, it can be shown that the distribution (concentration) of compound X in

CONCENTRATION OF X

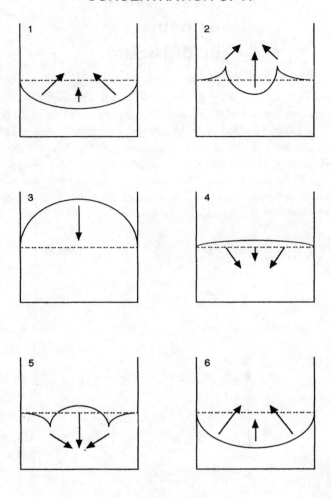

SPACE

FIGURE A.1
Cross section of a reaction vessel containing the Brusselator. The solid lines and arrows show the variations in the concentration of compound X as a function of space and time. The dotted line represents an invariant equilibrium situation.

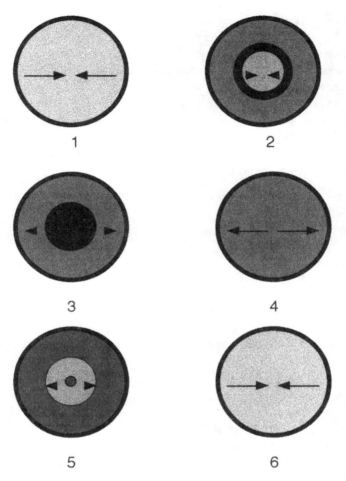

FIGURE A.2
The Brusselator reaction vessel seen from the top. Darker regions indicate a higher concentration of compound X. The arrows denote the
directions of the concentration wave.

the reaction vessel fluctuates in time and space. In other words, the reaction
mixture spontaneously acquires a spatial and temporal structure (order).

The fluctuation of the concentration of X as a function of space is shown
in figure A.1 at six different time intervals. Initially, the concentration of X
decreases in the center of the reaction vessel, followed by a wave (a moving
ring) that eventually makes the concentration of X higher in the center of the
vessel. The process then reverses itself, and a wave of concentration of X
leaves the center to reach the border of the reaction vessel. These oscillations

continue indefinitely as long as reactants A and B are fed into the system. Figure A.2 shows the phenomenon seen from the top of the reaction vessel. The Brusselator is not just a theoretical model; it represents very well the structures seen in the actual Belousov-Zhabotinsky reaction, a chemical reaction that displays moving, concentric rings of colored reactants (see appendix 2). Other dissipative structures show wavelike patterns in space that are stable in time. Such patterns are seen in developing embryos. The application of the mathematics of dissipative structures to living systems is still in its infancy and awaits multidisciplinary collaborations for potential fruition in the life sciences.

Appendix 2
Experiments for Educators

Some simple (and not so simple) demonstrations and experiments can be used to illustrate a few key concepts discussed in this book.

Genetic Drift

Chance as an evolutionary force can be illustrated with pieces of colored paper handed out to students. The differently colored pieces represent individuals in a population. The pieces of paper are picked randomly and color distribution is noted. The process is repeated for several "generations." Students record numbers of "individuals" of a given color present in each generation and graph the results. For details, see C. K. Omoto and P. F. Lurquin, *Genes and DNA: A Beginner's Guide to Genetics and Its Applications* (New York: Columbia University Press, 2004).

Selection

A good way to teach (artificial) selection is to compare the growth of bacterial strains on selective and nonselective media. These experiments require equipment and chemicals that are probably within the means of many high schools. Bacterial growth medium and pipette tips can be sterilized in a pressure cooker. The selective agents—antibiotics such as ampicillin and tetracycline—should be filter sterilized because they are temperature sensitive. Antibiotic-sensitive and antibiotic-resistant, plasmid-carrying *Escherichia coli* strains can be obtained from the American Type Culture Collection (ATCC). *E. coli* cells first grown in the absence of antibiotic(s) are later plated on selective medium, where the amount of growth is observed. Alternatively, students can collect bacteria present in their ears and nostrils (use sterilized cotton swabs).

Replica plating can be used to observe multidrug or single-drug resistance. With *E. coli*, gene-transfer-mediated resistance to antibiotics can be demonstrated through plasmid DNA isolation and transfer to sensitive strains. This step is equivalent to evolution in the test tube. The simplest gene transfer technique is the $CaCl_2$/heat-shock technique. Details of the techniques can be found in a variety of commercially available lab manuals and manufacturers' instructions.

Heat Flow and Thermodynamic Equilibrium

The hot coffee experiment described in chapter 5 can be done using a cup of hot water in a small Styrofoam box with a lid. The box should have two holes for the insertion of two thermometers. Students can graph water and air temperature as a function of time. This is in fact a genuine calorimetric experiment.

The opposite experiment can also be done, in which the cup holds ice instead of hot water. In this case, heat transfer takes place from the air in the box to the ice in the cup.

Dissipative Structures and Order out of Chaos

Oscillating chemical reactions can be used to illustrate these principles. These reactions oscillate in time (chemical "clocks") or in both time and space. These experiments yield stunning results that leave no student unimpressed. Several Web sites give detailed recipes for these reactions.

The *Oscillating Reactions—Chemical Waves* Web page by G. Dupuis and N. Berland (www.faidherbe.org/site/cours/dupuis/oscil.htm) is for French high school teachers (the URL shows the English version). It gives a very good theoretical introduction to oscillating chemical reactions, as well as practical details for conducting these experiments in the class room.

The following sites also give details on the Belousov-Zhabotinsky reaction, a reaction that epitomizes dissipative structures (see also appendix 1):

science.csustan.edu/stkrm/Recipes/Recipes-Oscillat-3.htm
www.musc.edu/~alievr/BZ/BZexplain.html

Liposomes as Pre-protocells and Trapping of DNA

These experiments are much more technically challenging and necessitate more complicated equipment, such as a microcentrifuge, a fluorescence microscope, and an electroporator, preferably connected to an oscilloscope. The electroporator can be homemade, however (see P. F. Lurquin, "Gene Transfer by Electroporation." *Molecular Biotechnology* 1997;7:5–35). Local colleges or universities may be willing to either lend or donate a fluorescence microscope, the most expensive piece of equipment needed for these experiments.

Large liposomes are made and manipulated as detailed in P. F. Lurquin and K. Athanasiou, "Electric Field-Mediated DNA Encapsulation of DNA into Large Liposomes" (*Biochemical and Biophysical Research Communications* 2000;267:838–841). A hookup to a vacuum line is needed to make these liposomes, and so is a hot water bath.

Transfer of DNA into preformed liposomes made in the presence of the dye ethidium bromide can be demonstrated by electroporation. This experiment mimics the trapping of nucleic acids into putative prebiotic pre-protocells through the effect of lightning, for example. Ethidium is a mutagen, however. If there are safety concerns, other fluorescent dyes that bind to DNA can be used. DNA is preferred to RNA in these experiments because of its much greater stability and ease of extraction (for extraction, see Omoto and Lurquin, *Genes and DNA*, cited above). These experiments are for advanced students because of their complexity. Students could also be involved in the building and testing of a simple electroporator. Such a project could take the best part of a semester.

P.F.L. would appreciate receiving comments on these proposed experiments. He can be reached at Lurquin@wsu.edu.

GLOSSARY

AIDS: acquired immunodeficiency syndrome, a disease in which the immune system is compromised after infection with the human immunodeficiency virus (HIV).

amino acid: an organic compound used to build proteins in living cells. There are 20 different natural amino acids found in proteins.

Archaea: a domain of life. Archaeans are a type of prokaryote often found in hostile environments. All members of Archaea are single celled.

Bacteria: a domain of life. Bacteria are a type of prokaryote. All members of Bacteria are single celled.

base: in this book, type of organic compound containing nitrogen, carbon, oxygen, and hydrogen atoms used by living cells to build DNA and RNA: adenine, cytosine, guanine, thymine (DNA only), or uracil instead of thymine (RNA only).

carcinogen: a chemical compound known to cause normal cells to become cancerous.

catalyst: an organic or mineral compound that accelerates chemical reactions.

chloroplast: a cellular body found only in plants and where photosynthesis takes place. Chloroplasts contain DNA.

chromosome: a cellular structure composed of DNA and proteins.

clade: a branch of a phylogenetic tree.

clone (v.): to isolate and make numerous copies of a single gene or a small set of genes from an organism.

creationism: the doctrine that states that God created the universe and life. Intelligent Design and creationism are very similar, if not identical.

cultural evolution: changes that occur over time and geographic space in cultural practices.

cystic fibrosis: a genetic (heritable) disease characterized by the malfunctioning of lungs.

Darwinism: a term rarely used today by scientists that refers to evolution by natural selection.

dating: in this book, the action of determining the age of biological and mineral specimens.

dissipative structures (or systems): physical or chemical structures that dissipate entropy in the process of self-organizing.

DNA: deoxyribonucleic acid, the blueprint of life, the molecule that contains genes. Four bases are used to make DNA: adenine, thymine, cytosine, and guanine. DNA also contains the sugar deoxyribose.

dogma: a belief authoritatively considered to be absolute truth.

drift (also genetic drift): evolutionary factor that changes gene frequencies in populations of living organisms by pure chance.

electromagnetic radiation: a type of radiation that is at the same time composed of light particles (photons) and combined, oscillating electric and magnetic fields. Visible light is a type of electromagnetic radiation.

electron: negatively charged subatomic particle found around an atomic nucleus.

entropy: in this book, a measure of order versus disorder. Entropy is calculated by dividing the quantity of heat in an object by its temperature.

enzyme: a biological catalyst that accelerates biochemical reactions.

equilibrium: in this book, a situation where chemical reactions or physical forces come to a standstill.

essence: in this book, the intrinsic and unchanging qualities of a thing that give it its identity.

Eukarya: a domain of life. Eukarya are cells and organisms whose DNA is packaged inside a cellular structure called a nucleus. Eukarya are also called Eukaryotes.

evolution: in a broad sense, the ability of all things to change over time.

fitness: a relative quantity that describes the ability of organisms to survive and multiply in a given type of environment.

flagellum: a whiplike structure present in some prokaryotic and eukaryotic cells used to propel these cells in a liquid medium.

fundamentalism: belief in the Bible or other sacred books as factual, incontrovertible historical records.

fusion: in physics, the action of merging two or more atomic nuclei together; in biology, the action of merging two or more living cells together.

gene: an element of heredity. Genes are made of DNA or, in some viruses, of RNA.

genome: the suite of all genes present in an organism.

glucose: a sugar whose metabolism produces energy.

gravitation (theory of): the theory that explains gravity.

gravity: the force that makes two material bodies attract each other.

Great Chain of Being: the ordering of living and nonliving things according to the putative absolute value of their essence.

histone: a type of protein associated with DNA. Histones are found in both Archaea and Eukarya.

HIV: human immunodeficiency virus, the virus that causes AIDS.

homology: degree of similarity shared by genes.

horizontal cultural transmission: transmission of cultural traits (language and religion, for example) between unrelated individuals, for example, from teacher to students.

hydrogenosome: a cellular body where hydrogen gas is produced biochemically.

hypercycle: an ensemble of interacting RNA molecules or interacting RNA and protein molecules where functions such as replication take place.

hypothesis: a proposition subject to verification or proof.

Intelligent Design: a doctrine that claims that a supernatural designer manufactured the universe and all that is found in it.

lipid: a type of molecule found in fats.

liposome: a spherical microscopic structure made from lipids, either in the laboratory or in nature.

LUCA: last universal common ancestor, hypothetical DNA-containing cells at the root of the tree of life.

metabolism: the suite of biochemical reactions that take place in living cells.

metaphor: a figure of speech normally used to simplify concepts by making reference to analogous, simpler concepts.

mitochondrion (pl. **mitochondria**): a cellular body, present in eukaryotes only, where oxygen is metabolized in order to produce chemical energy. Mitochondria contain DNA.

multiregional hypothesis (or **model**): the theory that modern human beings evolved independently from *H. erectus* several different times on several continents.

mutation: a heritable change in the base-pair sequence of a gene.

nucleotide: the chemical combination of a base, a phosphate group, and a sugar. DNA and RNA are long strings of nucleotides.

nucleus (pl. **nuclei**): in physics, a positively charged combination of subatomic particles (protons and neutrons) found at the center of an atom; in biology, the cellular body that contains chromosomes.

paleontology: the study of fossils.

phenylketonuria (**PKU**): a heritable disease characterized by the inability to metabolize the amino acid phenylalanine, whose accumulation in the body becomes toxic.

photon: a particle of electromagnetic radiation.

photosynthesis: the mechanism by which light is used to manufacture organic compounds in living cells.

phylogenetic tree: a treelike drawing linking organisms according to their evolutionary descendance. A pedigree is a very simple phylogenetic tree.

polygyny: the practice of a man having several wives at the same time.

postmodernism: a philosophical position that states that all explanations of the animate and inanimate world are equally valid.

postulate: an undemonstrated proposition accepted at face value.

prion: a type of protein that can change the shape of other proteins and make them assume pathological functions. "Mad cow" disease is caused by prions.

prokaryote: a single-celled organism whose DNA is not packaged in a nucleus.

protein: a string of chemically linked amino acids.

quantum mechanics: the highly mathematical theory that explains the behavior of subatomic particles and their interactions with electromagnetic radiation.

quark: an elementary particle present in neutrons and protons.

relativity (**theories of**): Einstein's dual theories that describe the equivalence between matter and energy, and explain gravity.

respiration: metabolic reactions involving oxygen gas.

ribosomes: small but complex cellular bodies where translation (protein synthesis) takes place.

ribozyme: a biological catalyst made of RNA.

RNA: ribonucleic acid, a large molecule, similar to DNA, where the sugar is ribose (instead of deoxyribose) and the bases are adenine, uracil (instead of thymine), cytosine, and guanine.

selection: in this book, a natural or artificial evolutionary mechanism. Natural selection operates in nature through environmental "forces" such a droughts, forest fires, volcanic eruptions, and floods. Artificial selection consists in selectively breeding plants and animals for desired characteristics, such as yield in corn, milk production in cattle, and shape in dogs.

sickle cell anemia: a heritable blood disorder characterized by malfunctioning hemoglobin.

stromatolite: layered, domelike structure where cyanobacteria and other organisms proliferate.

symbiosis: the action of living in very close proximity and cooperating at the biological level.

tautology: basically, a circular argument.

teleology: a philosophical position that affirms ultimate design and purpose in all things.

theory: systematically organized scientific knowledge of accepted principles. A valid theory must have explanatory and predictive value.

transcription: the action of generating RNA molecules by copying a DNA template.

transformism: the notion that nature, animate and inanimate, slowly changes over time.

translation: the action of generating proteins by decoding an RNA template.

uniregional hypothesis (or **model**): the scientific model that locates the origin of modern humans in Africa, and in Africa only.

vertical cultural transmission: the transmission of cultural traits (for example, language and religion) from parents to offspring.

FURTHER READING

The books and articles listed immediately below are nontechnical or semitechnical. Their reading does not require an extensive scientific background.

Behe, M. J. 1996. *Darwin's Black Box: The Biochemical Challenge to Evolution.* New York: Free Press.

Cavalli-Sforza, L. L. 2000. *Genes, Peoples, and Languages.* New York: North Point Press.

Cavalli-Sforza, L. L., and F. Cavalli-Sforza. 1995. *The Great Human Diasporas: The History and Diversity of Evolution.* Cambridge, MA: Perseus.

Chaisson, E. J. 2005. *Epic of Evolution: Seven Ages of the Cosmos.* New York: Columbia University Press.

Culotta, E., and E. Pennisi. 2005. Evolution in action. *Science* 310:1878–1879.

Dawkins, R. 1986. *The Blind Watchmaker: Why the Evidence of Evolution Reveals a Universe Without Design.* New York: W. W. Norton.

Dawkins, R. 2004. *The Ancestors' Tale: A Pilgrimage to the Dawn of Evolution.* Boston: Houghton Mifflin.

Dean, C. 2005. Scientists speak up on mix of God and science. *New York Times,* August 23.

De Duve, C. 1995. *Vital Dust: Life as a Cosmic Imperative.* New York: Basic Books.

Dyson, F. 1981. *Disturbing the Universe.* New York: Harper Colophon Books.

Frank, Thomas. 2004. *What's the Matter with Kansas? How Conservatives Won the Heart of America.* New York: Metropolitan Books.

Gribbin, J. 2004. *Deep Simplicity: Bringing Order to Chaos and Complexity.* New York: Random House.

Johnson, P. E. 1997. *Defeating Darwinism by Opening Minds.* Downers Grove, IL: InterVarsity Press.

Kerr, R. A. 2005. The Story of O_2. *Science* 308:1730–1732.

Krauss, L. M. 2002. *Atom: An Odyssey from the Big Bang to Life on Earth and Beyond.* Collingdale, PA: Diane Publishing.

Lurquin, P. F. 2002. *High Tech Harvest: Understanding Genetically Modified Food Plants.* Boulder, CO: Westview.

Margulis, L., and D. Sagan. 2002. *Acquiring Genomes: A Theory of the Origin of Species.* Philadelphia: Perseus.

Miller, K. R. 2000. *Finding Darwin's God: A Scientist's Search for Common Ground Between God and Evolution.* New York: Harper Perennial.

Monod, J. 1971. *Chance and Necessity: An Essay on the Natural Philosophy of Modern Biology.* New York: Alfred A. Knopf.

Mooney, C. 2005. *The Republican War on Science.* New York: Basic Books.

Omoto, C. K., and P. F. Lurquin. 2004. *Genes and DNA: A Beginner's Guide to Genetics and Its Applications.* New York: Columbia University Press.

Rennie, J. 2002. 15 answers to creationist nonsense. *Scientific American,* July 2002, pp. 78–85.

Scott, E. C. 2004. *Evolution vs. Creationism: An Introduction*. Berkeley: University of California Press.
Shanks, N. 2004. *God, the Devil, and Darwin*. New York: Oxford University Press.
Stone, L., and P. F. Lurquin. 2005. *A Genetic and Cultural Odyssey: The Life and Work of L. L. Cavalli-Sforza*. New York: Columbia University Press.
Stone, L., and P. F. Lurquin (with L. L. Cavalli-Sforza). 2006. *Genes, Culture, and Human Evolution: A Synthesis*. Malden, MA: Blackwell.
Wells, S. 2002. *The Journey of Man*. New York: Random House.
Whitfield, J. 2006. Base invaders: Could viruses have invented DNA as a way to sneak into cells? *Nature* 439:130–131.
Wilgoren, J. 2005. Politicized scholars put evolution on the defensive. *New York Times*, August 21.

More Technical Resources

Balter, M. 2005. Are humans still evolving? *Science* 309:234–237.
Balter, M. 2005. Are human brains still evolving? Brain genes show signs of selection. *Science* 309:1662–1663.
Chaisson, E. J. 2001. *Cosmic Evolution: The Rise of Complexity in Nature*. Cambridge, MA: Harvard University Press.
Chen, I. A. 2006. The emergence of cells during the origin of life. *Science* 314:1558–1559.
De Duve, C. 1991. *Blueprint for a Cell: The Nature and Origin of Life*. Burlington, NC: Neil Patterson Publishers.
Forterre, P. 2005. The two ages of the RNA world, and the transition to the DNA world: A story of viruses and cells. *Biochimie* 87:793–803.
Hogan, C. J. 1998. *The Little Book of the Big Bang*. New York: Copernicus.
Lurquin, P. F. 2003. *The Origins of Life and the Universe*. New York: Columbia University Press.
Noller, H. F. 2004. The driving force for molecular evolution of translation. *RNA* 10:1833–1837.
Noller, H. F. 2005. RNA structure: Reading the ribosome. *Science* 309:1508–1514.
Prigogine, I., and I. Stengers. 1984. *Order out of Chaos*. New York: Bantam.
Prigogine, I., and I. Stengers. 1997. *The End of Certainty*. New York: Free Press.
Stearns, S. C., and R. F. Hoekstra. 2005. *Evolution: An Introduction*. Oxford: Oxford University Press.

Web Sites

The pages listed below are in no particular order. Some promulgate Intelligent Design (ID) and creationism, and some oppose them. Some pages provide general information on philosophical and scientific thinking. All URLs were last checked in the winter of 2006. Needless to say, the Internet hosts innumerable other sites, chat rooms, and blogs on the issues of evolution, miracles, ID, and creationism.

www.accessexcellence.org/WN/SUA01/master_eye_gene.html: gives a summary of the discovery of a master gene determining eye formation.

www.talkdesign.org/faqs/Evolving_Immunity.html: presents an extremely detailed analysis of the evolution of the immune system, mostly for specialists.

www.health.adelaide.edu.au/Pharm/Musgrave/essays/flagella.htm: gives detailed information on the evolution of bacterial flagella, mostly for specialists.

www.stnews.org/archives/2004_december/books_authors_1204.html: offers a critique of ID followed by a response from ID adherents.

www.discovery.org/csc/: the official site of the Center for Science and Culture, the Seattle-based institution that promotes ID and its teaching.

www.icr.org/: the official site of the Institute for Creation Research. This institute conducts research on the "young Earth" hypothesis and offers degree programs in creationism.

www.csicop.org/si/: the site of the *Skeptical Inquirer*, a journal devoted to the study and debunking of pseudoscience (e.g., creation science, astrology, and ID) and paranormal phenomena (e.g., ESP, telekinesis, and spoon bending).

www.tufts.edu/as/wright_center/cosmic_evolution/index.html: the teaching site of Eric Chaisson, professor at Tufts and Harvard Universities. Chaisson's theme is evolution writ large, from the Big Bang, to human cultural evolution, to the future of humankind.

www.arn.org/index.html: the Web site of the Access Research Network, a creation of Phillip Johnson, one of the most ardent proponents of ID. This site makes it very clear that ID and fundamental Christianity are closely linked.

www.ncseweb.org: the Web site of the National Center for Science Education. This site actively opposes creationism and ID.

www7.nationalacademies.org/evolution/: this National Academies Web page clearly shows that evolution is overwhelmingly supported by the American scientific community.

www.talkorigins.org: although technical at times, this site provides thorough answers to creationist objections to evolution.

www.pbs.org/wgbb/evolution/: this PBS site provides multimedia tools for the teaching of evolution.

www.hyahya.org: the Web site of the Turkish Islamist creationist movement.

www2.truman.edu/~edis/writings/articles/hyahya.html: this page, by Taner Edis, physics professor at Truman State University, analyzes modern Turkish creationism.

people-press.org/reports/print.php3?PageID=988: gives the results of a poll conducted in July 2005 by the Pew Research Center for the People and the Press. The title of the poll is "Religion: A strength and weakness for both parties. Public divided on origins of life." This poll is largely devoted to public views of the creation/evolution debate.

The following three Web pages describe a dissipative system (recall that dissipative systems generate structure by dumping entropy into the universe) called the "Brusselator" (see appendix 1). These pages are for the mathematically savvy:

math.ohio-state.edu/~ault/Papers/Brusselator.pdf
mathworld.wolfram.com/BrusselatorEquations.html
cmp.caltech.edu/~mcc/STChaos/Brusselator.html

INDEX

Page numbers in **boldface** indicate figures

Abenaki, 18
Access Research Network, 168, 187–88
acquired characteristics, 105
adenine, 42, 119, 121
Africa, 18–19, 76, 85–86, 93
agriculture, 103–4
Ahmanson family, 182
AIDS, 75–76
Alaska, 98
aldol reaction, 150
aldosterone, 74–75
Altamira caves, 103
altruistic hypercycle, 123–24
altruistic ribozymes, 128
American Type Culture Collection
    (ATCC), 199
Americas, 90, 95–**97**
amino acids
    protein synthesis, 127
    and proteins, 119
    racemization, 58
    synthesizing in prebiotic soup, 117–**18**
    thioesters, 120
animal husbandry, 104
aniridia, 69
Anschutz, Philip F., 182
antibiotics, 71–73, 158, 184, 199
antigens, 60
anti-miscegenation laws, 12
Aquinas, Thomas, 32–33
Archaea
    endosymbiont hypothesis, 158–59
    evolution of, 142, 145–46
    fusion model of evolution, 155–**56**,
        157
    and histones, 154–55
    tree of life, 66–**67**
Aristotle, 32
asexual reproduction, 160
Asia, 98
Asimov, Isaac, 109
ATCC (American Type Culture
    Collection), 199
Athanasiou, K., 200–201
Australia, 36, 46, 90, 95–**97**
Australopithecus afarensis, 87–88, **91**
Australopithecus africanus, 90
autocatalytic, 195–98

Bacteria
    artificial selection experiment, 199
    endosymbiont hypothesis, 158–59
    Escherichia coli experiments, 170
    evolution of, 71–73, 142, 145–46
    fusion model of evolution, 155–**56**,
        157
    Michigan State University
        experiments, 151
    pleiotropic effects, 167–68
    tree of life, 66–**67**
bacterial flagella, 59, 62, 70–71, 134
banded iron formations, 149
base pairs. *See also* DNA; RNA
    DNA, 42–43
    homology, 64–66
    length of, 63
    mitochondria (mtDNA), 92
    mutation rates, 92–93
    mutations and sickle cell anemia, 46
    phylogenetic tree of life, 66–68, 91
    tautomeric shifts, 174
    trout, 68
Behe, Michael
    *Darwin's Black Box: The Biochemical
        Challenge to Evolution*, 15, 62
    genetic eye experiments, 69
    immune system, 60, 62, 70
    mousetrap metaphor, 79–80, 127
    perfection of organisms, 17
    statistical nature of genetics, 45
Belousov-Zhabotinsky reaction, 200
Bénard cells, 113–**14**, 191
Benedict XVI, 181
Beringia, 98
Bhagavad-Gita, 25–26
Bharatiya Jananta Party (BJP), 25–26
Bible, 28
bifurcations, 114–**15**
Big Bang theory
    endorsed by Roman Catholic Church,
        181
    and expansion of the universe, 140–**41**
    four forces of, 12–13
    Heisenberg uncertainty principle, 137
    and origins of life, 136
    thermodynamic disequilibrium, 142
    time of, 163–64

Bill and Melinda Gates Foundation, 183
binary oppositions, 20
biology, 136
bipedalism, 86–87, 89, 101
BJP (Bharatiya Jananta Party), 25–26
black holes, 138
Blind Watchmaker, The, 50
Boltzmann, Ludwig, 116
Borneo, 96
boron, 119
"bottoms-up approach," 169–**70**
Brahma (god), 25
brain size
    and culture, 190
    evolution of, 101–2
    fossil record, 89
    human genes and evolution, 90–91
    mark of humanity, 86–87
Brassica campestris (turnip), 167
Brassica napus (oil seed rape), 167
Brassica oleracea (cabbage), 167
Brusselator, 195–98
Buddha, 28
Buddhism, 27–28, 30
Buffon, Georges Louis de, 31
Bush, George W., 3, 180
"butterfly effect," 110, 114, 116

cabbage (Brassica oleracea), 167
calmodulin CAM gene, 44
Cambrian explosion, 161
caprylic acid, **126**
carbon dioxide
    fusion model of evolution, 155–**56**
    and micelles, **126**
    organic compound synthesis, 119
    prebiotic soup, 117
    rubisco enzyme, 78–79
carbon-14 dating, 55, 57–58, 103
carboxylic acids, 124–**26**
Cassini space craft, 172
CAT scans, 86–87
catalase, 148
catalysts, 119, 121
cattle, 105
Cavalli-Sforza, L. Luca, 105
cell membranes, 76
Center for Science and Culture (CSC), 15, 78, 82, 182–83
centrioles, 82

Chaisson, Eric, 140–**41**
chance
    and evolution, 16, 53, 107, 142
    Jacques Monod, 174
    and necessity, 173–76
    neutral theory of evolution, 50
    and perfection, 32
    probability, 174
    and radioactive decay, 110
Chance and Necessity: An Essay on the Natural Philosophy of Modern Biology, 174
chaos theory, 110, 142
Chauvet caves, 103
chimpanzees, 65–66, 101–2
China, 86, 96, 104–5
Chlamydomonas reinhardii, 160
chlorophyll, 113, 149
chloroplasts
    endosymbiont hypothesis, 157–58
    fusion model of evolution, 159
    photosynthesis, 59
    plant cells, 154
    rubisco enzyme, 78
Christian fundamentalism
    American public and evolution, 193
    culture war, 181
    Discovery Institute, 183
    and evolution, 28, 181
    impact on scientific research, 187
    in India, 26
    political connections, 3, 180
    and postmodernism, 183–84
Christianity, 26, 106. See also Christian fundamentalism
chromosomes, 92, **153**–54
cichlid fish, 167
citric acid cycle, 59–**60**
cladogram, 38–**39**
clay, 121, 124–**25**
climate, 97
Clinton, Bill, 182
cloning, 69, 74, 79, 170–71
co-evolution, 105, 107
Communist Party, 192
Constantine, 106
continental drift, 36
contingency, 175
contrasting traits, 40
corn (maize), 103, 152
cosmic rays, 58

cosmology, 135, 138, 142
creation myths. *See also* Genesis
    African, 18–19
    binary oppositions, 20
    Buddhism, 27–28
    Christian, 20
    Gilgamesh Epic, 5
    Hinduism, 25–27
    Islam, 21–23
    Judaism, 20, 23–25
    Korea, 27–28
    Native American, 18, 19–20
    and postmodernism, 183–84
creation science, 80–81
Creation Science Association of India
        Trust, 26
creationism
    confusion of facts and theories, 8
    definition, 4
    factions within, 193
    and fundamentalism, 30
    and Harun Yahya, 23
    impact on scientific research, 186–87
    Islamic beliefs, 22–23
    relationship to ID, 3–5, 15, 29
    and science education, 184–**86**
    as teleology, 52
    and William Paley, 15
creationists, 49–51, 56, 85
CSC (Center for Science and Culture),
        15, 78, 82, 182–83
cultural drift, 106–7
cultural evolution
    and agriculture, 103
    culture definition, 105
    emergence of, 91, 190
    horizontal transmission, 106
    and hot flashes, 78
    religion, 105–6
    vertical transmission, 105–6
cultural mutations, 104
cultural selection, 106
culture war, 181
cyanobacteria, 148, 150–51, 158
cystic fibrosis, 43–44
cytosine, 42, 121
cytoskeleton, 154

dairy cattle, 104–5
Daphnia pulex (water flea), 160
Darwin, Charles
    descent with modification, 34–35

horizontal transmission, 106
    and Lamarck, 33–34
    mutations (variants), 38
    natural selection, 42, 45, 50, 165
    naturalist investigations, 31
    and religion, 192
Darwinism
    as "belief" system, 10–11
    debate, 14
    Gallup Poll, 3
    gene frequencies and mutations, 47
    and Harun Yahya, 23
*Darwin's Black Box: The Biochemical
        Challenge to Evolution*, 15, 62
dating techniques, 34, 56–58, 151
Davenport, Charles, 11–12
Dawkins, Richard, 16, 50
de Broglie, Louis, 109
de Duve, Christian, 145
Defeating Darwinism by Opening Minds,
        189–90
Dembski, William, 15
Democritus of Abdera, 174
Denmark, 104, 193
deoxyribonucleic acid (DNA). *See* DNA
descent with modification, 34–35,
        38–**39**
determinism
    Big Bang, 136
    and evolution, 131
    Heisenberg's uncertainty principle,
        140–42
    and necessity, 174
    and science, 109
    and teleology, 111
Dharma, 25, 27
dinosaurs, 86
Discovery Institute, 3, 182–83, 192–94
disequilibrium, 116
dissipative structures
    Bénard cells, 191
    Big Bang theory, 142
    Brusselator, 195–98
    chance and necessity, 175–76
    experiment for, 200
    hydrothermal vents, 135
    liposomes, 125
    thermodynamic equilibrium, 114–**15**
dissipative systems, 116, 122
DNA. *See also* mitochondria (mtDNA)
    AIDS resistance, 76
    base sequence homology, 65–66
    dependability of technology, 107–8

DNA (*continued*)
  discovery of, 9, 42
  double-helix, 9, 42–**43**
  electroporator, 201
  and enzymes, 64
  gene duplication, 162
  gene regulatory networks, 165
  genetic gradients, 99–100
  and histones, 154–55
  Homo sapiens, emergence of, 91
  horizontal gene transfer, 146–47
  "invented" by viruses, 129–**30**
  and minicells, 169
  mutation mechanism, 42–**43**
  Neanderthals and modern man, 89
  neutral mutations, 40
  neutral theory of evolution, 50
  reverse transcription, 129
  and ribo-organisms, 145
  and RNA, 119, 142
  as software of life, 63
  tautomeric shifts, 174
  vertical gene transfer, 147
  Y chromosome, 93
Dooley, Kathryn, 179, 184, 189
double-helix, 9, 42–**43**. *See also* DNA
drift. *See* genetic drift
Drosophila melanogaster (fruit flies)
  genetic experiments, 69
  heart of, 166
  number of genes, 152
  reproductive cycle, 151
  reproductive isolation, 167
dwarfism, 37, 89
Dyson, Freeman, 12–14, 52

Earth, 6, 117, 119, 163. *See also* "young
    earth"
Edis, Taner, 22–23
Eigen, Manfred, 122
Einstein, Albert
  and Freeman Dyson, 12
  gravity, 7
  and Heisenberg's uncertainty principle,
    141–42
  postmodern theories on, 183
  and probability, 110–11
  and religion, 179, 192
  simplification, 55, 62
  theory of relativity, 52–53, 138–39,
    191
electromagnetic radiation, 136, 140–**41**

electrons, 136
electroporator, 200–201
Elohim, 79
embryonic hemoglobin, **163**
Empedocles, 31
Enceladus, 172
endoplasmic reticulum, **153**–54
endosymbiont hypothesis, 157–59
energy source for life, 113–15
entropy
  and the Big Bang, 140–**41**
  black holes, 138–39
  and chance, 173
  definition, 111–12
  dissipative system, 115, 175
  statistical concept, 116
enzymes, 63–64, 129
Escherichia coli, 170–71, 199
ethidium, 201
Ethiopia, 87, 90
eugenics movement, 11–12
Eukarya (eukaryotes)
  appearance of, 152, 160–61, 163
  descent from Archaea, 154–55
  formation of, 130, 142, 146, 151, 176
  fusion model of evolution, 155–**56**
  members of, 152
  and sexual reproduction, 159
  structure of, **153**–54
  symbiosis of mitochondria and
    chloroplasts, 158–59
  tree of life, 66–**67**
Europa, 172–73
European Space Agency, 172
evo-devo (evolution and development),
    165–66
evolution. *See also* natural selection
  acceptance of by U.S public, 193
  as cause of moral degeneration, 29
  censorship of, 179
  and cultural evolution, 103
  and determinism, 131
  early Greek theories, 31
  evo-devo (evolution and
    development), 165–66
  gene variant frequencies, 45–46
  and Judaism, 24
  Lamarckian explanation, 33
  multiregional/uniregional hypothesis,
    100–101
  naturalist investigations, 31–32
  punctuated equilibria, 161–62
  and religion, 192

second law of thermodynamics, 111,
    113, 139
  since birth of the universe, 163–64
  and teleology, 52
  "untamed chance," 16
extinction of species, 32, 38–**39**
extrinsic probabilistic events, 174–75
eye, 59–60, 69–70, 74
eyeless gene, 69

facts, 5–8, 29
fatty acids, 124–**25**
Feldman, M. W., 105
Feynman, Richard, 191
finches, 35–36, 39–40, 44
Fisher, Ronald, 45
fitness. *See also* natural selection
  AIDS resistance, 76
  and hypercycles, 123–24
  and mutations, 44, 174
  and natural selection, 35
  neutral theory of evolution, 50
  protein synthesis in pre-protocells,
    128
  RNA molecules, 134
  survival of the fittest, 51
flat Earth, 6
flatworms, 74
flightless birds, 37
floods, 19
Flying Spaghetti Monster, 4
Fore people, 106
fossils
  Cambrian explosion, 161
  dating techniques, 55–58, 151
  dinosaurs, 86
  emergence of life, 67
  human ancestors, 65
  intermediate forms, 184
  modern human migration routes, 95–98
  skulls, **91**
founder effect, 49
Four Noble Truths, 27
France, 193
Frank, Thomas, 181
free thinking, 179
free will, 188–89
Frist, Bill, 180
fruit flies. *See Drosophila melanogaster*
    (fruit flies)
fundamentalism. *See also* Christian
    fundamentalism

Darwinism as "belief" system, 11
Hinduism, 25–26
Islam, 28
Jewish, 28
and orthodox religions, 28
Puritans and cultural bottlenecks,
    106–7
root of creationism and ID, 30
fungi, 66–**67**
fusion model of evolution, 155–**56**,
    157–59, 173

Galápagos Islands, 34–35
Galileo, 171, 179, 181, 187–88
Gallup Poll, 3, 185
Galton, Francis, 11–12
Gandhi, Mahatma, 179
Gates Foundation, 183
gene pools, 45–46, **48**–49
gene regulatory networks, 165–66
gene transfer, 199
gene variant frequencies
  and evolution, 45–47
  four forces of, **48**–49
  Hardy-Weinberg theorem, 51
  human brain size, 101–2
  mitochondria (mtDNA), 92
general relativity, 136
genes. *See also* genetic drift; mutations
  in baker's yeast, 152
  brain size and evolution, 90–91
  and chromosomes, 92
  cloning, 170–71
  co-evolution with culture, 105, 107
  definition, 41
  and DNA, 9
  duplication and evolution, 162–63, 165
  genetic archaeology, 65–68
  and heredity, 105
  horizontal gene transfer, 146–47
  master switches, 161
  Mendel experiments, 11, 38, 40–41
  minimum number for life, 146
  protein synthesis, 128
  and race, 98–100
  resurrection of extinct, 73–75
  soil bacteria mutations, 73
  uniregional hypothesis of evolution,
    101
Genesis. *See also* creation myths
  binary oppositions, 20
  creation mythology, 18–19

Genesis (*continued*)
  fossil record and human evolution,
    107
  irreducible complexity, 4
  Jewish interpretations of, 23–24
  life spans, 85
  Maimonides commentary, 24
genetic archaeology, 65–68
genetic bottlenecks, 49, 94–95, 99–100
genetic drift
  and chance, 174
  and cultural drift, 106–7
  cultural evolution, 104
  and evolution, 64
  experiment for, 199
  human brain size, 102
  human evolution, 174
  migration routes, **48**–49
  mutation rates, 92–93
  neutral theory of evolution, 50
  physical characteristics, 99–100
  Y chromosome, 94
genetic gradients, 99–100
genetics
  emergence of *Homo sapiens*, 85
  and evolution, 83
  founder effect, 49
  and irreducible complexity, 168
  Mendel as "father," 40
  statistical nature of laws, 44–45
genome, 62, 64–65, 70
germ theory of disease, 8
Gilgamesh Epic, 5
glucose, 148
God of the gaps, 184–85
God the Creator, 10, 32–33
Golgi apparatus, **153**–54
Gould, Stephen J., 190
Grandmother Hypothesis, 76–77
gravity, 7, 12–13
Great Chain of Being, 32–33, 152, 189
Greeks, 6
guanine, 42, 121

Haldane, J. B. S., 45
Hanuman (god), 26
Hardy, Godfrey H., 45
Hardy-Weinberg theorem, 51
Harun Yahya, 22–23
Harvard University poll, 188
Haviland, William, 18
Hawaiian fruit flies, 167

Hawking, Stephen, 138
heart, 166
heavy-metal-resistant bacteria, 73
Heisenberg uncertainty principle
  communication and the general public,
    191
  and determinism, 140–42
  intrinsic probabilistic events, 174
  Planck mass, 138
  quantum mechanics, 137
helicases, 129
helium, 136, 139
hemoglobin, 44, 46, 149, 162–**63**
Henry VIII, 106
heredity, 105
Heritage Foundation, 182
Hinduism, 25–27, 30
Hinduism: A Cultural Perspective, 26
hippopotamus, 37, 89
Hirschfield, Brad, 24
histones, 146, 154–55
HIV (human immunodeficiency virus),
    75–76, 124
H.M.S. Beagle, 34
"hobbit" fossils, 88–89
Homo antecessor, 87
Homo erectus
  common ancestry of man, 39
  and extinct species, 90–**91**
  extinction of, 38
  and *Homo floresiensis*, 88–89
  and *Homo neanderthalensis*, 89
  multiregional hypothesis of evolution,
    100–101
  tool user, 87–**88**, 190
Homo floresiensis, 37, 88–89
Homo habilis, 39, 87–**88**, 90
Homo heidelbergensis, 87–**88**
Homo neanderthalensis, 85, 89, 101
Homo sapiens
  appearance of in Africa, 85–86
  chance and genetic drift, 174
  DNA evidence for, 91
  fossil record, **88**, 107
  fossil skull, **91**
  and *Homo erectus*, 87–88
  and *Homo neanderthalensis*, 89
  Homo sapiens idaltu, 90
  human migration route, **97**
  mitochondria (mtDNA) analysis,
    93
  modern humans appearance, 164
  number of genes, 152

uniregional hypothesis of evolution, 100–101, 108
Y chromosome studies, 93–95
Homo sapiens idaltu, 90
homology
  bacterial flagella, 70–71
  DNA sequences, 65–66
  gene regulatory networks, 165
  immune system, 70
  resurrection of extinct genes, 73–75
horizontal gene transfer, 146–47, 150, 159
horizontal transmission, 106
hormone receptor, 74–75
hot flashes, 76–78
hox genes (master switches), 161
human immunodeficiency virus (HIV), 75–76, 124
humans. *See also Homo sapiens*
  AIDS resistant, 76
  chimpanzees and DNA sequences, 65–66
  cultural evolution, 78
  Eukarya, 66
  genome, 63
  Khoisan (First people), 96
  migration routes, 95–98
Huxley, Thomas, 14–15
Huygens probe, 172
Hwan-ung (god), 27–28
hybridization, 167
hydrogen, 117, 136, 139, 155–**56**
hydrogen sulfide gas, 119, 151
hydrogenosome, 155–**56**, 157, 159
hydrothermal vents, 120, 134–35, 175
hypercycles
  cell membranes, 124, 145
  and chance, 174
  experimental results, 150
  Markov chains, 132
  and natural selection, 122, 131
  and pre-protocells, **130**
  ribozymes, 142
  RNA molecules, 123–**25**, 128
hypothesis
  definition, 9, 29
  origins of life, 116–17
  relationship to ID, 9–10
  verifiable nature, 80–81

Iceland, 193
ID (Intelligent Design). *See* Intelligent Design (ID)

immune system
  AIDS and HIV, 75–76
  antigens, 60
  irreducible complexity, 59–60
  nematodes, 70
  sea urchin, 70
  Viking marauder metaphor, 62
in silico (computer simulations), 175
In the Beginning (film), 28–29
in vitro evolution, 150–51
India, 96
Indonesia, **88**
inflation, 139
Institute of Advanced Studies, 12
Intelligent Design (ID). *See also* neocreationism
  Access Research Network, 168
  Behe book, 15, 45
  Center for Science and Culture (CSC), 15
  and creationism, 3–5, 15, 29
  dating techniques, 55–58
  evolution of, 4
  and Freeman Dyson, 12
  and fundamentalism, 30
  and genetics, 68
  and irreducible complexity, 16
  life on planetary systems, 173
  macroevolution, 71, 165
  microevolution, 71, 164
  mistakes in design, 76–78
  and President George Bush, 3, 180
  and probability, 111
  publishing history, 81–83
  Raelian cult, 79
  relationship to hypothesis, 9–10
  and the Republican Party, 3
  ribosomes, 132–33
  as scientific theory, 8–9
  second law of thermodynamics, 116
  as teleology, 52
  verifiable nature, 80–81
intrinsic probabilistic events, 174
irreducible complexity
  Access Research Network, 188
  and AIDS, 75
  aldosterone receptor gene, 75
  arguments for, 81, 83
  bacterial flagella, 59, 134
  cell membranes, 76
  cloning, 69–70, 170–71
  eye, 59–60

irreducible complexity (*continued*)
  and Genesis creation myth, 4
  and genetics, 168, 177
  ID and perfection, 16
  immune system, 64
  life on planetary systems, 173
  metabolic pathway chart, 59–**61**
  mousetrap metaphor, 80
  neutral theory of evolution, 50
  rhodopsin gene, 74
  ribosomes, 132–34
  and "specified complexity," 68
Islam, 21–23, 28
island dwarfism, 89
Israel, 90

Jacob, François, 31
Japan, 98
jellyfish, 66
Jesus Christ, 79, 106
John Paul II, 181
Johnson, Phillip E., 189–90
Judaism, 20, 23–25, 28
Jupiter, 117, 172

kakapo, 37
Kalahari Desert, 96
Kansas Board of Education, 3
Kansas City, 24
karma, 27, 28
Khoisan (San), 96
Kimura, Motoo, 49–50
Kinsley, David, 26
kiwi, 37
Korea, 27–28
Krebs cycle, 59–**60**
kuru, 106
Kwoth (god), 18–19

lactose tolerance, 44, 104–5
Lamarck, Jean-Baptiste de, 31–33, 35
language, 105
Lascaux caves, 103
last universal common ancestor (LUCA).
  See LUCA (last universal common
  ancestor)
leaf mustard, 167
lemurs, 37
Lévi-Strauss, Claude, 20
lichens, 157

liposomes
  "bottoms-up approach," 169–**70**
  carboxylic acids, 124–**26**
  experiments, 150, 200–201
  and micelles, **126**
  pre-protocells, 127
  RNA world, 142
Lord Vishnu (god), 25–26
LUCA (last universal common ancestor),
  67–68, 146, 158–59
"Lucy," 87–**88**
Lurquin, P.F, 200–201
Luther, Martin, 106
Lyell, Charles, 31, 34, 38
Lysenko, Trofim, 192

macroevolution
  gene resurrection, 74
  hybridization, 167
  and ID, 71, 165
  and microevolution, 168
"mad cow" disease, 106
Madagascar, 36–37, 89
magnesium, 149
Maimonides, 24
malaria, 46–47, 51
Margulis, Lynn, 158
Markov chains, 131–32, 135
Mars, 117, 172
marsupial mammals, 36
Marxism, 192
"master genes," 60, 69, 165
Mendel, Gregor
  experiments, 38, 40–42
  genes, 11
  and religion, 192
  statistical nature of laws, 44–45
Mesoamerica, 103
messenger RNA, 63
metabolic pathway, 59–**61**, 155–**56**
metabolism
  aldol reaction, 150
  definition, 63–64
  mitochondria, 92, 157
  and photosynthesis, 148
  pre-protocells, 128
  protocells, **130**
  and respiration, 149
  rubisco enzyme, 78–79
metabolites, 154
methane gas, 172
micelles, **126**

Michigan State University, 151
microevolution, 71, 164, 168
Middle Ages, 6
Middle East, 95–**97**
migration routes
  and genetic drift, **48**–49, 64
  modern humans, 95–**97**, 98, 108
  physical characteristics, 99–100
Miller, J.D., 193
Miller, Stanley, 117–**18**
minicells, 169
missing links, 89
mitochondria (mtDNA). *See also* DNA
  endosymbiont hypothesis, 157–59
  eukaryote structure, **153**–54
  function of, 92
  human migration route, 95
  inheritance of, 92–93
  Neanderthals, 101
  Nyctotherus ovalis, 157
  and respiration, 158
mitochondrion, 159
moksha, 25, 27
molds, 47
Monod, Jacques, 174
Mooney, Chris, 3, 181–82
Moral Majority, 182
mousetrap metaphor, 79–80, 127
Mozambique, 37
Muhammad, 21–22
multiregional hypothesis of evolution,
    100–101
mutations
  asexual reproduction, 160
  in bacteria, 71–73
  within cells, 164–65
  and chance, 53, 173
  chromosome doubling, 167
  and DNA, 42–**43**
  and evolution, 64
  finches, 39–40
  gene duplication, 162
  and gene frequencies, **48**–49
  gene pools, 45–46
  genetic archaeology, 65–68
  Hardy-Weinberg theorem, 51
  hormone receptor gene, 75
  hox genes (master switches), 161
  human migration route, 95–**97**
  LUCA (last universal common
      ancestor), 146
  malaria, 46
  "master genes," 165

Mendel experiments, 38, 40–41
microevolution, 164
minicells, 169
nature of, 42–44
neutral theory of evolution, 49–50
rate of, 92–94
ribozymes, 122
and sexual reproduction, 159–60
and skin color, 99
tautomeric shifts, 174
ultraviolet rays, 149
myoglobin, 162–**63**

NASA, 172–73
National Center for Science Education,
    193
National Institutes of Health, 83
National Jewish Center for Learning and
    Leadership, 24
National Science Foundation, 82
Native American, 95
natural selection. *See also* fitness
  and AIDS-resistance, 76
  bacterial resistance, 71–73
  and cell mutation, 165
  and chance, 174
  confirmation of, 36–38, 53, 81
  cultural evolution, 105
  definition, 174
  developed, 34
  endosymbiont hypothesis, 158
  extrinsic probabilistic events, 175
  and fitness, 35
  gene duplication, 162
  gene frequencies and mutations, **48**
  human brain size, 101–2
  and hypercycles, 124, 131
  liposomes, 124–**25**
  LUCA (last universal common
      ancestor), 146
  and mitochondria, 93
  mutations and evolution, 46–47, 64
  neutral theory of evolution, 50
  New Synthesis, 45
  and perfection, 35, 189, 192
  as process, 71, 103, 130
  and RNA, 122
  and sexual reproduction, 160
  and skin color, 98–99
  and Wallace, 38
  women's reproductive biology,
      77–78

Navajo, 19–20
Nazi Germany, 12, 186
Neanderthals, 85, 89, 101
necessity, 173–76
nematodes, 70
neocreationism. *See also* Intelligent
    Design (ID)
    age of Earth, 193
    dating techniques, 58
    goals of, 182
    ID and perfection, 16–17
    microevolution, 164
    publishing history, 81–83
    relationship to ID, 4
    and science, 107
Neolithic age, 104
neutral mutations, 40
neutral theory of evolution, 49–50,
    92–93
New Synthesis, 45
New York Times, 182
New Zealand, 37
Newton, Isaac, 7
Nile hippopotamus, 89
9/11 attacks, 23
nitrogen, 117
Noble Truths, 27
Noller, Harry, 133–34
nuclear fusion, 139
nucleotides
    hypercycles, 123
    pre-protocells, 128
    probability, 131–32
    ribosomes, 132–33
    and RNA, 121
nucleus, 66, 92, **153**
Nuer, 18–19
Nyctotherus ovalis, 157

oil seed rape (*Brassica napus*), 167
Okamoto, O, 193
Oktar, Adnan, 22–23
On the Origin of Species, 34, 39
opsins (light-sensing proteins), 69
organelles, 157–59, 173
organic molecules, 120, 122
Orrorin tugenensis, 87
osteoblasts, 55
oxygen
    Cambrian explosion, 161
    life on planetary systems, 172
    mitochondria metabolism, 92, 157

peroxisomes, 159
    and photosynthesis, 148–49
    primeval atmosphere, 117
oxygenase function, 78–79
ozone layer, 149

paleoanthropologists, 86
Paley, William, 15, 17, 127
Paranthropus, **88**
Paranthropus boisei, 90
Paranthropus robustus, 90
Pasteur, Louis, 8
Pauling, Linus, 179
Pax-6 gene, 69
pea plants, 40–41
peer-reviewed journals, 81–83
penicillin, 184
perfection
    Great Chain of Being, 32–33
    Lamarck hypothesis on evolution, 32
    and natural selection, 35, 189, 192
    neutral theory of evolution, 50
    of organisms, 16–17
    and teleology, 52
peroxisomes, 159
phenylketonuria (PKU), 40, 47
phlogiston theory, 110
phosphate group, 121
phospholipids, 169–**70**
photons, 140
photosynthesis
    chloroplast, 59
    definition, 148
    energy source for life, 113
    experimental results, 150
    hydrogen sulfide gas, 151
    life on planetary systems, 172
    and respiration, 149
    rubisco enzyme, 78–79
    in wheat, 64
phylogenetic trees
    definition, 66–68
    HIV studies, 75
    homology, 73
    LUCA (last universal common
        ancestor), 146
    mitochondria analysis, 93
    resurrection of extinct genes, 74
    tree of life, 151
    Y chromosome, 94
phytoplanktonic organisms, 147
pigs, 105

placental mammals, 36
Planck, Max, 7
Planck length, 137–38
Planck mass, 138
Planck time, 137–38
planetary systems, 171–73. *See also* individual planets
plants. *See also* individual species
   agriculture, 103–4
   cell composition, 157
   endosymbiont hypothesis, 158
   evolutionary time scale, 163–64
   fossil record, 162
   Great Chain of Being, 33
   hemoglobin-like genes, 163
   LUCA (last universal common ancestor), 67
   in Madagascar, 37
   metabolism, 78–79
   photosynthesis, 148–50
   reproductive isolation, 167
   rubisco enzyme, 78
   sexual reproduction, 160
pleiotropic effects, 167–68
pneumonia, 184
poliovirus synthesis, 168–69
polygyny, 94–95
Polynesia, 90, 96–**97**
population genetics, 45–46, 93, 101–2
porphyrins, 149
postmenopausal women, 76–78
postmodernism (PoMo), 183–84
postulates, 29
potassium-40, 57
prakrit, 25
prebiotic soup
   amino acid synthesizing, 117–**18**
   catalysts for, 119
   quantum probability, 175
   and ribozymes, 122
   and RNA, 121
   thioesters, 120
prehuman fossils, 87–**88**, **91**
pre-protocells, 124, 127, 128
Prigogine, Ilya, 109, 114, 195–98
primordial soup, 121–22, 135, 149, 150
prions, 106
probability
   and chance, 174
   and cosmology, 142
   fabric of nature, 110
   and ID, 111

Markov chains, 131–32
   in the prebiotic world, 175
   and radioactive decay rates, 110–11
   statistical nature of genetics, 45
Proceedings of the Biological Society of Washington, 82
prokaryotic cells
   emergence of life, 151, 176
   and eukaryotes, 152–**53**
   eukaryotic cytoskeleton genes, 154
   number of genes, 169
   and respiration, 149
   and ribo-organisms, 145
   symbiosis of mitochondria and chloroplasts, 158
proteins
   and amino acids, 119
   cytoskeleton, 154
   and DNA, 42
   eukaryote structure, **153**
   as hardware of life, 63
   heart, 166
   and histones, 146
   and metabolism, 63–64
   metabolites, 154
   replication, 121
   ribosomes, 132
   ribozyme synthesis, 127–**30**
protocells, 128, **130**, 201
Pseudomonas fluorescens, 167–68
Ptolemaic system, 171
punctuated equilibria, 161–62
Puritanism, 106–7
pyrite, 119

quantum mechanics
   and the Big Bang, 136
   definition, 136
   and Freeman Dyson, 12
   intrinsic probabilistic events, 174
   and probability, 137, 176
   uncertainty principle, 142
quarks, 11, 136
Quran, 22–23

race, 98–100
radioactive dating, 34, 57
radioactivity, 57, 110–11, 113
Raelian cult, 79
random genetic drift. *See* genetic drift

Reagan, Ronald, 182
reincarnation, 26–28
religion. *See also* Christian
    fundamentalism; fundamentalism;
    individual religions
  Christianity in India, 26
  creation myths, 20–28
  cultural bottlenecks, 106–7
  cultural evolution, 105–6
  and evolution, 192
  Great Chain of Being, 33
  and morality, 179
  vertical transmission, 105
religious right, 181–82
reproductive isolation, 166–67
Republican Party, 3, 181–82
Republican War on Science, The, 3,
    181–82
respiration, 149, 155–**56**, 158
reverse transcription, 129
Rhesus (Rh) gene, **41**–42, 45–46
rhesus monkeys, 65–66
rhodopsin, 74
ribonucleic acid (RNA). *See* RNA
ribo-organisms, 128–29, 145
ribose, 119, 121
ribosomes, 132–33, **153**
riboswitches, 150
ribozymes
  and chance, 174
  experimental results, 150
  hypercycles, 123, 142
  protein synthesis, 127–**30**
  riboswitches, 150
  and RNA, 121–22
rice, 63
Rig-Veda, 25
Rivista di Biologia, 82
RNA. *See also* messenger RNA; RNA
    world
  definition, 121
  and DNA, 119, 142
  hydrothermal vents, 134–35
  and hypercycles, 123–25
  and liposomes, 127
  and natural selection, 122
  operating system of life, 63
  poliovirus synthesis, 168–69
  ribosomes, 132–34
  ribozyme synthesis, 127–28
  transcription, 63, 166
  and viruses, 119, 127
RNA world. *See also* RNA

building blocks of life, 116–17
and chance, 173
expansion of the universe, 145
in vitro evolution, 150–51
liposomes, 142
primordial soup, 120–22
quantum probability, 175
reverse transcription, 129
second law of thermodynamics,
    125, 127
tree of life, 130
Roman Catholic Church, 171, 181
rubisco enzyme, 78–79
Russell, Bertrand, 10

Sagan, Carl, 3, 190
Sahara Desert, 98
Salafism, 22
samsara, 27
Saturn, 117, 172
Saudi Arabia, 22
Scaife, Richard Mellon, 182
Schönborn, Christoph, 181
science
  American public knowledge, 188
  communication and the general public,
    190–91
  creationism, impact on research,
    186–87
  and determinism, 109–10
  and facts, 7
  and free thinking, 179
  and hypothesis, 10
  neocreationist rejection of, 107
  peer-reviewed journals and validation,
    82
  politicization of, 181–82
  and probability, 111
  process of, 29–30
  and teleology, 17, 51–53
  and theories, 7
science education, 184–**86**
Science magazine, 101
"scientific materialism," 3
Scopes trial, 179
Scott, Eugenie, 193
sea urchin, 69–70, 74
second law of thermodynamics
  and evolution, 111, 113, 139
  and ID, 116
  RNA world, 125, 127
secular humanism, 11, 183

SETI (Search for Extraterrestrial
    Intelligence), 173
sexual reproduction, 159–60
Shroud of Turin, 57–58
Siberia, 96–**97**, 98
sickle cell anemia, 40, 46–47, 51
skin color, 98–99
social Darwinism, 11–12
Socrates, 179
soil bacteria mutations, 73
South Africa, 90
South Asia, 96
Soviet Russia, 192–93
species, extinction of, 32, 38–**39**
specified complexity, 68
Stalin, 192
State University of New York at Stony
    Brook, 168–69
statistical calculus, 110–11
statistical thermodynamics, 116
Stegodon, 88
stellar lifetimes, 13–**14**
Stenger, Victor, 13
sterilization, 12
stromatolites, 148, 151
sulfur compounds, 120, 134, 146
supernova, 139
survival of the fittest, 51
Sweden, 193
synthetic herbicides, 72–73

Tabaldak (god), 18
tautology, 50–51, 81
tautomeric shifts, 174
Tbx factor, 166
tectonic plates, 120
teleology
    Big Bang theory, 136
    *Defeating Darwinism by Opening
        Minds*, 190
    definition, 17, 50–52
    and determinism, 111
    and evolution, 53, 64
    and statistics, 131
Templeton Prize, 12
teosinte, 103
Thailand, 104–5
theories
    evolution of, 110
    experimental results, 56
    and hypothesis, 10
    in ID, 81

and predictions, 7–8
    scientific definition, 7–8, 29, 80
thermodynamic disequilibrium, 112–13,
    142
thermodynamic equilibrium
    after Big Bang, 139–**41**
    dissipative structures, 114–**15**
    dissipative system, 115
    emergence of life, 131–32, 143
    experiment for, 200
    hydrothermal vents, 175
thermodynamics, second law. *See* second
    law of thermodynamics
thioesters, 120, 128
thymine, 42
Titan, 172
Torah, 23–24
Tower of Babel, 5
transcription, 63, 166
transgenic organisms, 171
translation, 63, 132–33
tree of life
    DNA, 66–**67**
    LUCA (last universal common
        ancestor), 146
    prokaryotic cells, 147
    reconstruction of evolution, 151
    ribosomes, 133
    RNA world, 130
tree-ring dating, 57–58
trout, 68
tunnel effect, 138
Turkey, 22–23
turnip *(Brassica campestris)*, 167

ultraviolet rays, 149
uniregional hypothesis of evolution,
    100–101, 108
U.S. National Academy of Sciences,
    190
"untamed chance," 16
Upanishads, 25–26
uracil, 121
uranium-238, 57

variants. *See* mutations
Vedic science, 26
Vedism, 27
Venus, 117
Verizon, 183
vertical gene transfer, 147

vertical transmission, 105–6
viruses
  fusion model of evolution, 155
  horizontal gene transfer, 147
  invention of DNA, 129
  RNA as genetic material, 119, 127
vitamin D, 98–99
volcanoes, 120

Wallace, Alfred Russel, 31, 38–39
watchmaker metaphor, 15, 127
water vapor, 117, 172
Wedge Document, 192–94
Weinberg, Wilhelm, 45
Wells, Spencer, 85
What's the Matter with Kansas? How
  Conservatives Won the Heart of
  America, 181

wheat, 64, 167
Wilberforce, Samuel, 14
Wright, Sewall, 45

X chromosome, 93–94

Y chromosome, 93–95, 101
yeast, 152, 156, 160
"young earth"
  age of, 193
  creation myths, 20
  dating techniques, 56, 58
  Lyell investigations, 34
  naturalist investigations, 31

zygospore, 160

DATE DUE
